Television in the Age of Radio

Television in the Age of Radio

Modernity, Imagination, and the Making of a Medium

PHILIP W. SEWELL

RUTGERS UNIVERSITY PRESS

NEW BRUNSWICK, NEW JERSEY, AND LONDON

LIBRARY OF CONGRESS CATALOGING-IN-PUBLICATION DATA

Sewell, Philip W., 1970–
    Television in the age of radio : modernity, imagination, and the making of a medium / Philip W. Sewell.
        pages cm
    Includes bibliographical references and index.
    ISBN 978–0–8135–6270–4 (hardcover : alk. paper) — ISBN 978–0–8135–6269–8 (pbk. : alk. paper) — ISBN 978–0–8135–6271–1 (e-book)
        1. Television broadcasting—Social aspects—United States. 2. Television broadcasting—United States—History—20th century. I. Title.
    PN1992.3.U5S45 2013
    302.23′450973—dc23   2013010365

A British Cataloging-in-Publication record for this book is available
from the British Library.

Visit our website: http://rutgerspress.rutgers.edu

Manufactured in the United States of America

For Virgil and tinkerers of all eras

CONTENTS

ACKNOWLEDGMENTS

This book and its author benefited from a tremendous amount of support. I am especially indebted to my adviser, Michele Hilmes, for her counsel, encouragement, and wide-ranging interest in media and cultural history and to the members of my committee: James L. Baughman, Michael Curtin, Julie D'Acci, and Vance Kepley Jr. At key moments in this project and my life as a scholar, John Fiske, Paul Boyer, Thomas Schatz, Charles Ramirez-Berg, and Janet Staiger provided excellent advice and taught me about the scholarly life. I also owe a great debt to Grace Cook, Charlotte Maceo, David Wood, and Carole Buchanan, teachers who shared their critical curiosity and love of ideas. I am grateful to my fellow student colleagues, particularly Doug Battema, Ron Becker, Kelly Cole, Jennifer Fuller, Ruth Goldman, Josh Heumann, Derek Johnson, Elana Levine, Dan Marcus, Jason Mittell, Michael Newman, Paul Ramaeker, Rebecca Swender, and Billy Budd Vermillion, for their friendship and fostering of a community of intellectual ferment and support. Patrick Keating, Bill Kirkpatrick, and Shawn VanCour shared findings and insights from their own research and engaged me in lively conversations that sharpened my focus. Dorinda Hartmann was an exceptional source of intellectual encouragement, moral support, and good humor throughout this project.

At Washington University in St. Louis I have been fortunate to have remarkable colleagues who love media and ideas. Bill Paul, Charles Barr, Gaylyn Studlar, and Colin Burnett have each been generous with their unique intellectual talents and areas of expertise, and I am most grateful. Max Dawson, Doron Gallili, and Allison Perlman have helped me refine my thinking about early television, and it has been a pleasure to trade ideas with them at conferences and online. At Rutgers University Press, Leslie Mitchner has been a tremendously supportive and thoughtful editor, and Lisa Boyajian's gentle guidance through the mechanics of publication has been most appreciated. I also owe a great debt to the thoughtful feedback of my reviewers, who made this book better in manifold ways.

This book benefited greatly from the University of Wisconsin–Madison's University Fellowship, as well as from the Department of Communication Arts and the Helen K. Herman, Robert J. Wickhem, and McCarty funds for generous awards and grants. Similarly, Washington University in St. Louis provided leave time, research support, and opportunities to present my work in progress. This project would not have been possible without the dedicated work of librarians and archivists, particularly at the Wisconsin Historical Society and the University of Wisconsin–Madison library system. I am also grateful to Erik Gunneson and the staff of the Instructional Media Center for technical support and access to media. At Washington University our librarian, Brad Short, made sure I had everything I needed. Many thanks also go to my parents, who provided material support ranging from cash to cookies and large measures of encouragement and inspiration.

This book has shared a home with our ill-behaved but much beloved cat, Farnsworth, who kept me company through many a late night of writing, helpfully rearranging pages and adding spaces during strolls across the laptop while mercifully avoiding the catastrophic keys, mostly. The last and greatest portion of thanks belongs to my wife, Kim Bjarkman. Her work as a keenly constructive critic on this book is surpassed only by her steadfast support and ability to make me look at things anew.

Television in the Age of Radio

Introduction

The Substance of Things Hoped For

Pulp publishing mogul Hugo Gernsback kicked off the June 1927 issue of *Radio News* with an editorial proclaiming, "With the official recognition of Television by the Radio Commission, as well as the actual successful demonstration early in April by the American Telegraph and Telephone Co., it may be said that television has finally arrived."[1] This was not television's first moment of arrival, and it was far from the last. Gernsback's pronouncement and the editorial that followed do, however, point to some significant matters. First, that the United States' most widely read radio magazine and its editor-in-chief were heralding television's arrival several decades before it became a domestic commonplace testifies to a long period during which television existed as an object of conversation and imagination rather than a device in the home for (most of) the public. Second, the variance in capitalization between the first and second uses of the word *television* may be a sign of lax or eccentric copyediting, but it also hints at an uncertainty about usage that was in fact typical of articles about TV in the 1920s. Third, that Gernsback framed this arrival in terms of corporate display and governmental sanction suggests the matrix of institutional claims that would be made on and for the medium. Finally, since this was but one of many arrivals, Gernsback's declaration indicates that what credibly constituted television and its moment of accomplishment and recognition was subject to change and dispute. All of these circumstances stem from the roles that culture and language—particularly as manifested in systems of authority and evaluation—play in making and managing a social, technical, and economic phenomenon such as television. In the case of early television those roles were played on a number of stages as individuals and institutions thought and talked about television.

This book explores the very real impact that language and culture have on our world and how we live in it, taking as its case study the role that imagination played in effecting television as a technology, industry, and medium in the United States. In particular, it focuses on the ways in which culture shaped the understandings of and aspirations for television in the period from the mid-1920s to the late 1940s. Those knowledges and hopes matter not only because they worked to coordinate a host of human activities that were crucial to the development of television but also because they demonstrate some of the ways in which people made sense of and a place for themselves in industrialized modernity. Writing about television became a mode of public thought and speculation about intersecting systems of capital, gadgets, values, and power that not only worked to define or dispute television as a technology or industry or system of communication but also projected cultural concerns from one seemingly distinct domain of thought onto another. For instance, later in Gernsback's editorial he uses the example of being able to see opera or the president as an index of the medium's significance, thereby setting aesthetic and political goals for a technology that could not yet achieve them, while imagining television's users as people with serious tastes and interests. This was not random. Discourses of evaluation and systems of authority for talking and thinking about television were fashioned from a range of earlier habits of thought and allocations of cultural power in order to articulate a notion of what television should be.

The specific ways and circumstances in which such notions were developed and contested are the subject of the individual chapters that follow, but as a general matter, conceptions of what television should be were instrumental in both creating television and constraining its possibilities. On the one hand, they worked to facilitate the planning necessary for the development of television as a complex technical and textual system, providing goals and measures. On the other, working toward one specific notion often meant foreclosing alternatives, excluding certain uses and users, and quite often fashioning the medium in the interests of powerful institutions. Imagination has a repressive side. As communications scholar James Carey argues, "Once the blank canvas of the world is portrayed and featured, it is also preempted and restricted."[2] In both their productive and repressive aspects, considerations of television tied it to broader expectations about the modern world and deeply moored values. Television was imagined, disputed, and realized not in a freewheeling marketplace of devices and ideas but instead in a web of cultural, technical, regulatory, and aesthetic assumptions that sought to rationalize and control the meanings made of and by the medium. As these threads were knit together with specific gadgets and practices, they established an imagined understanding of television—as a technology, business, and system of communication—and its basic attributes, a shared definition as a set of aspirational norms that fairly quickly came to be thought of as television's essence. Through this process television would come to seem natural even as it was invented.

Distance Vision, Briefly

Many of the histories of early television in the United States have cleaved to narratives of invention and industry.[3] These strategies for storytelling have worked to inscribe television within metaphors such as races (with winners and losers assessed by clear-cut, meritocratic measures) and cultivation (where toil is rewarded) that serve to naturalize the conception of the medium as private property rather than a public good, but that does not make them any less compelling. Nor does it make them factually inaccurate. However, this mode of storytelling does limit ways of thinking about television and how it became part of our everyday lives. To understand these limitations, the established master narrative of early television as a specific series of technical milestones and achievements by inventors and institutions warrants a brief summary.

Television had been imagined in the form of crystal balls, magic eyes, and super telescopes for centuries, if not millennia, prior to the nineteenth century. With the midcentury invention of the telegraph, the relationship between time and space with regard to communication was forever altered, new notions of simultaneity developed, and certain editorial approaches to the management and synthesis of information replaced by new methodologies conforming to notions of objectivity and economy. Following the discovery of the photosensitive properties of selenium in 1872, rough schemes for distance vision exploiting telegraphic technologies were imagined and articulated. Quite simply, if an element's or molecule's electrical properties changed when exposed to light, this opened the door for translating the differential distribution of light, as in the image projected by a pinhole or lens camera, into some sort of electrical signal. Shortly thereafter, in 1876, Alexander Graham Bell used the mechanical force of sound waves to create an electronic signal that could be transmitted by wire and turned back into sound waves at the receiving end, establishing the basic technical precepts of the telephone.

By the early 1880s, complicated systems involving large arrays of selenium blocks accompanied by a commensurate number of wires were the first detailed imaginings of television. That is, these early schemes broke up an image into multiple picture elements—using the same principles as the ancient technology of the mosaic—each of which had a sensor linked to a specific channel or wire. For example, a tic-tac-toe grid would require nine (three by three) channels to display a game in which Xs and Os corresponded to black and medium gray. In 1884 Paul Nipkow in Germany reconceived the issue of television in terms of sequential scanning rather than an array of signals. Thus, the nine points on the three-by-three grid would be measured one at a time by a series of three holes in a spinning disk that would sweep across a row or column in a consistent manner, and the light source at the receiving end combined with an identical disk moving in synchronization would exploit characteristics of human vision to create the illusion of a constant image. A key advantage of this scheme was its efficient relegation of the signal to a single channel. However, neither the selenium sensors nor the light sources were responsive enough to varying input to create the illusion of moving images transmitted over space.

In the 1890s several individuals were working to exploit the electromagnetic phenomenon known as "Hertzian waves" to achieve wireless signaling. Oliver Lodge was the first to do so. Guglielmo Marconi followed and figured out how to turn it into a business, making a fortune from wireless telegraphy. Those working on picture transmission continued to work from the scanning principle, but most were working on wired systems, largely for transmission of still photographs. By the end of the first decade of the twentieth century, several inventors and scientists proposed using cathode rays or other forms of purely electronic scanning to overcome the dynamic and electrical hurdles posed by spinning-disk methods. Among these were Russia's Boris Rosing (and his student Vladimir Zworykin, a key player in the 1920s and 1930s), who devised a system with mechanical-image scanning on the transmission end and cathode-ray reception. Shortly thereafter, Alan A. Campbell Swinton, a British scientist and theorist, proposed a system with electronic scanning on both ends but did not build a working model.

At roughly the same time, voice transmission via Hertzian waves was made possible by certain inventions credited to Reginald Fessenden and Lee De Forest. The key was the modulation of the wave, that is, creating changes in a Hertzian wave analogous to the changes in a sound wave. The ensuing period saw the use of radio waves for point-to-point communication by commercial interests and some point-to-many uses by so-called amateurs. But quickly the United States and other nations began to require users of these electromagnetic waves to adhere to rules, particularly after the *Titanic* failed to hail nearby vessels as it sank (though partially blamed on interference from amateurs, the failure was almost certainly one of appropriate staffing of shipboard radio rooms). On the cusp of World War I, the spectrum was regarded as an unruly place needing order. With the onslaught of war, governments worldwide, including the United States, seized control of wireless communication and made use of a wide variety of patents to improve radio technology for military command and control objectives. Emerging from the war, radio in the United States navigated the Hertzian waves on a raft of intellectual and actual property that belonged to no single entity and in plurality to the British Marconi company. Finding these conditions to be contrary to the national interest, the United States expropriated Marconi's property and created a government-sanctioned patent pool cum service-and-manufacturing corporation, the Radio Corporation of America (RCA), whose principal members came to include the remnants of the American Marconi Corporation, General Electric (GE), American Telephone and Telegraph

(AT&T) and its manufacturing subsidiary Western Electric, Westinghouse, and United Fruit, which held certain patents and valuable ship-to-shore stations. By the early 1920s, Westinghouse's KDKA and AT&T's WEAF were developing business models for the profitable exploitation of *broadcasting*—a term adapted from agriculture to mean the transmission of a signal from a single point to multiple recipients.

Early aspirants to visual transmission had been interrupted by war. Indeed, Rosing's television dreams would be stymied in the Soviet Union, and his student Zworykin emigrated to the United States, where he eventually came to be credited as the inventor of television. In the early to mid-1920s, maverick inventors John Logie Baird in the United Kingdom and Charles Francis Jenkins in the United States began to pursue moving images transmitted over a distance and met with considerable success exploiting Nipkow's notion of scanning and refinements in photoelectric technology. Nevertheless, their systems produced what came to be regarded as "crude" images, as did the mechanically scanned efforts of GE's team, led by Ernst Alexanderson, and AT&T's team, headed by Herbert Ives. From 1927 to 1933 there was a flurry of commercial and consumer interest in television that, according to the standard history, faltered on mechanically scanned television's low resolution and dampened the public's appetite for TV in the years to follow.

Meanwhile, Zworykin and to a lesser degree Philo Taylor Farnsworth are credited with having conceived of electronic television—Swinton's and Rosing's earlier publications and inventions notwithstanding. Zworykin's work was frustrated by the blind injustices of corporate research, Farnsworth's by those of being a teenage farm boy in Idaho. Eventually, they both found moderately supportive backers, Zworykin at RCA and Farnsworth through a consortium of West Coast financiers. Given superior resources, a crackerjack legal team, little compunction, and some zealous overstatements by Farnsworth, RCA won most of the patent disputes but was for the first time in its history forced to pay royalties to inventor Farnsworth rather than purchase the patent outright. By the late 1930s, US television was essentially RCA television. There were disputes over color and requiring sets to be able to tune in channels in the ultrahigh-frequency (UHF) band, but for the most part television technology adhered to the standards developed at RCA in the 1930s until the rise of cable and the contemplation of high-definition television in the 1970s and 1980s respectively. Until the forced migration to digital television (DTV) for over-the-air (OTA) broadcasting, television in the United States was widely viewed according to standards rooted in the late 1930s.

Three points warrant elaboration here. First, this standard narrative of television history is generally critical rather than celebratory. Few outside of RCA and its affiliates have argued that the US television system that emerged was the best or fairest plausible outcome. Second, in this version of history, experimental television programming in the United States along with the significant broadcasting activities in Great Britain and Germany before World War II have been subordinated to technical, economic, and regulatory struggles, but none of the major works on this subject bypasses early programming entirely. Moreover, although this book complicates the tendency of earlier histories to characterize initial public enthusiasms as an obstacle to television's future commercial prospects, their description of excitement over lower-definition systems as a hindrance accurately captures the sentiments expressed by industry leaders such as RCA's David Sarnoff. Finally, while it would be historiographically convenient if American television had been imagined, invented, and domesticated entirely within the structures of the mature US radio industry, it is not so. While corporate participants in RCA's patent pool were intimately involved in television research, much of the crucial conceptual and practical invention occurred in independent laboratories of the United States, Great Britain, Germany, and France, and before that, the historically and legally remote late nineteenth century and pre-Soviet Russia. Consequently, many narratives of invention have a salutary tendency to consider television as a transnational phenomenon. However, there are other constructive ways of thinking about television that allow for a more expansive consideration of its development and import.

One of the key limitations of narratives of invention and industry is that they overemphasize television's status as a device, product, or commodity. In each of these identities, television takes on a seeming solidity that suggests an independence from broader social or cultural concerns in which its causes and effects are narrowly governed by rules of science, technology, or economics. This reductive habit of thought and representation is by no means unique to television. Tracing the "cultural origins of sound reproduction," the historian Jonathan Sterne notes a process he calls "technological deification," in which devices are thought of as transforming human history while themselves remaining aloof from it.[4] Sterne argues that the seeming agency of devices and the particular wide-ranging impact attributed to communication technologies stem from conflating a technology with a medium. In his scheme the former is "simply a machine that performs a function," while the latter is "a network of repeatable relations."[5] When we ignore the social relations that not only give a technology its meaning and sense of unity but also structure its use, we are liable to think of the power of those relations as residing in the device itself. Transposing Sterne's analysis onto our present inquiry into television, we can see that it would be a mistake to confuse the cathode-ray tube receivers or television cameras or transmitters that were refined in the 1930s with the already vibrant culture and business of broadcasting.[6] Instead, broadcasting informed the meaning and development of those devices from their anticipated uses to the technical standards that evaluated them, while the potential for and imagination of television prompted changes in broadcast practices, institutions, and audiences. Media do not simply erupt from the raw potential of gadgets, despite their tempting tangibility.

Likewise, in the case of framing television as a product or commodity, commonsense understandings of free markets, competition, and supply and demand obscure deeper cultural factors that bear on both institutions and individuals. For example, regulation by the federal government, the patent system, and the consolidation of the US electronics industry, among other forces, worked to forestall commercial television's introduction to the market for more than a decade. Significantly, they did so in accordance with what historians have deemed "corporate liberalism," an ethos of cooperation between government and business that sought to rationalize the social order and the economy in the face of the exaggerated collectivisms and individualisms enabled by industrial modernity. In his study of the regulation and corporate organization of US broadcasting, the historian Thomas Streeter finds that "the concept of corporate liberalism describes the affirmative values that guide decision making about major institutions" in the hope of building a relatively stable and seemingly fair social formation.[7] These values included "a faith in the power of expertise and of objective scientific knowledge to make manifest a transcendent, reified 'public interest.'"[8] Metaphors of science and technology, fields presumed to be socially and politically neutral, were used to frame rules for corporate behavior and strategies for interacting with the public. Broadcasting became a key site for the articulation of corporate liberal precepts in part because it was already imbued with "the aura of technology" but also because it provided an apt avenue for imagining and addressing the public as consumers, which was itself an institutionally useful way of "*conceptualizing social relations* in an industrial society."[9] Consequently, commercial broadcasting as an enterprise can be seen as both effect and cause of corporate liberalism's saturation of twentieth-century thought about the US political economy and its intersection with everyday life. Here, again, we see the workings of culture and values having significant impact on processes that are sometimes assumed to function according to autonomous laws of economics.

Nevertheless, there are limits running in the other direction—from science and technology and economics to the broader desires and demands of culture. Culture certainly affects the import ascribed to scientific discoveries or technical development and may work to shepherd resources to particular lines of inquiry or innovation, but it can make none of these things produce upon command. There are what the historian Hugh Aitken terms "supply-side constraints" on the available "stock of scientific and technical knowledge," in addition to such barriers as the availability of capital and infrastructure.[10] The best narratives of invention and industry tell us some very useful things about such hurdles and how people went about surmounting them. They also often helpfully foreground the agendas of institutions and individuals. Not only were such constraints and agendas part of the conversation about what television should be, influencing what was imagined or said about television, but they also often became the express subject of such speculation and aspiration—such as in discussions of how the sensitivity of photocells would put a check on television's resolution and restrict its possible content. In instances such as these the various participants in the discussion about what television was and should be worked to reconcile current limits with longer-standing cultural ambitions. In eschewing the narrow, stable identities suggested by narratives of invention and industry, we should not deny the specific constraints of science, technology, or economics but rather seek to consider them as necessarily bound up with issues of language and cultural power.

Evaluation, Authority, and Discourse

In considering how culture worked to make television and make it meaningful, this study employs a theory of discourse that holds language in general and specific utterances or statements in particular to be crucial in shaping not only cultural understandings of the material world but also human decisions and plans to refashion the world we perceive. This philosophical position is sometimes satirized as asserting that there is no reality and defended as observing that reality can only be imbued with meaning by language and the other systems of signs. While this may seem an insoluble dispute resting on matters of faith or philosophy at the level of the specific experiences of individuals, an examination of a complex cultural phenomenon such as television points to the sorts of contradictions and constructions that are both well-accounted-for by a theory of discourse and highly problematic for theories of essence. For example, assertions about the fundamental nature of television have repeatedly been rendered incoherent by technical and aesthetic choices that, as I demonstrate in the following chapters, were the products of political debate and industrial promotion—forms of discursive struggle. Thus, claims to the essence of television (or other media or human beings) are treated by this book as significant strands of discourse and objects of analysis, and the chapters that follow are in part an investigation of the cultural consequences of the presumption that there is a true and essential television waiting to be discovered by human activity.

Because this study contests the imagination and realization of television as a natural process, it analyzes the development of the medium in the United States in a manner that focuses on and hopefully illuminates concentrations of institutional and cultural power. Tracing the social construction of television in the United States up through the Second World War, this book emphasizes the role of evaluation and authority. The terms of evaluation such as quality, perfection, liveness, and entertainment are not objective measures (though they may be translated into quantifiable metrics like a specific number of scan lines). Instead, they are discursive formations, accumulations of meanings and habits of use in which there is no underlying essence of television or its attributes but rather a set of procedures for talking and thinking about them. Taking, for example, the discourse of quality, we can analyze the rules of formation by examining its different manifestations during this period and delineating the ways in which specific definitions of quality and television stood or fell with changes in the social and industrial context.[11] Quality was consistently a way of talking about what television should be, a way of organizing aspirational norms and unifying disparate interests around a presumably shared notion of the good. However, at different times notions of quality television stood for quite different things, including modes of production, duties to the public, specific genres, and relationships to other media. Moreover, different historical actors could seize on quite different meanings of quality in struggles for cultural or institutional power, such as when NBC's engineering and programming departments battled over the bounds between electrical form and content, wielding quite different articulations of quality. The disjunctures among these definitions of quality point to the ways in which television's seemingly stable cultural construction was in fact the product of a great deal of discursive work that remodeled conceptions of the medium's nature and uses to suit the demands of the moment, ultimately conforming television to the norms of sound broadcasting.[12] More broadly, these uses of quality demonstrate that evaluation is not necessarily derivative of extant form and practice. Rather, it can accompany and sometimes precede cultural forms such as media, rendering them culturally coherent and valorizing specific institutional relations.

Evaluative discourses link particular ideas, assessments, or beliefs to others, but these discourses are not exactly free floating, roaming how and where they may. Instead, their import and course of travel through culture are regulated by systems of authority and established circuits of knowledge and conversation. Systems of authority both deploy terms of evaluation and partly structure their circulation, ascribing legitimacy to some concepts while denying it to others. The allocation and use of authority most often relies on a mutually reinforcing network of institutional status, axes of cultural power, and learned literacies and behaviors. For example, historian Carolyn Marvin's study of the development of electrical expertise in the late nineteenth century found that the "electricians" claiming an exclusive right to speak authoritatively about electricity did not simply found their assertions on the ability to make electrical technologies work.[13] Instead, they insisted that would-be electricians be able to talk about electricity and electrical technologies in a particular way, and their discourse presumed that members of the group would be from the dominant side of the social order. Similarly, during the 1920s, white, technically or scientifically educated, middle-class men working for electronics manufacturers, the government, or certain publications typically enjoyed a greater baseline authority than someone who did not fit all of those criteria. However, these systems of authority were not entirely static. New discourses or speakers could sometimes gain at least limited legitimacy, as in the case of independent inventors such as Baird or Farnsworth. How much authority such interlopers might gain depended in part on the channels through which their words and ideas circulated.

Just as social status and technical and cultural literacies play a significant role in systems of authority, certain persistent circuits of discourse are maintained by disciplinary expectations, habit, and legal and commercial structures. In the case of early television, as various systems of authority intersected with disciplines such as the study of electricity and magnetism, signal engineering, or advertising and public relations, particular types of debates played out within groups of journals or at the conferences of professional societies or on the pages of the popular press. Circuits of discourse can be relatively autonomous or closed, governed more by internal norms than external pressures. However, no system will be entirely closed. For example, in his study of early wireless, *Syntony and Spark*, Hugh Aitken concludes that physical science of the late nineteenth century was relatively distinct from technology, which was in turn distinct from the economy, but there was a flow of information and other resources between science and technology and technology and the economy.[14] Although Aitken's model (deemed a "second approximation" that could be supplanted by a more nuanced third) posits a flow of outputs heading from science to technology to the economy, he expressly conceived of the linkages between adjacent spheres as forms of communication—outputs and feedback—in which the task of "translation" is crucial for the realization of scientific suggestion as a fact of everyday life.[15] The case of Marconi is instructive. He was less versed in science or its mode of expression than some of his rivals, and, as Carolyn Marvin notes, a "threatening outsider" to the British establishment, leading to skepticism on the part of Britain's scientific journals and a corollary vexation with Marconi's having circumvented their gatekeeping functions by seeking publicity in the popular press.[16] However, breaching this institutional circuit and translating scientific knowledge and technologies into the commercial enterprise of wireless telegraphy were among Marconi's key achievements. These feats also point to an emerging paradox in the circulation of discourse and systems of authority.

As the nineteenth century gave way to the twentieth, the pace and scale of the economy, technological innovation, and human social interaction increased in ways that were met with expanded systems of control that, perhaps counterintuitively, relied on and fostered various types of popularity. At a basic level, attempts to coordinate modernity—such as governmental regulation, the rationalization of production and consumption, or progressive reforms aimed at changing urban life—had to be explained and sold in vernacular terms. Moreover, some large corporations began public relations campaigns that sought to frame their institutional interests as being aligned with the public's. These campaigns were popular appeals, not in the sense of being populist but in that they discursively tied companies such as AT&T into the fabric of a desired modern life. As the historian Roland Marchand has found, advertising and corporate public relations worked as a kind of "therapeutics," in which products, services, and companies were imagined as resolving the problems of modernity by returning them to a human scale and expanding the consumer's individual agency.[17] On another level, science and technology were popularized as they became a source of content for a range of magazines targeting more or less popular readerships, from *Scientific American* and *Science Newsletter* to *Popular Science* and *Popular Mechanics* to Gernsback's *Radio News* and *Science and Invention*. These publications generally sought to leverage for themselves and their readers the cultural authority of science and technology, but they also provided liminal spaces for contesting the authority of institutions. With goals of selling subscriptions and advertising space, these magazines had incentive to explore ideas, devices, and uses that tickled their readership's fancy. Consequently, in the case of television, they sometimes served as contingent or subaltern circuits in which the medium's technical form and uses were discussed and disputed.[18] Still, the publications were tied into broader systems of authority, serving as key sites for the popular imagination of television as an orderly, modern combination of devices and social relations. This is part of the paradox. In order to sell ideas or commodities to citizens or consumers, the internal logics of science, technology, corporate planning, or governmental regulation were transposed into different, less restrictive registers that would resonate with at least a subset of the people.

Because television was imagined in terms of radio from the mid-1920s forward, developing popular understandings of the medium and disciplining public enthusiasm were of particular concern to radio's manufacturers, broadcasters, and regulators. Radio had developed within a corporate and regulatory structure that was built for long-distance wireless telecommunication and then relatively quickly retrofitted for broadcasting. At times these institutions were slow to respond to changes in practices and technologies, but with television the devices and uses were largely fitted to existing institutional models. As a result, considerations of not only content but also technical form and institutional structure were organized around appeals to cultural hierarchy in addition to the specific assertions of science, technology, or good corporate or governmental policy. Combined with the technocratic logics of corporate liberalism, the evaluation of television regularly drew on race, gender, age, and region to establish systems of status and value. As the chapters will demonstrate, this took place in discussions of technology, in which racist and colonialist imagery was used to stake out television's significance among other media, and it took place in discussions of content, where imaginings of what the audiences wanted were shaped by standards of female beauty and the perceived need to maintain distinct racial categories.

Significantly, the distinction between technical form and content was neither firm nor fixed in the imagining of television. From early on, anticipated content and the values and tastes of viewers were seen as necessitating specific technological choices. Presuming a popular, mass medium—particularly when the presumption was a synthesis of radio and cinema—fostered a set of evaluative criteria and favored a group of authorities that would have been quite different if television had been imagined and developed as a videophone. For example, it brought in issues of aesthetics and questions of quality that are the hallmarks of elaborated, shared systems of cultural production and consumption that are not generally considered germane to telephony. Moreover, imagining television as a popular, mass medium anticipated and worked to cultivate a particular type of user, one who thought of her- or himself as relating to television and its promised views of the wider world in specific ways. Not all users would take up those identities, but in this regard evaluative discourses and systems of authority worked to mold a medium that has regularly been regarded as doing constitutive work on the culture at large and the particular shape of modern life, impacting everything from the design of homes to the functioning of the consumer economy. In this way the cultural, political, and economic forces that bear on the meanings of television have counterparts that issue forth from the medium, forming a complex circuit of meaning and culture.[19]

The Affirmative Imagination of Television

This project is ultimately about the ways in which practices of taste, belief, and identity as articulated through evaluation and authority are crucial elements in the construction and experience of television. I find the affirmative imagination of television to be a process with substantive results, a clear example of the materiality of discourse. Televisual taste is a tool used both in the pursuit of power within the institutions of US television and in the construction, maintenance, and contestation of cultural hierarchy.[20] In mapping out the precepts and contradictions in these systems of taste and imagination that led to making television real, the primary objects of analysis in this study are statements made by critics, analysts, regulators, executives, inventors, artists, and viewer advocates as found in government documents, industry archives, academic articles, the popular press, advertisements, fan newsletters, and programming practices and planning. Each of the chapters examines a key facet of the social construction of television in the United States prior to 1948. Additionally, each of these uses of evaluation and authority in television's past provides critical insight into contemporary debates about television's future. The chapters are organized topically—focusing first on technology and standards, then expertise and enthusiasts, then institutional structure, and finally on programing—but have a rough chronological order that follows key shifts in the discourse on what television should be, leading up to its successful commercial introduction in the late 1940s.

The first chapter demonstrates how debates over television's name, uses, and technological standards rationalized the emergent medium by framing television's technical norms in concert with the prevailing cultural order through appeals to modernity, urban sophistication, the triumph of science over traditionalism and tribalism, and the utopian promise of an electrical sublime.[21] The first half of the chapter delineates the processes that marked some technologies as television-proper and others as outliers. Here, practices of definition worked to foster and foreclose the medium's possibilities. The chapter demonstrates how competing interests articulated their proprietary gadgets as essential to true television. These self-interested, teleological assertions framed television within cultural hierarchies of race, gender, and the hotly contested debates over Darwinism. Together, these processes established a conception of television that sought perfection rather than iteration, that saw the medium as driven by supposedly clear-cut technical progress instead of murky cultural contest. The often ignored cultural values that helped define television and its technical standards gave rise to a set of engineering and regulatory dispositions, an electronic aesthetic. The second half of the chapter analyzes those dispositions in engineering debates of the 1920s and 1930s in which quality hinged on notions of technological integration, progress, and elegance (all of which tied into broader public excitement and speculation about electricity). In particular, the discursive positioning of mechanically scanned and wholly electronic television depended on an emerging regime of knowledge and power that rephrased perfection in terms of quality and worked to valorize standardization, predictability, and thereby control.

The second chapter examines how conceptions of authority and audiences were framed in ways that contained the amateurs who had been influential in early sound broadcasting. The professionalization of engineering worked to discipline participation in broadcasting in general and television in particular, leaving a more constrained space for enthusiasm. These trends placed television within a more hierarchical system of distinctions between the assumed authority of inventors and regulators and the presumed passivity of the public. But, as can be seen in reader responses to contests and solicitations by enthusiast publications, there were alternative imaginings and practices of very early television by electronics enthusiasts and television amateurs. This chapter counters the notion of audiences (or audience fragments) condemned for passivity as inactive couch potatoes and finds instead a tension in their embrace of those hierarchical logics of television they claimed as their own. In effect, enthusiasts were offered contingent authority and status, and many bought in to this order. This pattern has intermittently erupted in television history, with recurrences ranging from amateur activity in the late 1920s to the quickly professionalized denizens of Web 2.0 today. Consequently, the early history of television, with the distinctions made among professionals, enthusiasts, and mere audiences, provides scholars and advocates of public involvement in television policy with significant insight into how the parceling out of intermediate degrees of cultural authority can effect broad stratifications and disenfranchisement.

The third chapter argues that the discursive construction of quality programming from sound broadcasting was used by regulators and established broadcasters to justify the commercial and regulatory structures that shaped television's slow rollout as a popular medium. Specifically, quality in sound broadcasting was defined in terms of business paradigms that rationalized commerce, justified commercials, centralized production and distribution, framed diversity in terms amenable to capital, and claimed audiences both as a source of legitimation and as wards to be uplifted. As a consequence, the emergent uses of quality with regard to television exacerbated the cultural concentration ongoing in radio. Here, notions of quality worked not just to benefit radio's established industrial interests but also to place national broadcasting within a paradigm that favored cultural stability. This stability was achieved by aligning the supposedly proper uses of broadcasting with an acceptance of the practices of the networks. These practices endorsed a consumer economy on a nationwide scale along with conceptions of gender and domesticity that both eased patriarchal tensions about messages coming into the home and broke the audience into markets. In grooming potential audiences and anticipating changes in the medium's commercial prospects and international growth, however, the custodians of US broadcasting cut off possible television futures. In a corollary push, the radio trade papers and general business press interpreted European experiments in television in a manner that celebrated the US paradigm and narrowed televisual potentialities. The chapter concludes with an analysis, pursued further in the next chapter, of the cultural consequences of television's delayed introduction. The development of television technique outside the public eye accentuated essentialist conceptions of television as a hybrid of cinema and radio and fostered an aesthetic hierarchy in which television would be found wanting. In contrast to either of those adjacent media, television was kept from meaningful commercialization for more than a decade, and both its institutional practices and aesthetic norms were developed around imported notions of quality that were relatively insulated from the market or public scrutiny.

The final chapter turns to conceptions of television's nature in relation to its anticipated audience during the period it was withheld from the public. These imaginations of the audience were promulgated through a diverse array of statements, including sociological speculations, aesthetic aspirations, corporate public relations, and internal debates among experimental broadcasters. As they influenced regulators, broadcasters, and sponsors, these imaginations bore heavily on the system and practices that would coalesce after World War II. Primarily, the chapter argues that the imagined relationship between television and its audience was reconciled by a conception of quality that held television's aesthetic nature and social obligations to be reciprocal. The prominent essentialism in prescriptive writing on television—predominantly generated by active and former experimental program producers—was both a pragmatic adaptation to the delays in making television broadcasting properly public and a set of plans posing as verities that worked to promote and simultaneously circumscribe the imagination of television.

Together, these chapters argue for an understanding of television's imagination as historically contingent and fractious, an ongoing discursive struggle that continues to shape the medium in profound ways that have ranged far beyond securing the appreciation of particular taste fragments. Affirmative values such as quality or the public interest have a productive nebulousness that has typically served the interests of institutional power. But that same vagary can also open up limited spaces for challenging entrenched power. In the face of technological convergence, ownership concentration, and the multifaceted phenomenon of globalization, American television is undergoing a shift perhaps as profound as its forestalled commercial introduction, and questions of quality have again been central to prescriptions for what television should be. The imaginings of television's qualities before its introduction were far from flights of fancy but rather acts of invention as real as soldering together circuits in a lab, and as we engage in contemporary evaluation of and speculation about convergence television, there are practical lessons from the past that demonstrate how the form and content of our mediated culture can be reimagined to translate aspirations into policy and hopes into substance.

1

Questions of Definition

By the early 1930s, "high-definition" electronically scanned television was said to be "just around the corner," but mass consumer investment in the technology did not pick up until after World War II. Throughout the 1920s and 1930s, public discourse on television was haunted by the twin ghosts of satisfaction and obsolescence. In the case of the former, the fear was that audiences/buyers would be satisfied with technologies that did not meet state or corporate standards, thereby frustrating the institutional designs of manufacturers, programmers, and regulators. In the case of the latter, the threat was that audiences/buyers would not be satisfied and indeed would be scared of immediate obsolescence, thereby forestalling the acceptance of the next technological leap. The specters of satisfaction and obsolescence held sway over imaginations of television's future as a consequence of notions of and desire for progress, stability, and quality.

The expectation that television would be a predictable or familiar thing in the future stemmed from the vast cultural work done to imagine a coherent communications system situated within a largely linear narrative of technological progress and subject to evaluation in terms of widely shared norms. But this cultural work obscured a series of struggles over television and its meaning. Although television today is used by billions of people to communicate with reasonable clarity and by thousands of institutions to generate vast income and considerable social control, television was conceived and continues to exist in a complex tension between consensus and dissensus, between concept and practice, embroiling it within ongoing cultural, material, and interpersonal struggles. Moreover, the lines of tension in these struggles are woven together such that substantive changes along one thread provoke changes in the others and require a near constant return to the loom to maintain a coherent tapestry, in which television tells a story and creates meaning. This television has consisted of not simply the programs we see but the systems that produce and distribute them and the technological artifacts themselves. Indeed, the semantic coexistence of and confusion among these three identities for television—program, system, and apparatus— demonstrate the interconnectedness of struggles over television and its meanings. Television is *made* to mean, both in its being designed to create meanings and the creation of meanings from it. However, these two types of meaningfulness are thoroughly enmeshed in historical contexts and material consequences that set the stakes in the debates over television.[1] The fabric of television cannot be freed from its fabrication. As the following pages will explore, what constituted television as both an ideal and a reality was quite variable in the 1920s, when different parties advocated distinct visions of the medium in accordance with their cultural and material investments. There were winners and losers in these debates, but what made and kept television more or less functionally meaningful was the development of contingent and fungible terms of evaluation such as a pragmatic conception of perfection. Thus, television came to exist in a framework that not only accounts for dispute but often has depended on it.

Such a framework was necessary because television is also the product of a shared imagination. Its cultural existence preceded the successful articulation of technologies to yield "distant vision" by a minimum of half a century. That television began as an idea or shared set of aspirations is an observation that was fairly common in commentary on television prior to its widespread introduction into the market. In the United States an exemplary instance is Richard W. Hubbell's *4000 Years of Television: The Story of Seeing at a Distance*, published in 1942, which traces aspirations to television from the ancient Egyptians and Assyrians, and the trope was fairly common in books and articles about television in the 1920s and 1930s.[2] The existence of media technologies in the imagination first was a wheel not so much reinvented as respun in the late 1980s and early 1990s by such historians of new media as Carolyn Marvin and Brian Winston, who accounted for the tendency of media technologies to be used in ways that restricted the particular medium's technological and cultural potential.[3] As a practical matter, it is clear that an idea must precede its rendering as an aggregation of wires, wheels, and tubes, but as these scholars demonstrate, that idea does not seamlessly translate into a technology's actual use. Moreover, in the case of television in the 1920s and 1930s, these ideas were often muddled and contradictory, sharing names, gadgets, techniques, or goals but depending on persuasion, coercion, and the vicissitudes of physics to bring television into focus.

This chapter maps out broad patterns of two interrelated negotiations over what constituted this thing called "television" in the 1920s and 1930s, before turning to the specific uses of quality in setting the technological standards that would hold until the digital era. The first set of negotiations took place in accounts of technologies that modern usage would not necessarily recognize as television. In these accounts the label *television* sometimes serves as an attention getter but more often as an organizing principle in the contentious process of naming and ordering the technologies, devices, processes, and people involved in the immediate transmission and reception of visual images over large distances. The second set of struggles involves the framing of television within a teleological discourse of media development in which television had a singular, rightful place among its sibling media all in the service of Man's progress (with the patriarchal conceit of having men stand in for all of humanity doing considerable cultural work). The remainder of the chapter explores the valorization of electronically scanned television and the concomitant derogation of mechanical television in the period prior to 1934.

At issue are overlapping questions of media historiography and public policy. The story of television technology tends to get told as a progress narrative, and this tendency is buttressed by the fact that television technology lends itself to measurement in terms of screen size, lines of resolution, brightness, color range, and a host of other criteria that make the improvement of television appear to be objectively demonstrable. However, the history of television technology can just as easily be told in terms of long periods where consumers are denied access to improvements punctuated by brief intervals in which new standards and technologies are compelled. During the initial period in which television technology was idealized and contested in the United States, key matters of public policy, consumer choice, and a competitive marketplace were cut off from rigorous public debate by regular recourse to the ostensibly objective technical standards and practices espoused by the discipline of engineering.[4] The public discourse on these technical questions was in fact interpenetrated by cultural assumptions about modernity and technology and industrial imperatives to leverage intellectual property and protect investments in infrastructure. Ultimately these discourses established a set of evaluative criteria that defined proper television technology and its uses quite narrowly around a broadcast paradigm. This set a pattern for later debates over television technology in the United States—a pattern in which the public's airwaves were to be reapportioned and the people's television sets subject to mandated upgrades and the threat of governmentally engineered obsolescence, all in the name of particular visions of workable technical excellence and a presumed need for a monopoly on the meaning of television.

What's in a Name?

The term *television* is thought to have been introduced in 1900 at the International Electricity Congress in Paris,[5] while schemes for wired transmission of still and motion pictures with names like *telescopy, electrical telescope,* and *telectroscopy* had been bandied about since shortly after the discovery of selenium's photoelectric properties in 1872.[6] Media historian William Uricchio found that the "public imagination" of electronically transmitted moving images had been thoroughly "anticipated and articulated" in the last decade of the nineteenth century.[7] As such a system became technically feasible, wide-scale usage of the term *television* in the American popular press came with a cycle of rising and waning publicity from 1925 to 1934 (see figures 1 and 2).[8] The period prior to 1935 includes what historian Joseph Udelson has called "the first television boom" and was characterized as a period of "optimism and enthusiasm, as well as . . . muted misgivings," lasting from 1928 to 1933.[9] This period was also a moment of foreclosure of possible futures for television, defining certain uses, content, and social relations as not television.

That foreclosure was productive in defining television, even to the point of getting writers and readers comfortable with the name *television,* which was subject to dispute and fairly regularly set off in quotation marks as a gesture of contingency. For example, in 1912 the *Literary Digest* noted, "Plans for 'Television' by electricity crop up frequently, and yet we have not thus far seen anything at a distance by means of any of them," and again in 1926, "'Not impossible, but very unlikely,' is the verdict by Dr. Lee De Forest, the distinguished inventor of radio-apparatus, upon 'television,' which we are occasionally told has actually been accomplished."[10] Likewise, in 1925 *Time* reported, "A London report declared that one J. L. Baird, inventor, had perfected 'Television,' a device to enable a person talking over a telephone to see his antagonist. It may be so, but Thomas Edison's experiments in that direction were not successful."[11] Though certainly not ubiquitous and more likely to be found in general interest news magazines than radio-enthusiast or scientific publications, the setting aside of the term *television* through the use of quotation marks is striking in articles on television from the early twentieth century, and especially those of the 1920s.[12] The uncertainty heralded by this bit of punctuation anticipated a series of contests over what television would be.

Prior to 1926, a magazine article ostensibly about television was as likely to describe a system or device for still picture transmission as one for the reproduction of moving images at a distance. This is partly a result of the journalistic practice of placing mention of an exciting, idealized medium in an article primarily concerned with the incremental improvement of an established, associated medium. Specifically, various methods for still photograph or document transmission had been available since before the First World War, but postwar articles sometimes used the teaser of television to spice up reports on the latest developments in "photo-telegraphy," "tele-photography," and facsimile technologies.[13] Moreover, working on the model of the cinematograph, still-picture

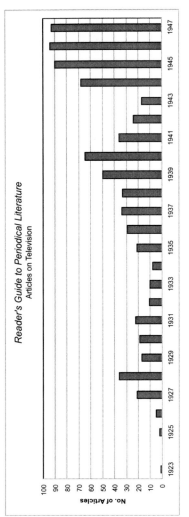

Reader's Guide to Periodical Literature
Articles on Television

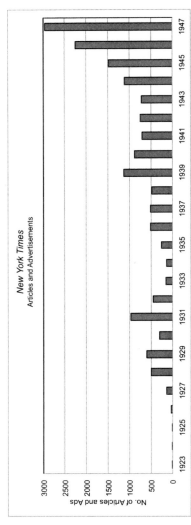

New York Times
Articles and Advertisements

FIGURES 1 AND 2. The three peaks in publications correspond to the enthusiasm and publicity around mechanically scanned television and the early Farnsworth and Zworykin demonstrations, RCA's introduction of its television at the 1939 World's Fair, and the eventual successful launch of television after World War II. Charts produced by author.

transmission was considered a necessary precursor to successful moving pictures, and it was unclear what the electrical and mechanical barriers were to leaping from one to the other. This pattern of discussing television as a concatenation of stills can be seen at least as early as pre–World War I submissions to *Scientific American*.[14] Significantly, because television schemes dating as far back as Paul Nipkow's 1884 invention of the scanning disk relied on breaking an image into picture elements for sequential measurement, transmission, and display, this notion of a television frame as a still picture is inherently metaphorical.[15] Although scholars like Sean Cubitt and Philip Auslander have used the absence of the frame to speak to television's ephemerality,[16] in these uses of the 1920s the metaphor of the frame worked to anticipate television as part of an iterative path of technological development while likening it to the cinematograph.

Nevertheless, there was a debate about whether still transmission was part of television or merely its precursor. These declarations of what is or is not television were part of the contest for discursive authority to define the medium and its uses. In the camp that denied still transmission, the salvos would take the form of a simple assertion such as radio author Alfred Dinsdale's "The process is known as photo-telegraphy. It is not television."[17] On the opposing side there were often reassurances combined with explanations that anticipated other imaginations of television. For example, in 1929 J. H. Morecroft, a radio engineer, columnist, and past president of the Institute of Radio Engineers, described still-picture transmission enthusiastically: "This process is really television. . . . Instead of gazing into the fabled crystal sphere, however, [the viewer] would look at some kind of chart, ink marked or photographic, upon which the distant scene would be reproduced."[18] However, even these articles proceeded to detail the technological differences between still and motion pictures.

A common form of comparison between still and moving versions of television occurred in attempts to quantify the difficulty of transmitting moving images compared to stills by means of calculations that applied the silent-cinema standard of sixteen frames per second to still-photo transmission's time requirements to demonstrate the need to increase transmission speeds by several orders of magnitude. For example, Morecroft went on to argue, "Now, if we imagine that such pictures could be reproduced in one tenth of a second instead of twenty minutes, wireless vision would be achieved" (206). Television inventor Ernst Alexanderson, who in contrast argued for a firm distinction between what he called "radio photography" and television, nevertheless used the interpolation of still-photo transmission and silent-cinema standards to postulate the viability of television, albeit with one thousand times the bandwidth taken by radio photography.[19] As General Electric's chief research engineer, Alexanderson had good reasons to believe in and want television to adhere to motion picture standards. Both men were arguing for television's possibility, but Alexanderson and GE had a financial and strategic stake in defining television in terms of the moving image. Alexanderson's research and patents were of more potential value in such a system because they showed promise of superseding the limits on scanning and transmission speed of older devices. Accepting still-picture transmission as television could potentially undercut the development of a moving-image system and the sale of the devices that system would need.

Still-picture transmission was not the only front in the discursive struggle over television's manifestation and meaning; there was another competing technological vision that had to be defined as "not television." Charles Francis Jenkins, inventor of several key motion picture projection technologies, had intermittently attempted to apply his work on optics and motion pictures to the "problem of television" since the late nineteenth century and directed his energies toward television in 1920 after developing the prismatic ring, which allowed for significantly increased speeds of motion picture photography.[20] Jenkins's early efforts yielded several types of moving images that were vigorously disputed in terms of the thresholds for what could be called television. Jenkins's first demonstration of moving image transmission was a small model windmill with slowly turning blades, and soon afterward, he began demonstrating a system that produced small, moving silhouettes or "shadowgraphs" from human scale models in 1925.[21] W. B. Arvin of *Radio News* said of the windmill demonstration, "It was the first time in history that *real television* had been demonstrated."[22] In contrast, three years later Lee De Forest, inventor of the audion tube, argued in *Popular Mechanics* that "real television" was at least a decade away and required full shading rather than "small, poorly illuminated, coarse-grained, unclear silhouette and half-tone effects."[23] De Forest was, in some sense, correct in his characterization of the images produced by mechanically scanned, narrow bandwidth, moving picture transmission schemes, and certainly in his asserted aspirations for television. However, the common, contemporary reference to and cataloging of silhouette and shadowgraph transmissions as television testifies to their having once been thought of as television and to the quite effective disciplining of the discourse by authorities such as De Forest. This and other disciplinary acts worked both to foreclose and to produce possible futures for television, as well as to facilitate a significant act of historical erasure in which mechanical television is bracketed out of mainstream histories of television.

In addition to the related, successful efforts to mark these two alternative systems of picture transmission as "not television," various parties interested in framing television's future worked relatively unsuccessfully to introduce terms as an alternative to or subcategory of television. The name *television* was found wanting because of its mixed etymological heritage—*tele* being Greek, and *vision* being Latin—with the British *Wireless Magazine* suggesting the pure Greek *teleopsis* as the replacement.[24] Likewise, *Living Age* found the verb *televise* less than sonorous, calling it, "a word which makes us wince, and which we hope will eventually be changed."[25] Critics also expressed dissatisfaction with the term *audience* since those partaking of televisual entertainment would be using their eyes rather than or along with their ears. Thus, terms such as *visience, looker in, tellser, sightener, noisivisioner, radiospect, perceiver, lookhearer, scanner, televist, teleseer, viseur,* and *lookstener* were put forward and largely rejected.[26] This linguistic fastidiousness had a practical rationale among reporters and editors in the still standardizing and consolidating publishing business, and it had a cultural impetus stemming from a backlash against the coinage of advertisers, businesspeople, and the rise of mass culture.[27] However, these terminological disputes were not simply symptomatic of grand-scale questions of cultural authority as played out according to the proper rules for word coinage. As the historian Carolyn Marvin found, such skirmishes over terminology were fronts in cultural struggles between strata in the electrical hierarchy that were further inflected by questions of class and nation.[28] These disputes also worked to privilege particular technologies and practices as being television proper, with others being marked as subsidiary or corollary.

Such hierarchical relationships were often established through incremental linguistic cues and finally overt pronouncements to create and reinforce distinctions that were linked to the valuation of various technical schemes, content, and people. For example, in 1925, W. G. Walton asserted, "Television or the radio movie . . . is the transmission and reception of pictures by electricity in such rapid succession that a motion picture effect is obtained."[29] Here the author made no effort to distinguish *radio movie* from *television,* and usage throughout the article treats the terms as synonymous. By 1926, Orrin Dunlap explained how Vladimir Zworykin's work on the photoelectric cell would "make television and radio movies possible."[30] The *and* in this usage indicates two different things rather than two different terms. The emergent definition of radio movies was that they were filmed content that was later scanned and transmitted. The desire to cement this distinction is evidenced in Hugo Gernsback's 1927 proclamation, "There exists some confusion in the public mind because there has appeared in the press the unfortunate term of 'radio movies,' which is a totally different thing from television."[31] Such calls for educating the public underscore the fact that names matter in imagining and ascribing value to emergent media.

As with stills and moving silhouettes, the stakes in the dispute over radio movies were not simple terminology but strategic advantages in selling competing visions of television's future. For Jenkins, who regularly worked from filmed content, this definition further ostracized his efforts and inventions from the utopian imaginings of television during the first boom, a boom that incidentally overlapped the Crash of 1929 and put mechanical television inventors and entrepreneurs in a financial bind. It also set the technical bar considerably higher since transmission of filmed images was much less daunting than direct scanning of live scenes for wired or wireless transmission. Far from being mere word games, these disputes were stacking the discursive deck to effect a specific technical articulation of television, one that, not coincidentally, was agreeable to the established interests in the US electronics and entertainment industries.[32]

Television's Telos

As television's cultural and technological identity had been asserted through processes of naming, it was further defined through evaluative discourses of progress, perfection, and practicality that worked to establish it within systems of social, scientific, and communicational order. The late 1920s and early 1930s saw regular debates over what was real television, actual television, perfect television, and practical television. In essence, this period marked the consolidation of a notion of what television should be, a *telos* in which television would reach its true purpose: fitting properly into larger discourses of progress, assuming its natural place in an order of media in service to society, and coherently reconciling the calls for perfection and practicality that would allow for a quality consumer and social good. In each of these instances television was tied to broader systems of thought about modernity and how to be a proper modern, scientifically minded, and urbane subject. As the medium was defined with increasing coherence, it was inscribed within a network of social relations and cultural power, where television stood as both product and index of a fairly approving vision of the modern world—a medium and a way of life that were somehow meant to be.

Television came into focus in an era when notions of progress held particular sway. From the growing influence of Progressivism in regulatory thought to beliefs in the positive effects of scientific and technological change, acts of affirmative imagination were apt to be framed in broader conceptions of progress. This may seem inescapable since planning demands thinking not only about a future but the sort of future one might want. Additionally, progress is a compelling story line, a powerful tool for organizing ideas, and a key means for placing historical events and artifacts in a system of order. However, understanding the present or the past in terms of progress has several pitfalls. Such narratives tend to valorize the present as both the apex of development and a necessary step toward a better future. They often frame the ideas, technologies, or ways of life that lost cultural, commercial, or political struggles as dead ends or false starts, thereby effacing conflicts and treating their outcomes as natural.

Moreover, in the 1920s and 1930s, notions of progress were bound up with the specific cultural and organizational values of the professional managerial class, the members of which would hold considerable sway over television as not only various types of authorities but also anticipated early adopters. Television was evaluated in ways that affirmed those values.

Critics and commentators consistently placed television in the scheme of science and its orderly progress, employing two interrelated but distinguishable strategies. The first was to speak of television within the broadly teleological and taxonomic vocabulary of science and engineering—a triumphalist language that saw scientifically driven modernism draining the swamps of superstition and religion with Western man at the forefront, indeed the ever rising pinnacle, of biological, social, and technical evolution. A second strand of discourse more directly placed television's technical elaboration within discourses of orderly engineering processes and an incremental timeline for its introduction as a consumer good. This latter trope was an argument for thinking about progress in a particular way—a way of being savvy about technology and modernity—while the former more generally placed television within narratives of human and scientific advancement.

The period of lower-resolution television's introduction as a functioning technology was suffused with an expansionist vision of science and engineering in which the whole of nature and human experience could be rendered explicable and thus perfectible.[33] This was the time of Darwinian theory's political triumph in the "monkey trial," in which Dayton, Tennessee, high school teacher John Scopes was tried for illegally teaching evolution. Although he was found guilty, he was defended in such a manner that creationist and populist opposition to Darwinisms, both biological and social, were made to look ridiculous and squarely opposed to reason. Significantly, articles on television in science magazines were often juxtaposed with reports of recent decisions by state legislatures and school boards or further evidence of evolution. For example, in a 1927 issue of *Science News-Letter*, the article "Televisionary" shared a page with "Literalism and Illiteracy" and "'Monkey War' Collapses," placing the political progress of evolution beside the technical progress of television in the grand march of science against a backdrop of ill-educated fundamentalists in "'backward' counties," particularly in Tennessee.[34] The juxtaposition of television's progress with testaments to evolutionary discourse's consolidation of its dominance placed television within a larger milieu, where exclusivity and monopoly were considered natural results, where survival was evidence of fitness, and where the displacement of that which came before was an inevitable and necessary fact of progress. All of this was very flattering to those on top.

Parallel to the attempt to fit the fauna into a taxonomy that held man as the zenith of biological progress, the early twentieth century saw attempts to reconcile the relationships among various fields of physical knowledge whereby chemistry, optics, electricity and magnetism, and statics and dynamics could be brought together under a single set of principles, the so-called Grand Unified Theory. For many of these theorists, Albert Einstein among them, this was expressly an attempt to demonstrate the orderliness of the universe.[35] Television, with its reliance on the photoelectric effect, the explanation of which earned Einstein his Nobel Prize, occupied an intriguing place as a technical synthesis of diverse sciences. Reporting on moving and still-picture transmission for *Radio News*, John Arnold noted, "Many branches of human knowledge have been levied upon to furnish the appliances of this art; for picture transmission is a group achievement, the product of many workers in various fields of thought, in which individual genius has played only a contributory part."[36] Arnold specifically invoked electricity and magnetism, mechanics, optics, and chemistry as fields essential to the realization of television. Across a range of publications, television was portrayed as a practical manifestation of scientific integration, a technical corollary to the push for unified theory. In addition to the push for theoretical unification, congruent efforts emerged within the individual sciences in which phenomena were categorized and placed in ordered relation to one another. A striking, graphic example from 1926 was *Scientific American*'s "Tree of Electricity" (see figure 3).[37] The aforementioned dispute over what to call television was still ongoing, and thus it is referred to as a "visible: wireless (future)" on the "signals" branch. Significantly, this scheme works to place applications in relation to one another and as the outgrowth of scientific knowledge rather than the product of tinkering with the combination of extant technologies or negotiating competing interests. As the historian of technology Carroll Pursell notes, "As the nineteenth century turned into the twentieth, more and more technologies became transformed by science, and the centralizing effects of modern life gathered them into systems for more effective management. The way in which the nation dealt with natural resources and work, the government of cities, and even the generation of technological change itself became heavily infused with the methods, results, and spirit of the sciences." Pursell argues this infusion ultimately narrowed the range of technical practices, and as is further explored in the next chapter, it progressively left them "open only to those who were scientifically trained and formally permitted to enter them."[38] The "Tree of Electricity" proposed by *Scientific American* suggests that there is a singular correct technical answer to the "problem of television," and this notion would become crucial in regulatory demands for standardization. Thus, television would be the logical and unique end of the correct application of scientific theory and engineering practice.

Nevertheless, few engineers and inventors were thoroughly blinkered by the discourse of progress. Far from it; they cogently argued for the complexity of

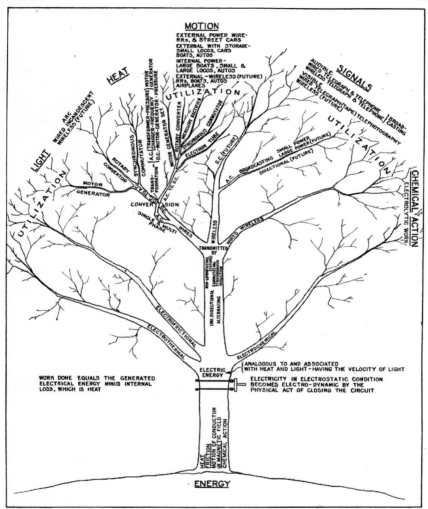

A Tree of Electricity

It is impossible to clearly delineate all the ramifications of electricity. We give, therefore, only the principal applications to show their inter-relation

FIGURE 3. "A Tree of Electricity," published by *Scientific American* in 1926, imagines an organized and natural growth from physical phenomena to specific technologies. This taxonomy recalls genealogical family trees, suggesting heredity and degrees of kinship. Courtesy of Memorial Library, University of Wisconsin–Madison.

technological innovation, among other things because it was and is hard. A particularly detailed and ambivalent statement on the nature of progress was made by Carl Dreher, an RCA engineer and *Radio Broadcast* columnist, who wrote, "We are so constantly bombarded with the idea of 'progress,' nowadays, that we are apt to conclude that it is a notion of universal validity, which has always existed. This is an error."[39] Dreher further philosophized about the assumption of "happiness [as] the aim of life," opining that men of the past were as or more free and "doubt[ing] if I am happier than they were, all the way back to *Pithecanthropus Erectus*. So much for progress in that sense." Yet he found progress narratives to have a compulsory power in the age of machines: "As soon as machinery enters the door, progress breaks in at the window and sits down in the best chair. There are no perfect machines. . . . Some, however, are better than others. . . . If you build one machine, you must shortly build another and better one, or someone else will. And so Progress has you by the neck." He concluded by noting that progress's apparent universality was a result of selective attention and application, but a proper understanding of progress as incremental improvement could be applied to radio and, in later articles, to television. As Dreher's comments about men's happiness hint, such a proper understanding was tied to particular ways of being a man.

Concurrent with the earliest television demonstrations by Jenkins and Baird was the push for an ethos of engineering professionalism in radio-enthusiast publications, which attempted to dispel the notion that methodical approaches were effete by articulating an endorsement of engineering in expressly masculinist terms, whether favoring the inventor or the engineer. For example, a *Radio News* "hammatorial" argued, "They seem a long way apart, the hammer and the slide rule, but they are brothers under the skin, although one is the younger and has a reputation for midnight oil. As a matter of legal fact, they are both joint heirs under their father's will, and their ancestor is none other than old man Advancement himself."[40] Likewise, J. H. Morecroft of the Institute of Radio Engineers (IRE) invoked sound broadcasting's patrilineage of inventions—the Fleming valve, the De Forest audion, the Armstrong regenerative circuit—in arguing for the engineering ethos of incrementalism as articulated through a story of gradual progress.[41] The historian Jonathan Sterne found that a "male-birth model of technological history" not only made "good news copy and patent applications" asserting "ownership and authorship" but also worked to naturalize media technologies, imposing coherence by heralding "singular moments of birth," stamping out alternate articulations of gadgets and media identities.[42] Patrilineal litanies such as Morecroft's performed those functions, but they also called for a professional modesty that recognized the iterative nature of scientific and social progress.

Because these calls for modesty were themselves a form of cultural power play, we should not be surprised to find that they could simultaneously be bullying. For example, in 1927 *Radio Broadcast* used a recent screening of *Metropolis* to tie "the mechanical advance of civilization" to Bell Telephone Laboratories' concurrent television demonstrations, enthusing that the lab had perfected television as one of the "extraordinary scientific tools of modern life."[43] The article further lauded AT&T's engineers for "actually accomplishing what others have attempted" and impugned inventors such as Baird for secrecy and a lack of demonstration in the United States. It followed up by situating the development of television within a framework of institutional common sense: "These Bell Laboratories men . . . are content to let the other fellows do the talking while they iron out the trouble." They were men of action, not men of words. The piece concluded by noting the rampant speculation about television and asserting "time, not prophesy, will tell what use the world will make of this distance-conquering eye." Simultaneously praising the men of AT&T for their incrementalism and castigating Baird for his lack of full disclosure, this article worked to espouse a professional reserve marked as manly, reframing Baird's (and Jenkins's) winning the race to transmit transient images as an overreach.

This set of cultural values—patience vs. avidity—would come to be mapped on one of the predominant discursive tropes of the lower-resolution-television era, that of television's being "just around the corner." Claims that television was "just around the corner" were a hallmark of the first boom. Udelson's history of early television highlights this trope in discourse, but analyzing it as a site of struggle is beyond the scope of his analysis.[44] In particular, the purposeful discursive struggle between "just around the corner" and the "distant future" warrants attention to the two positions' roles in articulating television's "progress" as part of an emerging master narrative of technical and cultural evolution that was troubled by contradictions between the probable and the possible, the normative and the exceptional, and continuity and disruption.

By late 1928, the tension was decisively framed between the two poles of "just around the corner" and the "distant future." Reporting for *Radio Digest*, Harold Brown noted the confusion resulting from contradictory reports claiming on the one hand "a console combining a phonograph, a Radio receiver, a silver screened speaker and a moving picture that speaks, sings and plays!" to be "no farther away than just around the corner" and on the other television being "something for the 'far distant future.'"[45] Here, the notion of television as imminent was dismissed as superstition and an errant belief in science as a "great magician" rather than the rational system favored by experts. While "the corner" was regularly remarked on in popular reportage on television, it increasingly came to be discussed as a problematic belief of fans who were thought to be subject to flights of fancy and manipulation by unscrupulous hucksters. Retailers and manufacturers invoked the corner to dispel it and its supposed contribution to the cooling demand for sound sets.[46] Meanwhile, engineers and other experts used the "corner" as a form of shorthand to signify public naiveté about the proper place of television in the order of science and media technologies. For example, Theodore H. Nakken, designer of the transmitting system employed by *Radio News*' station WRNY, asserted in the *New York Times*, "To the layman not conversant with the facts in the case, [television] appears to be a development of the last few years. As a matter of fact, television is not new at all. As far back as 1873 the solution to the problem of sending pictures through space seemed to be just around the corner."[47]

A particularly elaborate form of reasserting the notion of orderly progress was a 1932 hoax that drew analogies between sight broadcasting and time travel and worked to establish a sense of televisual reason and understanding while using the "around the corner" discourse to signal the prank to insiders. In this instance *Radio Digest* published an article in February 1932 titled "Just Around the Corner, Reincarnation: Transmuter Rejuvenates," which opens with the claim, "Now that television is an old story, science is on the verge of announcing another great discovery."[48] The article went on to describe how a man being televised suddenly was transformed into a character with late nineteenth-century costume and affect. This article played the joke close to the vest, never disclosing whether the claims of time travel are a complete fabrication or a report on a televisual illusion perpetrated by clever implementation of lighting schemes to give the appearance of two different period costumes. Thus, the expert enthusiast was asked to recognize time travel both as beyond the means of electrical communication and as a potential trick effect of television production.[49] However, the crucial joke in this article was the mockery of the "just around the corner" discourse. Readers were invited to think of themselves as knowing better and being willing to wait on television of the future rather than getting caught up in the enthusiasm of television of the moment. Equally significant, however, was the promise of television as being a distant eventuality, the fruit of responsibly delayed gratification, of submission to order. In essence, the "just around the corner" discourse and its contradiction with claims of television in the "distant future" worked to place the technology's development within a rational timeline governed by contemporary scientific prejudices. Thus situated, television was both brought into a more coherent imagining and cut off from possible alternatives. These acts of definition and delimitation were significant in a field dependent on investment capital, regulatory sanction, and popular embrace.

The Order of Media

In addition to television's place in narratives of scientific, evolutionary, and civilizational progress and the articulation of a timeline on which televisual progress could be tracked, television was also inscribed into a set of presumed relationships with other media and human perception. Television's progress and perfection would come to be judged largely in terms of its fulfillment of the expectations set by this web of relationships. Arguments seeking to place television within this system of order pursued two routes to roughly the same set of conclusions. The first route established a hierarchy of media by asserting a hierarchy of the senses. The second founded its quite similar hierarchy of communication technologies on supposed technical specificities as they intersected with not only the senses but presumed social needs and temporal advantages. At the end of both routes, television would be held to contradictory standards drawn from sound broadcasting and cinema, thereby setting up some of the industrial and aesthetic tensions that would define television as both obvious—a seeming textbook solution to technical and social problems—and wanting. The two paths are worth retracing as they point to the challenges and opportunities posed by writing about television drawing on analogies to the senses and present technologies.

In articulating television's role in the media's march to mimic human perception and its proper place among other media technologies, perception was discussed both authoritatively (whether correctly or not) and humorously. Thus, in an article mocking television with a joke about the imminence of transmitting smells, the author also argues for the primacy of sound broadcasting through an appeal to an unattributed study, which claimed, "It appears that when a man dies the senses usually fail in the following order: smell and taste, sight, touch, and hearing. The significance of this to broadcast listeners is obvious. In the physiological turmoil of dissolution, when the individual is no longer responsive to odors, tastes, spectacles, and contacts, he can still harken to his favorite broadcasting station!"[50] However, differences in perception were not idle questions in debating television's future for several reasons. First, there was the significant set of challenges posed by the differences between sound and sight. As Edgar Felix of *Radio Broadcast* noted, "an eighty-piece orchestra . . . blends into a single, though highly complex, sound wave consisting of variations of air pressure, involving frequencies no higher than ten or fifteen thousand per second," whereas, to this day, all methods for picture transmission via electromagnetic signals involve breaking the image into pieces.[51] Likewise, the article by Nakken about television's having been "around the corner" for half a century took great pains to root television's slow going in the differences in perception.[52] Although these differences are real—the eye and ear are different, as are the patterns of compressed and rarefied air and reflected light we experience through them—such appeals to perception situate television within particular conceptions of human nature and a hierarchical way of thinking about the senses.

As the statements about the differences between sight and sound attest, it was and still is a cultural commonplace to contrast the two senses. A centuries-old pattern of thought and expression that the historian Jonathan Sterne identifies as "the audiovisual litany" ascribes to the two senses quite distinct attributes and roles in human experience and culture. Broadly, this litany has held vision to be the sense of rationality and detachment, with visual metaphors such as the Enlightenment serving to advance what he calls "the visualist definition of modernity." Meanwhile, sound was regarded as the sense of immersion and closeness, "as manifesting a kind of pure interiority."[53] Sterne persuasively demonstrates the flaws in this conception of the senses, as well as its too little examined roots in Christian theology, but for our purposes what is most important is the litany's pervasiveness and the cultural work it performs, often leveraging those hidden values. The assertion of sound being the last remaining sense and the possibility of radio offering deathbed comfort repeats certain articles of faith and frames radio as a medium of intimacy. Appeals to the complexity of image transmission dovetailed with conceptions of sight as the rational sense, the sense of grids, perspective, and maps. Television's claim on the visual aligned it with presumed truths about the origins of modernity in the rationality and detachment of science and philosophy. Those truths both bolstered the emerging definition of television as it should be and were buttressed by acts of imagining the medium.

In addition to framing television in terms of rationality and advancement, discussions of perception tended to frame communication technologies as analogues for human organs and, in doing so, doubled down on a notion of sensation as distinct from the social. Hearing and seeing may seem like raw anatomical processes, but in fact they, and even more so listening and looking, are developed within and by culture and experience. As Sterne notes, "the very capacity to relate to the world through one's senses is organized and learned differently in different social settings."[54] Which sights or sounds we attend to and which we ignore are the product of culture. Additionally, Sterne demonstrates that social relations have directly borne on scientific and technological understandings and uses of the senses through such practices as dissection, attempts to mimic anatomy with talking and hearing machines, and even the use of "excised human ear[s]" in experiments by inventors such as Alexander Graham Bell.[55] Such practices bespeak a disposition toward human bodies and organs (particularly the bodies and organs of others) as machines that do work. Here sensation is understood in terms of productivity. Almost simultaneously, the body and its parts are abstracted. Other materials are enlisted to do the work of flesh and bone. What remains are the cultural understandings of work and the naturalizing power of the imitation of anatomy.

The common trope of describing televisual apparatus in terms of the eye and retina was not simply an act of explanation but also one of legitimation. In reporting on AT&T television, *Scientific American*'s Louis Treadwell asserted, "The analogy of television with the function of the eye is exceedingly close. The surface of the retina is composed of infinitesimal spots which are individually connected and run back to the optic nerve."[56] Similarly, Zworykin's iconoscope was said to have been directly modeled on the human eye. *Popular Science* enthused, "Just as the human eye's retina is composed of innumerable rods and cones that respond to light, so Dr. Zworykin's artificial retina is a mosaic of millions of microscopic photo-electric cells."[57] By linking television technology to the anatomical mechanisms for human sight, the devices were placed in a system of anthropocentrism that worked to elevate those technologies that most resembled our organs.

These appeals to the human body also subtly assuaged the anxieties fostered by the uncanniness of seeing at a distance. More explicitly on this front, Hollis Baird (no relation to John L. Baird) stretched contemporary theories of perception and argued that scanning was nothing new and a function performed by the eye in taking in complex images: "Thus, while television may seem to be a far cry from any human parallel, it actually follows the human eye more accurately in its procedure than does a camera which takes in all at once a complete picture."[58] Baird's use of scanning to discuss shifting attention is something of an outlier in terms of drawing analogies between televisual processes and human perception. Indeed, scanning was more commonly discussed as dissimilar from natural vision, with mosaic approaches being the key analogy for the retina, which *Science News-Letter* called "the original television transmitter in our own eyes!" and contrasted with mechanical scanning.[59] While these two examples employed divergent conceptions of human sight, they both worked to assert that television should fit the natural order.

H. Baird's contrast with photographic processes notwithstanding, by far the most common assertion of television's dependence on human perception involved the alleged phenomenon of "persistence/retentivity of vision," long associated with the cinematograph and thereby providing an additional means to place television within a familiar system of order. Author after author explained the basics of creating transient images by invoking the cinema to explain the "lag" in human perception that allows samples to stand in for a constant image and moreover fool the eye into seeing motion.[60] This was a significant element in the process of bringing television into an analogical relationship with cinema—a relationship in which for most of the twentieth century it was consistently defined as the low other. At the same time that television's excellence was staked to the mimicry of human perception, as well as its capacity for liveness and simultaneity, the device was persistently drawn into a comparison with cinema in which its image and stylistics would regularly be found lacking. As Uricchio notes, simultaneity was indeed so valued in nineteenth-century imaginations of moving image systems that the as yet unbuilt (and not then named) television partially defined the medium of film "as much by what it could as what it could not do."[61] Although Uricchio's research into this earlier era rebuts the historiographic tendency to presume "the primacy of film as a moving-image medium,"[62] by the 1920s, in the United States, film had staked out its identity and the relative high ground in an aesthetic media hierarchy. Consequently, arguments about good television would be skewed toward liveness and ability to capture the real rather than beautiful or poetic expression.

The second route to establishing an order of media was equally reliant on hierarchizing the senses, while also bringing in elaborate interpretations and speculations on the uses of various media and the meanings to be made of human experience. Thus, Carl Dreher's exemplary *Radio Broadcast* article, "The Place of Television in the Progress of Science," claimed, "Sight and hearing are the two principal senses of the higher animals. The other senses are quite limited in range and contribute less to the picture of the universe which man, especially, must try to construct for the purposes of his life."[63] In this article Dreher argued against what he clearly regarded as an overly enthusiastic and ill-informed report on the 1927 AT&T demonstration. He called for "thought on the subject of what roles may best be played in the drama of modern life by such scientific applications as television, telephony, the phonograph, talking movies, aural broadcasting, and allied inventions." To that end Dreher went on to provide detailed tables asserting the relations among media and their appropriate uses. In the first (see table 1), he assayed the "characteristics of the principal sense- and intelligence-reproducing inventions," a group of inventions from which wireless technologies, such as radio, were purposefully absent.

His chief concern along this axis was the "transitoriness of life" and a means for preserving and disseminating excellence: "In this way, John Barrymore and Caruso, alive and dead, are spread over the earth. . . . Essentially, therefore, motion pictures, phonographs, and their synthesis, the talking picture, are means of, first resisting the passage of time, and secondly, overcoming the spatial and energetic limitations of certain special human beings whose performances are of great interest to their fellows." In contrast, Dreher declared

	TABLE 1	
Sound	*Nature of Utility*	*Light*
Phonograph	Permanent record	Photograph (static) Motion Picture (kinetic)
Telephone	Rapid reproduction at a distance	Television

that "by means of the telephone and televisor we project ourselves, sensorially, through space." Thus, the "'permanent record' group" existed to conquer time, while the "'tele' group" worked to conquer space.[64]

Dreher's second axis once again situated television within a technological lineage, a child of "telephoto [facsimile] systems, and the motion picture art." In the order of media, he saw greater and lesser lights: "The fundamental inventions . . . are the telegraph, the camera, and the phonograph. The others are elaborations and cross-breedings." Broadcasting and wireless telegraphy barely rated because he considered them a subset of telegraphy and telephony; the use of the spectrum would "result in profound differences in social application of the arts in question, but the metaphysics remain the same." In dismissing social relations and appealing to metaphysics, Dreher asserted an ontological relationship between media and their use: "All these inventions are, in the last analysis, means by which human beings secure agreeable or necessary sensations, in the absence or because of the unavailability of the original sources of those sensations, owing to the movement of time and non-movement of space." In either case, Dreher presumed an original that existed independent of mediation. In conflating the original performance with the person of the performer and underlining that bodily appeal with the possibility of the voice and image persisting after death, Dreher avoided the subtle fact observed by philosopher and social critic Walter Benjamin that the production of an original changes with the advent of mechanical or electrical reproduction in that the original is now in fact also a product of reproducibility.[65] Cleaving to this notion of a preexisting original would become particularly significant in evaluative standards of liveness and acceptable image resolution, but it is also worth noting as an attempt to frame technologies that promised to reorder time, space, and the social in human terms.

That the humans in question, Caruso and Barrymore, already stood as symbols of aesthetic excellence neatly swaddled this reassurance that "the progress of science" was in fact the progress of man in the trappings of high culture. Dreher made this point more expressly with another distinction that would remain particularly significant in making sense of electronic media: "When agreeable sensations are involved we are dealing with entertainment; when the sensations are necessary, rather than merely pleasant, we speak of utility. There is no sharp dividing line. Broadly, one sustains life; the other helps make it worthwhile. Let us hope television will do both."[66] This distinction between information and entertainment was already a crucial pillar in the structures of evaluating and regulating US media, and it would have profound consequences for television as its quality would come to be assessed in terms of its potential to provide uplifting entertainment.

In case there was any doubt about the beneficiaries of uplifting entertainment, illustrator Franklyn F. Stratford provided a depiction of Dreher's taxonomy of media uses with the phonograph spreading the good word or *aria* (see figure 4). The racist and colonialist ideology is right on the surface, with the

"THE WAX DISCS MAY BE CARRIED TO DISTANT POINTS"

FIGURE 4. In illustrating *Radio Broadcast's* 1927 piece "The Place of Television in the Progress of Science" with the phonograph, the modernity of the West is evoked by the juxtaposition of media technologies with supposedly primitive technical have-nots. Not only are media technologies depicted here as indexes of modernity but also, in keeping with the colonialist imagination, as tools for projecting civilization. Courtesy of West Campus Library, Washington University in St. Louis.

phonograph serving to ease the "white man's burden" of civilizing the world,[67] but in many ways the illustration worked as a distillation of the discourses that established television's place in the progress of science. Music scholar Timothy Taylor finds such depictions to be a common trope in early 1920s discourse about radio, shoring up the medium's supposed modernity "by juxtaposing it to peoples thought to be premodern."[68] The illustration can be seen as part of an ongoing trend of what Taylor calls "technological imperialism," in which the possession or lack of technologies serves as an index of modernity and cultural worth.[69] Built on the representation of supposedly premodern peoples, this meaning of technological lack could then be transposed into other registers and onto other classes, groups, and nations. It is not surprising that television would, as we will see in the following pages, be enmeshed in a set of discursive tensions composed of designations of primitivism and crudity coupled with ideals of perfection and practicality, which competed and colluded as heirs to progress, the demanding taskmaster that promised continual improvement yet no satisfaction.

Primitivism and Perfection

The network of progress narratives that enmeshed television promoted the notion that there was an essential television that was temporarily obscured by contemporary crudities and awaited perfection, or at least its practical approximation. The first step in valorizing this essence of television that would be realized in the future was to emphasize television's lack of refinement in the present. Thus, alongside *Pithecanthropae*, Hottentots, and Tennesseans, television of the 1920s was also regularly described as crude or primitive. In particular, the representatives of General Electric and RCA were quick to point out current television's defects. For example, Alexanderson's report on his own work for GE stated, "The images . . . are so crude that they have no practical value."[70] Certainly 1920s television was crude and primitive by the standards of televisual progress of the twentieth century, but equally if not more significant were the commercial and cultural interests served by the designation.

Early commercialization of television posed a definite threat to established radio manufacturers and a potential danger to higher definition television sales by creating public disillusionment. Consequently, the very large electronics manufacturers espoused a restrained development and commercialization of the medium. In particular, advocates of electronic television such as RCA, its subsidiaries like NBC and eventually RKO, and its parents like GE were invested in staving off mechanical systems as crudities and forestalling television's revolution of what they hoped was a stabilizing radio industry until their own patented electronic technologies and infrastructure were ready.

If concern for the radio business model partially underwrote attributions of crudity, so did notions of good scientific and industrial engineering practice. While the large electronic manufacturers had incentives to maintain the radio status quo, this does not mean their research scientists and engineers were just disingenuously pursuing corporate interest when condemning 1920s television. Mechanical television, with its tinkerer inventors and clunky contraptions, offended modern scientific sensibilities. *Radio Broadcast* quoted the German scientist and inventor Max Dieckmann as claiming, "With electrons I think I have the real instrument for television. Electrons are almost weightless and can travel at any speed we need. All mechanism has a weight and inertia that in my opinion will always drag down efforts at perfect television."[71] For Dieckmann, "perfect television" was "the reception of images as fine as published photographs," which stood in contrast to the contemporary possibility of "crude television." Similarly, British scientist Alan Campbell Swinton hailed mechanical exhibitions as "magnificent" but found them to be relatively pointless and something of a distraction.[72] He called for abandoning mechanical television research and focusing instead on "the ultimately more promising methods in which the only moving parts are imponderable electrons." As Dieckmann and Swinton had been pioneers in electronic systems and consequently had reputational (and in Dieckmann's case intellectual property) investments in electronic television, they too were invested in mechanical television's crudity. This strand of discourse portrayed television with moving parts as a sort of Frankenstein's monster, an ungainly and seemingly unnatural imitation of televisual potential. Electronically scanned systems would eventually surpass mechanically scanned television, but during the time that electronic systems were closing the gap, this translation of engineering aesthetics into scientific fact and the language of crudity and perfection helped to stymie further innovation and public adoption of television.

In addition to claims about the fundamental basis for scanning the television image, assertions of crudity were tied to calls for tight regulatory control and licensing of only a few, relatively wide bands in the higher frequencies. For example, RCA's Alfred Goldsmith, quoted in *Science News-Letter*, argued, "A narrow band of frequencies assigned to television would permit the transmission only of unpleasantly crude images of restricted dimensions, and would therefore at once block the development and public appreciation of the new art."[73] While Jenkins and De Forest called for continued transmission in the broadcast band to maximize experimental television's geographic reach and potential audience, *Science News-Letter* summarized the RCA position, as given to the Federal Radio Commission (FRC) by engineer Julius Weinberger that "successful commercial television involves the transmission of distinct images of at least two human figures, and that a crude reproduction of a single face did not come within the qualification."[74] Weinberger consequently argued that the bandwidth demands precluded television's placement in the broadcast band, not incidentally maintaining a status quo highly favorable to RCA. Alexanderson's, Goldsmith's, and Weinberger's proclamations about what is needed to overcome crudity all speak to the notion of a perfect form for television, an essence in need of achieving. That is, crudity and primitivism worked to create a standard of perfection by signifying perfection's absence.

This was buttressed by the articulation of crudity and the primitive to evolutionary or developmental discourses in general usage and in the specific case of television by their role in spelling out a future for television based on an organized program of research and regulation, a vision that called for a timeline similar to the popularization and commercialization of sound broadcasting. Thus, Goldsmith invoked crudity in support of his claim that "a fair parallel is to compare television in its present state of development with ordinary broadcasting in its condition in 1921."[75] Similarly, *Science News-Letter*'s James Stokely compared the first television boom to the successful broadcast boom of the early 1920s, finding similar patterns of sporadic enthusiasm and technical (and formal) crudity: "The present state of television is almost identical."[76] As it happened, in 1929 television was twenty rather than ten years away from rivaling the state of radio at the time, but then again, television diverged from the radio track at roughly this same moment. While many of these reports were enthusiastic about television, by linking television's present state to earlier radio, they also had the potential to cool public enthusiasm for the television of the moment and suggest to both the public and their regulatory protectors the degree of improvement to be gained by patience, thereby helping to effect the derailment. There were, of course, significant innovations that came with delay, but the schedule of these improvements' introduction and the commercial and regulatory context in which they occurred were shaped by a standard of perfection.

These instances of tying crudity to a timeline for television are examples of but one subset of the ways in which the timeline for television was consistently articulated in terms of perfection. Whether placing perfection five or ten years off or "just around the corner," these statements established a notion of television's development as having a recognizable end and often specifically referred to that end as perfection.[77] This, in turn, was part of an even broader articulation of television in teleological terms that ranged from simply positing perfect television as the answer to crudity and the result of evolution to specifically articulating perfection in terms of television's uses.

Commentators presumed several specific uses of television that would require this perfection. By far the two most significant of these were conceiving of television as a visual supplement to the telephone (point-to-point) and, in the alternative, imagining it as a means for broadcasting (point-to-many) and viewing entertainment, information, and important events from the comfort of home.[78] Each of these presumed uses required a translation of meanings and social relations from existing media onto television. Telephony and broadcasting had both gone through periods of definition where alternate uses and meanings stemmed from what scholars in the sociology of technology call the "interpretive flexibility" of technological artifacts.[79] While telephone technologies had once been used for broadcasting-like purposes, by the 1920s the telephone had a fairly stabilized identity built around switched networks and individualized communication.[80] Likewise, as the media historian James Hamilton demonstrates, broadcasting had undergone several key shifts in meaning: from an agricultural practice with connotations of resistance to rationalized, capital and technology intensive methods of sowing crops; to a means of distributing evangelizing or reformist messages through pamphlets and other literature that sought to enlighten or transform the individual and society; to a system that served "as a means of achieving social solidarity via the centralized distribution of entertainment devices" that still required cultivation or mastery over the forces of nature.[81] According to Hamilton, broadcasting of the 1920s, though still bearing vestigial yet significant connotations of its earlier meanings (uncertain, popular, spiritually and socially transformative) and still not entirely stabilized, had at least settled into two related patterns, the distinction between "makers and audiences" and "a form of sociality paradoxically collective in its pervasiveness and individualized in its experience."[82] The articulation of television to the telephone or broadcasting would frame transmitted moving images according to the social and commercial logics of either medium, even as it opened those media up for redefinition and flexible interpretation. Thus, perfection could be rather different depending on the articulated medium, its attendant cultural values, presumed uses, and infrastructure.

Interestingly, for telephonic uses the technical barriers to higher-resolution mechanical scanning were diminished by fewer bandwidth limitations, and questions of perfection were a less pressing concern than recognition and constructing a solid business model and technical infrastructure. Indeed, in *Radio News* H. Winfield Secor described the Bell demonstration as consisting of "practically perfect reproductions."[83] For those who imagined visual broadcasting, however, questions of perfection harried predictions of television's imminence.

At this point television's technical perfection was primarily imagined in terms of its ability to present a wide range of shot-scales and to capture scenes under natural light. As the examples above attest, a host of articles decried mechanical television's limited shot-scale and in particular its reliance on close-ups. At the close of the 1920s the key comparison was between radiovision and the cinematograph.[84] Some of the earliest articles on television following Baird's and Jenkins's successful demonstrations invoked the motion picture as the salient comparison. For example, Dinsdale's aforementioned 1926 article in *Radio Broadcast* said of Baird's work, "The results are not yet as perfect as those seen on the motion picture screen, but such rapid progress has been made that the writer has no doubt in his mind that before long absolute perfection will be arrived at."[85] By 1930 the terms of comparison with the cinematograph were well established. In *Scientific American* Dinsdale argued for evaluating "the present television apparatus and methods" in terms of a future standard based on film:

"My guess is that television, for home entertainment purposes, will have to be capable of embracing a field of view, either indoors or outdoors, as extensive, complete, and flexible as is at present coverable by means of a motion picture camera, and the detail presented will have to be comparable with that of the motion picture also."[86] He reasoned that television must meet that standard because it would either compete with motion pictures as an entertainment form or provide a means of distribution for theatrical exhibition. Abetting this move to set the cinema as the key reference point in evaluating television's perfection was a set of assumptions about the public and television's commercial prospects, which were briefly mentioned by Dinsdale in this article but had been increasingly elaborated throughout the late 1920s.

These instances posited commercial release of television receivers as the logical end of television's course toward perfection. In some instances commentators proposed a contingent perfection, a balance between perfection and practicality as in Hugo Gernsback's statement: "If television apparatus is perfected to such a degree that it becomes a commercially practical instrument, the telephone companies will not hesitate to make an attachment that can be used on your desk or home telephone."[87] Notably, Gernsback, who distinguished radio movies from television, did not at this moment conceive of television as decisively a point-to-many device but rather saw a kind of Jazz Age Skype as one of television's possible futures and perhaps more practical because of the bandwidth available over wires. It's also worth noting that Gernsback imagined television as a device that would be separate from the sound unit, as a component rather than an integrated audiovisual box. This perspective was shared by many others. For example, in discussing a broadcast version of television, A. P. Peck noted, "[First,] the grade of perfection that the pioneers desire has not been reached, and the apparatus therefore is not on the market for general distribution. Secondly, this new development will not render present receivers obsolete. The reception of radio pictures calls for a separate receiver from that employed for the reception of voice and music."[88] Peck worked to simultaneously allay anxieties about prematurely passé purchases and acknowledge the fact that television was not inherently a singular appliance. Much work would be done over the following decade to "black box" television, to take the many devices involved in constituting the television set of the later twentieth century and make them seem like one thing, despite the fact that "set" implies an aggregation. This had much to do with the desire and perceived need on the part of manufacturing and broadcasting firms to deal in and with a discrete consumer product in a defined network of social and economic relations. RCA, its confederates, and peers had a plan to extend the radio model in a regulated and decisive fashion.

However, a group of television inventors (primarily independents like Jenkins) and their partners in broadcasting were in the process of launching an assault on this business model, deploying both pragmatic counterarguments to the rhetoric of perfection and the opportunity to buy television receivers and watch programming. Many of the counterarguments came from Charles Francis Jenkins, who called attention to the regulatory restraints placed on experimental television by the FRC and pointedly remarked on the philosophical absurdity of a standard of perfection. For instance, Jenkins praised the AT&T demonstrations, hailing Ives but then noting, "It must be remembered that any worker can obtain beautiful detail if given a sufficient number of communication channels, whether through space or over wires. The question of available communication channels is one which has seriously handicapped all of us engaged in developing an economical solution of television."[89] In a typical example of the latter, Jenkins was quoted as arguing, "We are repeatedly told that it will be from five to ten years before the public will have perfect television. One might just as truthfully say a thousand years, for perfection is never attained."[90] Several years later, in an article titled "What Constitutes Perfect Detail in Television?" William Hoyt Peck, another mechanical television inventor, further argued that purely quantitative measures of image resolution rested on unstated assumptions and proscriptions for screen size and distance from which the image would be viewed.[91] These theoretical arguments were accompanied by the establishment of regular mechanically scanned television broadcasts designed for enthusiast and public consumption, as Jenkins, Experimenter Publications/*Radio News*, and others sought to grow television on a model similar to sound broadcasting in the 1920s.

By late 1930, Jenkins and CBS in New York, Hollis Baird's Shortwave and Television Laboratories in Boston, and the Chicago Federation of Labor and the Western Television Corporation in Chicago were working to attract audiences with regularly scheduled entertainment programming via transmitters and receivers relying on mechanical scanning.[92] Throughout the early 1930s Jenkins and Western Television in particular pushed for limited commercialization. Jenkins attempted to use his broadcasts to promote his television receiver kits with the argument that it was a necessary adjunct to his experimental work.[93] The FRC did not concur. Vinton Hayworth, the manager of Chicago experimental station W9XAP, argued, "As seen from a production man's angle the fly-in-the-ointment of better presentation is the hesitation of the authorities to license television stations (that are now operating) for commercial sightcasting."[94] *The Review of Reviews* deemed the FRC's position on commercialization one of the "two great obstacles in the way of high quality home television."[95] Specifically, the problem was that experimental broadcasters had to rely on regularly licensed sound stations to provide audio for their sight broadcasts, but they were not allowed to transmit the video portion of popular commercial sound broadcasts, the content most likely to attract established radio audiences. Thus, W9XAP relied on WMAQ, the *Chicago Daily News* commercial station, but it could only provide sight service for the generally less popular sustaining programs. In Hayworth's words, "Our difficulty at W9XAP is conjoining with WMAQ. . . . If WMAQ's time is sold, then according to Federal Radio Law, W9XAP must go its own way transmitting a silent picture. And we do insist that silent television has served its purpose, which is mainly: 'Television is practical and practicable.'"[96] But it wasn't perfect.

The FRC steadfastly refused to license any form of commercial television broadcasting or simulcasting and simultaneously argued that lack of sustained public interest justified deferring commercialization. It held in its annual report for 1932 that most telecasts were "limited" to close-ups of one or two people, and the commission asserted, "This type of program, while of interest because of its novelty and usefulness for experimental work, has a very small amount of sustained 'look-in' interest."[97] Basing much of its argument on "what the public has been led to expect in the way of entertainment," the FRC declared that television programming could not live up to the standards set by "the technical improvements made during the last few years in sight-and-sound motion picture technique." Here the appeal is to "the mind of the public," which the commission presumes to know but cannot possibly trust with making decisions about watching commercial programs or purchasing receivers, and the standard is again the cinematograph. As mechanical television died on the vine, these two preoccupations with the public's desires for entertainment (however conflicted in conception) and with the approximation of other art forms, particularly cinema, would drive the shift from evaluative criteria rooted in notions of perfection and progress to the more fungible questions of quality and public interest.

Pondering the Electron: RCA and the Electronic Aesthetic

Within this framework quality was invoked alongside calls for progress, practicality, and perfection. Eventually, quality—in the sense of a quality good—would serve to negotiate among cultural and engineering ideals and commercial and consumer demands for practicality. In this, the edifice of television's technical quality rested not only on the aforementioned cultural work to articulate an essence of television but also on two precedents: the relatively uncontroversial uses of quality in engineering and commercial discourse about television and the radio industry's investment in *quality* as a marketing term from the mid-1920s on. As mechanical television was being dispensed with as a crudity, however, quality was also a central element in a technological aesthetic defining true television as electronic. The central proponents of this aesthetic in the United States were the engineers and executives of RCA and its subsidiary NBC, which adopted and inflected the discourse in the interests of their intellectual property and business models, but the various strands of thought and expression came to permeate the evaluation of television in the 1930s, becoming a form of common sense. By 1935, proper television would be electronically scanned and analog encoded and would remain so until digital's rise as the means to HDTV. Throughout these processes the definition of television's possible content and uses was further narrowed along lines that framed it as a device for one-way, centralized broadcasts of content evaluated by cinematic image standards. Questions of access, flexibility, and more radical notions of the free market were largely left unasked, while the policy implications of seemingly neutral issues of image quality or signal quality governed the development and release of US television.

During the 1920s and 1930s, television's quality was discussed primarily in terms of fidelity and image resolution. This had significant precursors in sound broadcasting's discourses of tone quality, selectivity, and power, as there was a fairly robust debate among radio enthusiasts and experts before the consensus prioritized tone over other sonic characteristics.[98] A general assessment of television's image reproduction in the 1920s tended to express a current standard of recognition and then articulate notions of progress. For example, *Science News-Letter* reported, "At present most of the radiomovies are in pantomime only but increase in 'picture quality' will come with experience and perfection of transmitting methods."[99] Other accounts anticipated amateur and enthusiast interest but warned of low quality, as in *Radio Broadcast*'s report: "Some stations are now on the air with television, and some are getting ready to go on, so that dyed-in-the-wool experimenters will find it hard to resist the temptation to set up apparatus to receive the broadcasts—even though their quality and program interest is negligible."[100] Beyond these general assessments, engineering and enthusiast reports tended to evaluate image quality quantitatively.

From early on there was a fairly strict equation of quality and quantity of dots per inch or of lines of resolution. This stemmed in part from the standards for evaluating facsimile systems. For example, an early report on television and still photographs by wire reported, "The quality of photographs transmitted by this system can be made especially good for magazine use. By increasing the speed of transmission, photographs can be sent at greater speed, for use in newspapers."[101] The print metaphor held for much of the 1920s. For example, after contrasting the "poorest of newspaper reproductions" on "cheap newsprint" with those of "this magazine and other popular ones on good paper," glossy *Radio Broadcast*'s R. Clarkeson argued that even with the lowest standard, "for an image of one foot, which wouldn't give much of a view of a spectacle such as a ball game, there would be 360,000 dots."[102] The resolution he describes is slightly better than the standard for the United States in the latter half of the twentieth century, but his analysis of the relationship between resolution and image size gets at one of the most bedeviling problems for 1920s television. The television sets and kits available for the home provided a small image that posed problems for any sort of group viewing. As Clarkeson noted in a later article, one could use a magnifying lens, which would "enlarge the image and decrease the quality but make the picture more easily seen by a group."[103] Clarkeson and others saw these issues of resolution and screen size as insuperable barriers to mechanical television, which could not move fast enough nor keep any picture element lit long enough to provide what they considered a quality picture.

The advocates of electronic television, particularly the employees and affiliates of RCA and NBC, seized on many of these discursive threads as they engaged in the process of externally fending off the challenge posed by mechanical television and internally debating what quality television would be. Despite claims about the quantifiable nature of technological quality—in its most reductionist form, the equation of a greater number of scan lines with higher quality—much of the evidence from NBC displays a dependence on the motion picture as a defining standard for evaluating the image. In a memo to NBC's president Merlin Aylesworth regarding the Western Television Corporation, NBC executive C. W. Horn stated, "Before television can claim popular fancy it must be sufficiently developed so that it can compete with ordinary quality motion pictures."[104] As RKO's fellow subsidiary under parent RCA, NBC was well poised to exploit film-image standards and, moreover, had a substantial disincentive to prematurely move into television and potentially compete with its corporate sibling, the weakest of Hollywood's integrated majors. Motion pictures were the basis for comparison within the research and development departments at NBC and RCA. In a paper on the workings of the iconoscope, a cathode-ray tube (CRT) basis for television image capture, Vladimir Zworykin noted, "The sensitivity of the iconoscope, at present is approximately equal to that of a photographic film operating at the speed of a motion picture camera. The resolution of the iconoscope is high, much higher than necessary for television of the highest quality."[105] Although Zworykin provides a quite detailed comparison and analysis of the number of picture elements involved in film and television, motion picture resolution—a resolution that standard-definition television would never reach—is simply assumed to be the standard. Setting the motion picture image as the standard for acceptable television picture quality is a far more historically specific question than counting the scan lines. Of course, for NBC, RCA, and Zworykin much of the argument was about shoring up the iconoscope as a core television technology and the privileging of electronic as opposed to mechanical television.[106]

In addition to the importation of benchmarks from the cinema, electronic television was held superior in terms of notions of liveness and immediacy as being essential to quality broadcasting. Zworykin provides a brief history of methods for image scanning in his 1933 paper: "This [scanning] involved purely mechanical complications in construction of sufficiently precise scanners, difficulties in increasing the number of picture elements and particularly in obtaining sufficient light. This last limitation actually introduced a stone wall which prevented the increase of the resolution of the transmitted picture to obtain the necessary quality and practically excluded all hope of transmitting an outdoor picture—the real goal of television."[107] Zworykin and others solved the scanning-speed challenges of mechanical television with an electronic scheme involving the CRT, which could achieve greater scanning speeds and, even more significant, did not require as much amplification. Zworykin regarded the most important gain of the CRT system as the constant polarization of the picture element when not being scanned by the electron gun.[108] In his paper he states that the CRT is "the only factor whereby real television can be achieved, if we understand by this term not only the transmission of a picture of limited definition under artificial conditions but the actual transmission of a picture of high resolution under reasonable or natural conditions of illumination."[109] In considering the ultimate goals of television to be the reproduction of views outside the studio, Zworykin echoed earlier conceptions of fidelity. As Sterne argues, regarding the dominant discourse of sound fidelity, "it is the measure of sound-reproduction technologies' product against a fictitious external reality."[110] In such a scheme the medium is evaluated in terms of fidelity or quality by its ability to be undetected. Consequently, the relative value of the medium is staked to its ability to efface the conditions and very fact of production. Devices do not do this on their own. Instead, processes of culture and language teach, cajole, and seduce us into thinking of the often very present indices of their production—such as scan lines or frames—as unremarkable.

Beyond fidelity, Zworykin's call for television to transmit "natural" or "outdoor" scenes posits liveness as essential to television. In fact, throughout Zworykin's writing on television there is paramount concern for relaying images immediately. This emphasis on live programming was an important concern for NBC throughout the 1930s, as shown by the company's investment in mobile broadcasting and remote broadcasts of such events as the World's Fair and the World Series. Obviously, such notions of quality played into NBC and RCA's superior intellectual property positions and established business practices in electronically networked sound broadcasting, but they also exploited a particular concept of television as a cultural institution, which could communicate with the nation immediately. This was not only a key element in attempts to forge national identity in an amalgamation of states inhabited by a heterogeneous mix of people but also a central tool by which broadcasting carved out a semirespectable place in American cultural hierarchies.[111] The presumed need for liveness relied as much on a set of assumptions about the audience as on notions of an order of media as described earlier by commentators such as Dreher, but the early work to inscribe expectations for television within a limiting taxonomy of uses served to naturalize what were essentially industrial and regulatory choices.

The link between electronic television and quality was further underwritten by quasi-aesthetic discourses of integrity, coherence, and elegance suggested by the scientific and commercial discourses detailed earlier in this chapter. Yes, you could kluge together a spinning disk and an array of photocells, as did Baird and Jenkins, but that was a mode of invention that harkened back to the tinkerer's contraptions—a mode that was inimical to the recently ascendant disciplines of engineering and scientific management. The lack of integration and the reliance on users required by mechanical synchronization were an affront to what Carroll Pursell identifies as the core values of these disciplines—efficiency, conservation, and organized research.[112] Moreover, mechanical television ran counter to what James Carey and John Quirk, drawing on Leo Marx, term "the rhetoric of the electrical sublime," in which the tensions of modernity and industrialization are seen to be mediated by the revolutionary promise of electricity.[113] Electronic television won this stage of what Udelson terms "the great television race" as much because it was a better fit culturally as because of a core technological superiority.

None of this is to say that electronic television did not offer specific technical advantages over mechanical television—in particular, it helped address thorny issues of speed, resolution, brightness, and what we might call user-friendliness. Nevertheless, the institutional construction of television technology at NBC and RCA during the early 1930s further demonstrates the ways in which this complex object/concept called television was invented as much through ideas about what it should be as the properties of a specific photoelectric cell. Moreover, these struggles over television's essential quality during the first boom set the pattern for the introduction of television technologies, a pattern the media historian William Boddy sees as marked by corporate obstructionism, regulatory high-handedness, and paternalistic assumptions about television's users that would be repeated in the buildup to the 1939 introduction of television at the New York World's Fair, in the corporate-government collaboration on the National Television Standards Committee (NTSC), and again in the television boom and freeze of the late 1940s and early 1950s with questions of color and UHF intermixture.[114] In each instance the institutions and individuals claiming authority over television eschewed both open architecture and the highest possible resolution, while arguing for standardization in the name of rational production and marketing. In the end the evaluative discourses such as contingent perfection, orderly development, and quality were used to install a set of technological standards regarded as mediocre for most of its half-century on the market.

The Problem of Historical Erasure

Mechanically scanned television is little remembered, and when it is, it is often subject to a way of thinking about the relationship between the present and the past that affirms the present. In his history of early television, for example, film and television director Michael Ritchie asserted, "Mechanical television died simply because it wasn't good enough. There was no conspiracy of big corporate monopolies; no Lone Ranger inventor stymied by short-sighted moguls. It just stank. The receivers sold for an affordable price, but people eventually were willing to pay a lot more for a cathode-ray receiver because it was real television and not some flickering fad in a hundred-dollar box. It would be nice to conclude that electronic-television pioneers learned something from their mechanical TV predecessors. They didn't. Electronic TV evolved separately."[115] It would be nice to conclude that a superior technology won a fair fight, as Ritchie claims, but the standardizing of television was a process of technical brinkmanship and diplomacy, imagination and negotiation, conspiracy and consensus that was fundamentally wed to a shared set of aspirations for television drawn from the well-cultivated popular imaginary. Yes, mechanical television was lower resolution than electronic television.[116] Yes, two decades later and after the nadir of the Great Depression there was a better market for higher-resolution, electronic television. Yes, the inventors of mechanical and electronic television came from two different pools. But Ritchie's assertions of causality are unprovable and may blind us to more significant questions.

We cannot know whether mechanical television would have failed on some sort of free market; broadcasting and electronic communications were by no means an unconstrained field of activity. There may not have been a confederacy of executives and bureaucrats gathering specifically to plot mechanical television's doom, but relatively centralized planning and standardization were regarded as good and proper under the ethos of corporate liberalism. The FRC made choices rooted in a protectionist conception of the public interest to deny commercial mechanical broadcasts. Executives and engineers at RCA, GE, and AT&T valued orderly development of an electronics and communications market in which they were dominant rather than a scramble to introduce a new medium. Whether mechanical television would have, should have, or could have succeeded does not matter so much as the fact that its failure came at a moment when preventing a more spectacular and public failure was seen as good policy. This approach to regulation and planning (and its justification through the evaluative discourses discussed in this and the following chapters) set the stage for the television to follow, while taking restraint of public choice as a given.

Mechanical television practice—and somewhat paradoxically the FRC's rationales for withholding regulatory sanction—also worked to tie television to a broadcast model. The technologies, practitioners, and even the aesthetics may have been different, but CBS, Hollis Baird, Jenkins, WRNY, the Western Television Corporation (WTC), the Chicago Federation of Labor (CFL), and Don Lee were engaged in broadcasting for home reception, commercial or not. The standards for granting licenses and denying commercialization drew on assumptions about broadcasting and entertaining audiences. As the next chapter will demonstrate, these acts of definition and regulation disciplined and slowly expunged other modes of interacting with television. If we regard a medium not simply as a technology but rather as a set of articulated social relations, values, institutions, and gadgets, then the endgame of mechanical television in the United States articulated the medium of television in terms of broadcasting to a much greater degree than a videophone or theater television. And this primacy of broadcasting would matter greatly for the television to follow.

The general thrust of television history treats mechanical television as a detour, with many histories barely addressing it at all.[117] This erasure is not solely a product of later history writing but in fact began almost immediately. In 1934 the *New York Times'* Orrin E. Dunlap quoted RCA-Victor vice president W.R.G. Baker as stating, "It may be said that one of the difficulties has always been in deciding just how 'good' a television picture in someone's living room would have to be to be considered a successful permanent means for providing entertainment. . . . There were a number of engineers and scientists who felt that the systems with which they were working represented 'television' . . . and any of them who urged the setting up of commercial services did so because they seemed convinced that nothing but inferior pictures would ever be available."[118] Acting as what modern journalism critics would call "a stenographer to power," Dunlap did not contradict these claims about the beliefs and intentions of inventors he had reported on throughout the late 1920s and early 1930s.[119] He went on to convey Baker's belief that "it is fortunate that 'television' of the 1930 variety was never introduced in a serious way" and that this television "would have been a novelty with no enduring or permanent value, and any systems set up would have certainly been discarded in a very short time."[120] Thus, contentious policy decisions were silenced and their results attributed to good fortune. By 1938, Frank C. Waldrop and Joseph Borkin wrote *Television: A Struggle for Power*, a story of television's history and present in which Charles Francis Jenkins's name never came up.[121] This silencing was never absolute. For example, Hubbell's *4000 Years of Television* gave Jenkins and the ancient Assyrians roughly equal coverage, but the story of television was the story of electronically scanned television's refinement and progress.[122]

The neglect of mechanical television in these histories is a testament to the power of evaluative discourses to legitimize television of the present and the affirmative imagination of its future. But those discourses were not solely—and sometimes not even primarily—directed at television. They were, and some still are, ways of talking and thinking about the modern world and how we interact with it. As the historian Lisa Gitelman observes in her study of writing machines, historical erasure of certain prior technologies is a function of the logics of progress and success and failure that help structure our sense of modernity. Those logics provoke a process of forgetting, in which successful technologies are regarded as part of a series of steps toward a better future while vanquished machines are written out of history and memory. This forgetting is not a mere side effect, not an incidental absentmindedness about what came before. Rather it helps sustain a sense of progress and modernity. As Gitelman notes, "As moderns and consumers, we have been conditioned to think that technologies supersede each other one by one, the present ever liberating us from the past."[123] The near and long-term historiographic pruning of the presumed dead branches of the tree of science and technology is thus a productive repression, enabling a sense of streamlined, iterative development.

But the liberation from the past that ostensibly ensures modernity constitutes a strange sort of freedom. Most baldly, not everyone wants to leave the past behind. Some people hold on to traditions, and they hold on to artifacts long after they have come to be considered outmoded.[124] While such obduracy in others may help the rest of us to feel modern—perhaps while averting our gaze from our own cherished rubbish—we are hemmed in as well. Among other things, this pattern of thought and representation has emphasized consumption over use. Conceiving of the public primarily as consumers has of course been productive for capitalism, but presenting the products of culture as there to be *used up* rather than *used* also frames the past and present in terms of exhaustion. The implication is that we must always be moving on, and this articulates a constrained way of thinking about past, present, and future while justifying systems that diminish certain types of risk by restricting choices. My next chapter will examine the systems of authority that set some of those limits and the words and behaviors of people who sought to test or transgress them.

2

Engendering Expertise
and Enthusiasm

The era of mechanical television was not just a moment of setting standards
and definitions that conformed to the sociocultural order. At the same time
that the medium's technical identity was being pinned down, television became
an important front in attempts to stabilize the relations among institutions,
enthusiasts, and the public—particularly the radio public—by means of several
interrelated systems of authority. Significantly, early television presented a paradoxical problem in which social and technical change was, on the one hand, a
more or less welcome harbinger of modernity and, on the other, a destabilizing
threat to a coalescing cultural and communicational order. The forms and practices of identity described for and claimed by experts, ascribed to or disputed
by amateurs, and presumed of audiences sought to rein in such instabilities,
adapting the patterns, pleasures, and penalties of inclusion and exclusion from
broader social life to the specific logics of radio and television.

During the decade prior to the Baird and Jenkins demonstrations of 1925,
electronic media in the United States had undergone at least two significant
industrial reorganizations that were accompanied by elaborations of a comple-
mentary regulatory framework. The first key industrial change was the formation of a national monopoly to manage US wireless telecommunications through
RCA, bringing the twin benefits of not being beholden to a subsidiary of British Marconi and consolidating the intellectual property portfolios considered
necessary for a truly excellent system. The second was the rapid displacement
of that point-to-point paradigm by broadcasting, which forced RCA and its confederates to renegotiate not only their contracts but also their understandings
of and arguments for an orderly approach to electronic communication. Over
the same period a rough political consensus emerged that wireless communication demanded coordination through government regulation. Congress claimed

authority over radio through the Radio Acts of 1910, 1912, and 1927, as an exercise of the constitutional power to regulate interstate commerce, and the general legislative prerogative to protect public safety.[1] After the 1927 act, introduced during a supposed time of "chaos" brought on by successful court challenges to previous regulatory schemes, the newly created Federal Radio Commission issued a series of orders and station reallocations that worked to contract the number of sound broadcasters and further the dominance of the commercial, sponsor-driven model of broadcasting in the United States.[2] These reorganizations and the developing regulatory system were molded, as broadcast historian Thomas Streeter has shown, by corporate liberalism's attempts to rationalize and legitimate a particular vision of technical and social order in which the technical and the social bled into one another and the former became a means for understanding the latter.[3]

As we have already seen, debates about television's supposed nature were tied to understandings of social relations, but appeals to and exercise of authority over television also directly articulated a faith in society's functioning as a sort of machine. As Streeter found, "metaphors of technology" conceived of the social world in terms of discrete parts that could be effectively balanced and integrated to keep the overall system in good working order. Leveraging the supposed political neutrality of machines, what constituted good working order became a sort of common sense, while whom that order benefited was spun in corporate liberal discourse through a particular conception of the public and its interest. While corporate liberalism certainly functioned ideologically to obscure the material and cultural stakes of decisions such as winnowing the number of broadcasters, it also facilitated compromise among institutional actors and mediated conflicts within capitalism and liberal thought. Thorny issues such as the contradiction between "individual freedom" and "the social good" and the public's existence as both a political force and a market for goods and services were framed as matters of alignment, calibration, and balance.[4]

As the precepts of corporate liberalism converged out of public relations and regulatory policy, the proposed agency of the public was limited. The public was thought and discussed not in terms of its rights but its need for a particular type of communication. This line of thought posed the public less in terms of freedom of expression and consumption than being able to opt in or out of a centralized communication and social system framed in paternalistic rhetoric and organized in the interests of corporations like RCA and AT&T.[5] By the time of the 1927 Radio Act, the notion of a "public interest" that could be discerned independent of political partisanship or private interest had become entrenched in regulatory thought. Moreover, as Mark Goodman and Mark Gring argue, influential members of the US government who were more or less aligned with Progressivism conceived the act with a greater emphasis on corporate responsibility and stability than freedoms of expression on the parts of citizens.[6] Whether conceived of as corporate liberals or Progressives, members of the corporate-regulatory circuit of authority habitually transposed conflict-laden political and cultural questions into administrative or technical matters, the purview of experts.[7] In this manner the regulatory regime could pretend and consider itself to be neutral despite the considerable political, economic, and cultural consequences of its decisions.

As technical authority merged with regulatory power, it carried with it literacies, norms, and internal hierarchies of the system of electrical expertise that had developed in the late nineteenth century. Even as corporate liberalism aspired to a functionalist neutrality, the heirs to the group historian Carolyn Marvin calls "electricians" persisted in policing the bounds and expounding on the values of their identity as electronic authorities. Although some elements of that identity stemmed from the assumed dominance of white, patriarchal masculinity, Marvin found that "late-nineteenth-century electricians constituted a self-conscious class of technical experts seeking public acknowledgment, legitimation, and reward in the pursuit of their task. Their efforts to invent themselves as an elite justified in commanding high social status and power focused on their technological literacy, or special symbolic skills as experts. They distinguished themselves from mechanics and tinkerers, their predecessors, and from an enthusiastic but electrically unlettered public by elevating the theoretical over the practical, the textual over the manual, and science over craft."[8] Such tactics of distinction persisted with technical elites in the twentieth century and were further underwritten by processes of institutionalization through education and governmental or corporate agency.

The tinkerers were never entirely vanquished, however, and were somewhat revitalized by the culture of amateur experimentation in wireless. Moreover, as a market for both electronics and stories about sound and visual radio, electronic enthusiasts were an essential constituency in successfully projecting authority over wireless. At the same time in the mid-1920s, easy to use, consumer-ready, and decorous radios came to be seen as the feminized and simplified use of wireless. For some users this redefinition, commodification, and feminization of the radio receiver was unwelcome, provoking dreams of new frontiers for enthusiast practice and mastery in television. As these cultural trends converged, representations of and thought about television and expertise sought to conscript and discipline electronic enthusiasms. In doing so, a persistent strategy was to explain the system of authority and televisual order in terms not only of technocratic standards and institutional legitimacy but also of gender and generation—a particular framework in which metaphorical and actual claims about women and children propped up certain knowledges, practices, and technologies as the domain of men.

This chapter performs an archaeology of the opposition between the proposed identities of authorities and audiences for American television in the 1920s and early 1930s. It examines television's framing within a paradigm that shrank the liminal spaces that had been occupied by amateurs in early sound broadcasting. The discursive trends of the mid-1920s placed television within an increasingly hierarchical system of distinctions between the authority of inventors, engineers, and regulators and the presumed passivity of the public. These distinctions were framed in terms of gender and age in both figurative explanations of policy choices and literal descriptions of radio's and television's authorities and users. This period saw an increasing professionalization of radio and television and in particular began to build narratives buttressing institutional norms that would benefit the established powers in American radio. Nevertheless, as the rest of this chapter details, the developing system of American broadcasting had to court and control television enthusiasms. In defining user relationships to television, questions of age and gender would remain key, but the alternative imaginings and practices of very early television by television amateurs and electronics enthusiasts both embraced and contradicted such norms. These contestations spoke not only to the other things television could be but also to the different ways in which the people could make television their own and (complicating overly optimistic visions of alternative media uses) the contradictory means by which groups sought to foreclose on others' claims to competing visions of television. Attempts to rationalize and regulate television and its uses ultimately drew heavily on patriarchal presumptions and paternalistic values, and even those attempts to act out against paternalism relied regularly on gender and other hierarchies to distinguish electronics enthusiasts from mere listeners and would-be lookers-in.

Authority and Invention

By June 1927, television had by almost all definitions been demonstrated publicly. Whether John Logie Baird, Charles Francis Jenkins, Ernst Alexanderson, or Herbert Ives—to name only the prominent Anglophonic inventors—gets credit is a matter of considerable historiographic debate, and no small measure of national prejudice, and ultimately stands or falls on the definition of television employed. As much as the struggle over television prior to 1935 was about defining evaluative terms, however, it was also about who had the authority to use them. Television was brought into being as a set of technological artifacts and practices by inventors, industrial research scientists and engineers, manufacturers, capitalists, experimenters and amateurs, and governmental regulators. The degree to which each of these parties were able to dictate the terms of television's cultural existence, and particularly its prospects for popularity and commercial success, depended in part on their ability to wield at least one of several types of author-ity in the public sphere. These assertions of authority relied on a specific set of tropes and tactics, which heeded the workings of deeply embedded cultural hier-archies but also stressed the distinctive modes of discourse that would become part of the standard repertoire of televisual power plays: disciplining invention, institutionalizing electrical expertise, and marginalizing users and audiences.

Individualist conceptions of invention presented something of a problem for the circuit of authority being formalized around wireless. As radio was being defined and regulated as a corporate enterprise and communal activ-ity, the achievements of individual inventors disrupted notions of coordi-nated innovation and suggested compelling counteridentities to the emergent dichotomy between agents of organized industry and mere users or consum-ers. Inventors like Baird and Jenkins demonstrated that there were other paths both more competitive and cooperative than the favored corporate route to technological development. Working outside the strictures of the electronics giants, these inventors sought to leverage their early achievements to establish not only the priority required by intellectual property law but also the cultural and industrial legitimacy of having gotten there first in order to define the medium.[9] Moreover, their journalistic surrogates presented a scrappy model of innovation and publication in which the inventors were ready to stand up for themselves and their devices.[10] For example, *Radio Broadcast*'s Alfred Dinsdale first noted the inability of most "investigators" of television "to back their claims by an actual demonstration," before both tweaking and asserting authority with his praise of Baird: "Unheralded by claims, and scoffed at by many skeptical 'authorities,' Mr. J. L. Baird has arrived with his apparatus, the result of years of patient effort, and has actually given demonstrations innu-merable to scientists, press men, and curious visitors."[11] It would seem difficult to deny the authority claimed by demonstrating a television device, and, in large measure, it was difficult, but only for a short period in the mid-to-late-1920s. Baird and Jenkins had produced a referent for the sign "television," and this gave them some indisputable power. Moreover, they had the compelling exemplar of sound broadcasting's collaborative interaction between inventor and users to argue for a relatively open and popular development of distance vision. Jenkins, in particular, envisioned a host of individual inventors as the means to televisual development. Although they could not be silenced in their attempts to articulate a vision for television's future, however, in the long run the inventors, investors, and institutions that enjoyed these early successes in the struggle for authority would lose out to claimants to scientific and engi-neering expertise and guardianship of the supposedly benighted public.

The first step in this process was to discipline conceptions of the genius inventor and make it serve the interests of modern industry. Some of the key

heroes in the mythology of American invention were industrialists and innovators in corporate research, Thomas Edison being the foremost example. But
as the historian Susan Douglas has noted, the mythology of the inventor as a
man with a Horatio Alger work ethic and technical skills to match held considerable cultural purchase, especially within the field of radio, where inventors like Marconi and De Forest achieved dramatic innovations without the
backing of large-scale corporate research.[12] This myth was specifically linked
to cultural constructions of the masculinity of radio amateurs. Imaginings of
radio and television users in terms of gender were crucial in asserting authority
over broadcasting, but first, the rearticulation of technical accomplishment in
terms of serving the civil order and civilization in general, as well as fulfilling
the promise of science—concepts themselves enmeshed in gender and other
cultural hierarchies—deserves attention.

One strategy, the assertion of television as a shared aspiration, worked to
frame the inventor's accomplishment as a more modest realization of a common dream. For example, General Electric research engineer Ernst Alexanderson used a scene from the George Bernard Shaw play *Back to Methuselah* (1921),
in which a future British leader uses a device to communicate by sight and voice
"with his various cabinet ministers several hundred miles away," to demonstrate television's shared imaginary invention.[13] Alexanderson asserted, "The
new things that civilization brings into our lives *are not created or invented by any-
body in particular*."[14] Theorizing a mixture of destiny and prescience, he averred
that engineers and inventors simply render imminent ideas "practical." Alexanderson's observation on the nature of technical innovation, when considered
on its own, is probably best regarded as a display of humility and thoughtful circumspection by a widely respected inventor. Personal intention aside, however,
this statement was delivered by the head research engineer for one of the largest electronics manufacturers cum intellectual property concerns in the United
States. In that context it was part of a larger discursive pattern that can be traced
from nineteenth-century utterances such as "necessity is the mother of invention" and "invention is 90 percent perspiration and 10 percent inspiration" to
statements in the early 1930s that sought to integrate specific technological
innovations within a story of incremental rather than radical change.[15] That is,
the individual genius theory of invention, while certainly congruent with the
broad structures of capitalism and appeals to the entrepreneurial spirit, posed
a quasi-populist threat to the ideological and financial bases of oligopolistic
industry and consolidated commerce in the United States, and as a result, it was
brought under systems of control.

The thrust of this discursive push was to put the unruly genius in a bottle
and advocate mastery of invention through professionalism, as established
by the pursuit of education, organized and corporately funded research, and

careful expression of modest innovation in the disciplinary languages of science, engineering, and law. As the nineteenth century moved decisively into
the twentieth, the conception of the inventor as provident outgrowth of boyish enthusiasm and the free market was gradually supplanted by theories of
invention that were more friendly to large-scale corporate capitalism and the
hybrid market-command economies that would characterize American mass
communication practice in the twentieth century. Following Jenkins's predictions, American television would see a small fleet of "boy" inventors such as
Hollis Baird, Ulysses Sanabria, and most notably Philo T. Farnsworth founder
while trying to gain a beachhead from which to compete with the established
and better capitalized manufacturing firms. In the main, they would fail, and
invention would become the purview of organized corporate research. Likewise,
between 1927 and 1933, *Popular Science*, *Popular Mechanics*, *Radio Broadcast*, and
Radio News, among others, encouraged modes of amateur experimentation and
popular reception that would ultimately be rendered incoherent by their failure
to maintain relations between television practitioners and the public in keeping with the rapidly coalescing orders of televisual commerce and regulation.

Science and invention were to be placed in a commercialized public
sphere. In 1927, Herbert Hoover, at the time secretary of commerce, declared
that "the day of genius in the garret has passed, if it ever existed," and "the
greatest discoveries of the future will be the product of organized research
free from the calamity of such distraction" as child care, cooking, and teaching.[16] Science was to be freed of domestic shackles to serve industry. Moreover,
Hoover's call for this peculiar emancipation drew what were becoming increasingly salient distinctions between "pure science research" and its application
through invention and engineering. Thus, while *Science News-Letter* celebrated
Hoover's address with the headline "Free Geniuses, Says Hoover," the thrust of
his message worked toward undermining the genius in favor of organization
and professionalism. By 1933, H. Olken, in a *Scientific American* article praising
"Invention—A Coming Profession," stated the new wisdom bluntly: "Invention is
regarded the world over as a matter of genius—a rare mysterious ability to create. Such is not the case; invention is not a rare and mysterious faculty present
only in geniuses, but a faculty which all intelligent persons possess."[17] Arguing
that "inventive faculties . . . can be provided by proper education," he returned
to the trope of opportunity: "There is an urgent need in modern industry for
an abundant, constant, and dependable supply of inventions. In other words,
modern industry demands the services of an inventing profession." Invention
was to be professionalized, and Olken went on to argue that, based on contemporary practice, the professional requirements of invention were and should
remain distinct from engineering. Most commentators, however, saw a need for
electronics enthusiasm to conform to technical discipline broadly construed.

One method for imposing this discipline was an appeal to the imperatives of intellectual property law. In *Radio News*, for example, Jay Hollander tried to persuade amateurs to be more professional by citing the US Patent Office's need for conformance to engineering standards in the submission of data when he described a typical experimenter complaint: "But the main dirge has to do with a number of failures of ideas in the hands of their originators, only to result in extreme success in the laboratory of a neighbor."[18] The author argued that a thorough engagement with theory and expression of ideas in the language of science is necessary for the experimenter or amateur to protect priority for intellectual property purposes. In another piece, Hollander reminded enthusiasts of the imperative of "doing things up to a proper scientific brown with the proper garnishing of notes and curves" and dangled the hope of riches through royalties before concluding that "the moral of this tale is: Be a scientist first and an operator afterward, instead of *vice versa*."[19] In these 1925 articles, Hollander envisioned the supplementation and even supersession of amateur sound-radio practice with science.

Nevertheless, he still argued for practices specific to the radio amateur's practical needs and sense of identity. For example, in describing the proper process of documentation he also argued for the application of science in terms of efficiency, describing good notes as "a very definite and concise essay on the operation of certain apparatus being used in an effort to make certain improvements of the known methods" that would provide "clarity of purpose" and "make the end just seventeen and three-quarters easier to gain." Wryly invoking amateur frustrations with their spectrum and time allocations, he recommended, "Come on, the old physics and the reports of the Royal Society are pretty interesting. Read 'em while waiting for the broadcasters to finish."[20] In calling for attention to professional standards, Hollander confronted one of the broader cultural challenges faced by the advocates of amateur radio, the portrayal of the amateurs as immature boys and therefore illegitimate claimants to authority in radio.[21]

Yet the relationship between a deligitimated boyhood and other modes of masculinity was necessarily complex as a result of both the heterogeneity of amateurs and enthusiasts and a continuing appeal to fun. For example, while exhorting the amateur to grow up, Hollander put forth his argument in a playful, masculinist mode suggestive of juvenile adventure literature, hailing his readers as "hearties" or "gents" and commanding, "Now, me bucks, lean low and let me whisper a first-rate panacea into your stretching ears." He then followed with a worry that such amateur practices as pinning the call letters of stations to the walls of the radio "shack" looked like childish play with the alphabet and opined, "The ham should seek more pertinent fields where his great energy and ingenuity will produce something more valuable to future generations than mere wall paper. *Ergo*, let him start some real science."[22] These attempts to use science to reconcile amateur art and identity with the imperatives of capitalism ran up against two obstacles: the desire to be an "operator" first (along with a corollary predilection for defying authority) on the part of many hams and the prior and jealous claim on science by the fraternity of engineers.

By the late 1920s, the boy in the radio shack's journey to being a man in the lab was increasingly tied to education and credentialing as an engineer.[23] The promiscuity of letters offered by a world of call signs was replaced by the veneration of a far smaller pantheon of acronyms such as IRE and EE. While the Institute of Radio Engineers was central to the regulation of sound and visual broadcasting practice through the setting of standards and the FRC's dependence on its engineering staff,[24] the underlying gatekeepers to engineering were educational institutions. The historian of technology Carroll Pursell argues that with the growing influence of science, engineering, and scientific management, technical practices that once enjoyed a diverse constituency became, in the early twentieth century, the narrow purview of those with access to a particular form of scientific training and credentials.[25] By the late 1920s, radio-enthusiast publications were brimming with advertisements for "Study at Home" training, enticing would-be inventors with such courses as the Radio Institute of America's "Achieve Success in Radio," the National School of Visual Education's "Movies Teach You Electricity," and the National Radio Institute's "Be a Radio Expert."[26] These advertisements told of the riches and class ascension to be won through the technical training of correspondence courses, but these promises were also accompanied by articles that sought to distinguish between fandom and technical handiwork, on the one hand, and university sanctioned engineering and science, on the other. The mundane version of this distinction was attention to credentials and honorifics, but more overt and pointed articulations of the hierarchy that held the scientist in esteem above the operator came into play as amateurs sought or were encouraged to seek a college education.

It is worth pausing here for a moment to clarify several points before moving on to the specific manifestations of the college argument. First, it would be a mistake to view advocacy of a college education as simply cover for buying a title that confers status. Education is a disciplinary practice that works to produce a specialized subjectivity more apt to produce statements and artifacts that conform to a given discursive regime. That is, we should expect a trained electrical engineer to be both more likely to develop electronic devices that subscribe to professional and industrial utility and more able to describe an invention in terms that garner it scientific and legal legitimacy. Nevertheless, we should recognize that the past is full of people who fashioned gadgets that worked but did not properly fit the technological identities proscribed by a particular discursive regime, and these people tended to be pushed aside, both by their contemporaries and by history. Second, while journalists, inventors, executives, and others who deign to speak for and about technology need to establish credibility, the systems of discursive authority that underwrite the practice of establishing credibility were somewhat one-sided in this instance, conferring greater authority to intellectual property holders, university- and government-sanctioned experts, and the agents of large electronics interests than the users who bought or built their sets and were, in legal theory, the owners of the air. Third, although discursive authority did not somehow trump physics, the goals, standards, and limits set by scientific, legal, and commercial authority narrowed the scope of what was possible far more effectively than the so-called "laws" of physics ever could. Fourth, these discursive limits are not insuperable, but they are quite strict. Fifth, and finally, in describing these contesting claims to authority, I find it more productive to think in terms of a multivalent discursive struggle over the power to speak for and about radio and television technology than to rest in the reductive oppositions set forth by various parties involved in the struggle. That is, while some advocates of university engineering education sought to marginalize radio amateur and fan practice in favor of maintaining the prerogatives of science and industry, the binary distinction drawn by their statements certainly did not account for the diverse continuum of radio practices. Likewise, the snugly tailored identities offered by those discourses did not necessarily wear comfortably on the men and women invested in them.[27]

Nevertheless, the push to make the university the seat of technical authority was well under way by the late 1920s. Articles in the enthusiast press giving advice to the young man seeking to enter the radio profession demonstrate the ways in which institutionalization worked to discipline both technical practices and ways of being. For example, in 1928 Carl Dreher of *Radio Broadcast* surveyed professors of electrical engineering at nine universities on behalf of readers who wanted to work in radio. He characterized these readers as "young men who feel the need for adding to their knowledge but lack formal preparation," possessing little understanding of what university study meant.[28] He further asserted, "The relation of radio engineering to the more fundamental divisions of technology is also frequently misapprehended, the importance of radio being naturally exaggerated in the minds of some of its devotees." Certainly, readers who lacked access to institutions of higher education would likely lack the necessary information to translate their interest in radio into a meaningful course of study, but with his claim to know the minds of radio's "devotees," Dreher pushed well beyond science's systems of knowledge and into the realm of cultural stereotype, however well intentioned.

In this article Dreher, despite claims to equanimity, clearly favors what he calls the "broad-training policy" of general scientific education as put forth by Prof. J. H. Morecroft of Columbia University. Morecroft averred, "It is extremely foolish for a young man to specialize in a specific branch of engineering work before he is well aware of his aptitude and of the opportunities awaiting him in any special field."[29] Although the underlying philosophy may be pedagogically accurate, its expression points to a power dynamic that extends beyond that of teacher and student, positioning radio's fans as fools. Morecroft further justified Columbia's policy by noting that it fit the personnel demands of corporations: "Our largest communication company, for example, does not desire to have men trained in specialized communication theory and practice." In this plan, communication engineering and the application of science to sound and sight transmission comes at the end of or even following a course of study. Dreher concludes approvingly: "The philosophy underlying this attitude is that industry is so highly specialized that it is hopeless to give a man more than the broad fundamentals at school. . . . But if at some time a man wants to learn something special in a superficial way, no harm is done, provided he knows what he is getting, and does not take it for more than what it is."[30] While tacitly acknowledging that radio enthusiasm was often a deeply felt and personal practice rather than an abstract application of professional skills and values, Dreher unambiguously favored placing his hypothetical student in the position of seeking a job rather than fulfillment. He framed the question in careerist terms, asserting the economic advantages of pursuing a degree in engineering rather than radio training through extension programs.

In a *Radio News* article fifteen months later, Dreher took the argument further, hypothesizing two aspiring radio practitioners—John, the operator, and Tom, the engineer. Taking both protagonists from high school through further education, employment, marriage, and terminal job opportunities, Dreher argued for Tom's life path. In Dreher's hypothetical, Tom has the resources to buy an education in a "first-rate electrical engineering course, with a degree of specialization in radio and audio principles, acoustics, telephony, and the like," that is, a general degree in communications engineering.[31] Unsurprisingly, Tom, the man with the greater resources, particularly technological and cultural capital, is recognized to have better prospects. His superior earning potential is justified by his ability to comprehend and coordinate a wide range of technical endeavors:

> As specialization increases his gift of integration becomes more and more valuable. If Tom has that gift, there is no reason why his income should not grow—he may be good for $20,000 a year, say, when he is forty. . . .
> He need not know where the wires run on all the terminal boards, but he must know the salient weaknesses (even more than the strong points) of the equipment which is built or operated under his jurisdiction, and he must know the strengths and weaknesses of his men just as thoroughly. In other words, an engineering executive is not a man who coordinates a

lot of things he knows nothing about, but an engineer who coordinates a
lot of things about which he knows the salient facts.[32]

Indisputably, being born with resources has its advantages; nevertheless, the
discursive work being performed to laude technical training while steering
radio enthusiasts away from pursuing a course of specialization is striking,
especially in its reliance on hypothesizing the radio professional and holding
him to imaginary career goals, where salary seems to be the measure of a man.
Moreover, in holding "administrative ability" to be the climactic skill—the mark
of maturity—Dreher's abridged bildungsroman neatly described the synthesis
of technical expertise, bureaucratic efficiency, and rationalized sociality valued
by corporate liberalism. This way of being a modern man offered both agency
and acceptance in a cohering social and technical order. Those comforts were
not on such easy offer to other identities as radio and television regulation was
formalized through legal and especially technical doctrine.

Vanquishing the "Freak Whistle and Confusion"

Vesting power in engineering and then using that authority to set corporate or
public policy based on predictions about content, consumption, and culture
was typical within the systematic advocacy of cultural hierarchy by the major
firms and regulatory bodies as culminated in the 1927 act. As evaluative discourses ran this circuit of authority, they carved out a distinct channel in which
established forms of social dominance reinforced contemporary understandings of the electronic order as a realm of efficient technical administration.
Within the regulatory framework erected on the foundation of the Radio Act of
1927, a clear hierarchy was set forth, distinguishing "prominent persons" from
"the public," from "the listeners," and from "the fans."[33] Moreover, within the
group at the top there was an interlocking coalition of corporate, legal, and
technical interests that put forth the majority of voices at the early hearings
where the future of American broadcasting was to be regulated.

Forty-six "Prominent Persons Offer[ed] Suggestions" at the public hearings held March 29 through April 1, 1927, shortly after the commission was
appointed.[34] Roughly equal numbers of commercial broadcasters (six) and representatives of electronics manufacturing firms or associations (eight), along
with their engineers (six) and attorneys (eight), made up just over three-fifths
of the witnesses. Of the rest there were several representatives of educational
(three), labor (one), and religious (one) broadcasters, spokespersons for wired
communication companies (two), as well as several agents of government
bodies (three) and an assortment of interested parties from publishing, trans-
portation, and citizens groups and radio societies (seven). Notably, the only
person identified as an inventor was Charles Francis Jenkins, who was there to

advocate for immediate opening of the airwaves for television broadcasts by experimenters in collaboration with an unknown host of amateurs. In contrast to most other witnesses, Jenkins hoped to replicate the environment of popular technological and programming ferment that characterized the utopian imaginings and realizations of early sound broadcasting in the United States.

This was not to be. While television enjoyed a brief moment of regulatory sanction as a popular art in the early days of the FRC, it came under increasing fire for its encroachments on sound broadcasting and its failures to live up to higher-resolution imaginings. Although the FRC initially allowed for some experimental television transmissions in the AM broadcast band during late 1928, these were limited in duration and banned from the period between 6:00 and 11:00 p.m.[35] The purpose of the time restrictions was to prevent television signals from disrupting nighttime radio by subjecting listeners scrolling the dial to the high-pitched tone that resulted when a video signal was decoded by an AM radio. For some on the commission these restrictions did not go far enough. Chairman Robinson dissented and invoked "the best engineers," specifically citing claims by the Bureau of Standards' Dr. Dellinger and RCA's head engineer, Dr. Goldsmith, to argue, "All necessary experimentation to forward and perfect television could take place between the hours of midnight and six in the morning. Why disturb that which the public has become used to, by freak whistle and confusion? The forwardness of manufacturers could well be curbed for the present."[36] Chairman Robinson's position quickly won out, and on January 14, 1929, the FRC issued General Order No. 56, pushing television on the broadcast band into a smaller time allocation, 1:00 to 6:00 a.m.[37] By 1930 the articulation of federal policy on television had been relegated to the FRC's engineering division, which declared, "The commission did not recognize visual broadcasting as having developed to the point where it has real entertainment value," and pinned licensing and frequency assignments to the degree to which an applicant "was a qualified experimenter and could be expected to contribute to the advancement of the art."[38] This statement set the pattern for the remaining policy statements by the FRC, placing television under the jurisdiction of the engineering department and refusing to make affirmative statements about the specific characteristics that would constitute "real entertainment value." This policy created substantial disincentives to the "advancement of the art" by rendering television's commercial prospects entirely speculative in the midst of the drastically adverse investment climate brought on by the Great Depression. Independent, entrepreneurial television was unlikely to take root and grow.

As we saw in the first chapter, television's affirmative imagining took place within a tightly defined set of expectations drawn from specific analogies to what were considered adjacent arts and sciences. Moreover, the imagining of television was also constrained by discourses of legitimacy that sought to render television a specific act of educational, corporate, or governmental authority. Nevertheless, the very fact of invention and demonstration opened up sites for struggle over television's future and attempts to harness its utopian potential for popular ends. This is why early announcements of successful television demonstrations display a schizophrenic compulsion to assert television's impossibility or impracticality. For example, a *Scientific American* article titled "Practical Television Demonstrated" claimed that financial and logistical barriers "render entirely imaginative any predictions as to the commercial possibilities which this demonstration portends."[39] Here, television was both technically achieved and impossible as commercial practice. Consequently, these very acts of imagination—of engineer and user, of content and system— were themselves often working to delimit televisual possibilities.

Attempts to confine and lock down televisual practice trumped bold imaginings and the adventurous embrace of populist potential, all in the name of consumer safety. While boyishness was mobilized as a source of idealized pleasure for the male engineer or radio enthusiast, it was simultaneously used to strip noncommercial practitioners of their claims to the spectrum. To start, it is worth noting that advocates for specific uses of the high frequencies persisted in relying on the image of the child to justify their particular recommendation—following the pattern noted by media historian Susan Douglas. For example, Dr. Dellinger, in calling for a "factor of safety" in the development of the high frequencies for sound transmission, asserted that the public was misled by "sensational reports": "It is true that a boy in the United States will occasionally communicate with a boy in Australia, using 50 watts or even 5 watts. But such communication is of no use commercially."[40] Although Dellinger's use of "safety" is more in keeping with the need for certain technical tolerances to ensure successful transmission under a wide array of circumstances, he moves directly to the trope of protecting the public from misinformation, or at least misinference, by the boy who cried DX. In a similar vein Dr. Goldsmith argued for relatively wide bands in the high frequencies for experimental television as "clearly the minimum basis of a true television service of permanent interest to the public. It may be anticipated that uninformed or nonconservative television broadcasters would transmit an endless series of wobbly, blurred, fuzzy or silhouette pictures, with bad flicker and of limited area. This would be called 'television,' but would truly be no more a useful example of television than a child's wavering drawing is a masterpiece of art by Rembrandt. 'Television,' so called, from irresponsible sources will benefit only the oculists of the United States in proportion as it ruins the eyesight of the public 'lookers-in.'"[41] Here, childish "television" must be developed into a useful art by responsible parties with the interests of the public and its health at heart. These presumptions stemmed from conceptualizations of the public as naive and in need of guidance.

Many of the declamations on television terminology that I detailed in chapter 1 used the device of the uninformed member of the public to assert linguistic authority over distance vision, and they persisted into the late 1920s and beyond as both a common imagination of the audience and a gambit in public relations by electronics firms. The broadcast audience served as a particularly effective screen onto which institutions could project their interests because in some very significant ways they were already a product of the imagination. As the media scholar John Hartley argues, audiences are "invisible fictions," stories that get told about the aggregate of actual viewers in order to impose the semblance of commonality.[42] Hartley finds that a key mode of imagining the audience is "paedocratization," in which the audience is constructed as feminine and childlike and thus needing corporate and government protection.[43] Although Hartley wrote of a later era, there is congruence between the "paedocratic regime" he describes and the logics of early twentieth-century corporate liberalism. Moreover, this discursive tack allowed institutions to frame assertions of authority and self-interest as necessary protection or education of the public. For example, in December of 1928 D. E. Replogle lamented on behalf of the Radio Manufacturers of America (RMA) that "terminology and medium of transmission are points in which the public should be instructed." He argued that the public misunderstood the nature of most television demonstrations, as they conflated wired television with the more difficult radio transmission and misapprehended the difference "between sending photographs by radio, the sending of images from motion picture films, and the far more difficult feat of actual television."[44] Replogle's comments were part of a larger effort in the late 1920s by the RMA, the National Electrical Manufacturers Association (NEMA), their members (the major manufacturing concerns), and several leading science and business journalists both to curb public enthusiasm for television and define television in terms that would complement or at least not subvert their interests.

Foremost among these interests was the growth of sound broadcasting and the instruments necessary for its growth. Television posed a threat to a still consolidating commercial broadcasting order, for which hard work, or at least consistent effort bellying up to the regulatory trough, was only beginning to pay enormous dividends. In this context the established manufacturers spun defensively with regard to television. For example, the spokesman for NEMA moved to save radio's hold on the airwaves from the threat of pictures, arguing that "the interest of the listener should be carefully safeguarded."[45] A key technical concern mobilized by the sound broadcasting interests was the "freak whistle" that occurred as a result of still picture signals being demodulated by a radio receiver. For example, NEMA argued for experimentation only in "obscure hours" because "the broadcasting of television and still picture signals, being of a disagreeable character when reproduced through the loud speaker, should not be permitted to intrude at any time upon the listener's regular tone entertainment service."[46] This line of argument is typical of the careful framing of the public interest and the notion of service occurring during the late 1920s as radio's corporate and regulatory order was coalescing.

Manufacturers and regulators further asserted that protecting the public interest meant preserving the public's future ability to be interested in television by keeping it out of view in the present. In this vein H. Davis, vice president of Westinghouse, lauded broadcasting for public service and teaching "the public to expect the very highest grade of programs and quality in program transmissions," while worrying they would not "be patient enough to pass through another similar gawkish period of evolution with television," as had occurred with radio.[47] Thus, he concluded "that the gawkish period in the development of television should be passed in the laboratories." Similarly, the aforementioned dissent by Commissioner Robinson argued for saving the public from its enthusiasms and worried that the premature consumer "is so likely to be so disappointed that he will not only damn the Commission" but also "junk his new-fangled contrivance for which he has paid the advertised price," thereby spoiling the future potential for television.[48] Robinson's concerns, like those expressed in the previous few paragraphs, can be understood simply as expressions of cautious or conservative industrial and government policy. What stands out in all of these comments, however, is not so much the claim that television is inchoate, but a set of assumptions about the public's need for guidance, particularly as those assumptions were informed by a reconceptualization of broadcasting's public as audience members and consumers rather than users—like the radio amateurs—or citizens.

Some commentators did confront the examples of sound broadcasting's relatively open early history, baldly proclaiming that radio's current public was less worthy of evaluating television than that which had responded to wireless telegraphy several decades prior. Thus, Lawrence W. Corbett argued in *Radio Broadcast* that Marconi "appealed to a far more critical public (and then only to highly-trained engineers) than Baird" and asserted the latter was "aided by colorful and exaggerated reports in a general press that knows nothing more about his invention than the fans who will be expected to invest in his televisors."[49] This despite a body of amateurs catered to by multiple enthusiast publications—including the one publishing his article—which hailed their readership as technically competent and a body constituting a substantial intermediary group between experts and consumers. As a result of the entrepreneurial development of a readership for radio matters, the group of existing and cultivated amateurs, experimenters, enthusiasts, and fans was undoubtedly larger than those earnestly engaging with Marconi's invention; moreover, they were steeped in several decades of expectations about seeing at a distance.

Nevertheless, the public was assumed to be too fickle and inattentive to machinery, and not coincidentally television's presumed public was insinuated to be overwhelmingly female. Alongside the broadcasting boom, representations of the gender, age, and presumed expertise of radio's users underwent a steady shift. The historian Richard Butsch found a shift in cover art for *The Wireless Age* from photographs of devices to illustrations of female listeners in familial or romantic settings beginning in 1922.[50] While this reimagination met with a backlash in some radio magazines such as *Radio News*, it tracked with a shift in the conception of the radio industry.[51] In 1929 Orrin E. Dunlap claimed in the *New York Times* that "radio is now sold as a piece of furniture rather than as an electrical machine. The artistic touch has been promoted, because dealers assert that women now do more purchasing than men, and they insist on radio as a piece of furniture that will adorn the home."[52] After citing studies that found women to be in the supermajority for purchasing decisions, Dunlap related this to decor: "That is why radio has been beautified and why the console cabinets with built-in loudspeakers are more in favor than they were several years ago." Dunlap pursued his inquiry into the market for radio receivers further, asking rhetorically, "Is television around the corner? If I buy today will my set be obsolete next September? The answer given this question a year ago applies today: 'Television is in the laboratory stage.'" After defining the buyer as a woman, he chided her naiveté and told her not to hold out for visual broadcasting. The gendered dichotomy between imaginings of the audience from source to source is striking. *Radio News* and *Radio Broadcast* addressed their audience as men and presumed male operators of the radio and television.[53] In contrast, *Radio Digest* and the general interest magazines were far more likely to conceive of radio and television as occurring within a domestic sphere that was inherently feminine or, in the case of others such as Dunlap in the *New York Times*, likely to repeat the developing industrial-regulatory logic in which the core of radio users were construed as passive listener/consumers considered vulnerable by chauvinist stereotypes. Both gendered imaginings offered the user/listener some type of power and agency, be it as a junior partner in technological development, a privileged adept, or the final domestic decision maker. But, whether referred to as a public to be protected, listeners/lookers-in to be pleased, or fans to be tolerated, the audience was imagined in the interests of institutions.[54] As we will see in the next section, the difference between imagining the audience and engaging the audience's imagination can create spaces for challenging authority and the vision of a passive television public.

Technical Populism

The emerging system of authorities was not without its dissenters. As power presented itself, it offered the opportunity for defiance. This defiance came in several forms: technical populism celebrating the lone inventor, or the inventor-amateur dyad, with its attendant disregard for credentials and claims to privilege further leavened by humor and hoaxes that established contingent popular expertise; contests that incited alternative imaginations of television and the technical order; and spying that focused on secretive television experiments. Each of these cases testifies to the shortcomings of a televisual order in which enthusiasts lacked a means to participate. But attempts to enlist enthusiasts into an alternative order did not categorically reject television's development as an asymmetric system of communication. While some interested inventors invoked the democratic potential of amateur involvement to further their own alternative visions of sight broadcasting, they maintained the hierarchy of inventors and amateurs. Similarly, the more direct hailing of enthusiasts to imaginative or active involvement in television did not argue for a radical democracy of access but rather for practices that would set the home experimenter apart from the lowly consumer.

In the 1920s, concurrent with the rise of the major radio manufacturing firms, a fairly thoroughly articulated discourse of technical populism was espoused by several key figures in US radio enthusiast publications. This discourse defied the ongoing institutionalization and standardization of broadcasting, imagining invention and innovation as a freewheeling process in which superior ideas and creative energies would triumph. It promised a contingent form of status to the enthusiast, who was typically imagined as male. Its central tropes condemned the conservatism of the large manufacturing firms, celebrated the individual as the locus of significant innovation, and called for opposition to regulatory pressure and the authority of the manufacturers. The technical populists recognized that users and aspiring users could act as what historians of technology Ronald Kline and Trevor Pinch describe as "agents of technological change."[55] As Kline and Pinch observe, uses are not wholly determined by design or regulation but rather are shaped by context and culture in concert with individual identities and inspirations. Moreover, such uses exert a reciprocal influence on an emergent technology as both a set of articulated gadgets and an associated group of cultural practices. The chief advocates of technical populism engaged with this particular conception of users and aspirants in part as an act of lay theorization but also in an attempt to cultivate potential markets and allies in their attempts to profit from early television.

The most distinctive—and probably most significant—technical populist was Hugo Gernsback, publisher of electronics-enthusiast and science fiction magazines. He unflaggingly hectored radio manufacturers, experimenters, and audiences on their roles in making radio better (sometimes better meant more democratic, sometimes more selective).[56] Compared to the more reserved *Radio Broadcast* and *Radio Digest*, with their respective emphases on engineering and program content, Gernsback's *Radio News* used a distinctive blend of exhortation, humor, and fancy to articulate a range of amateur involvement, including individual invention. In an exemplary instance of this populism one Gernsback editorial argued, "If a new invention does make its appearance, in a majority of cases it does not originate in the big research laboratories, but rather comes from independent outsiders. The Armstrong regenerative circuit, for instance, was invented in a college laboratory. One of the most important inventions of recent years, the television system of Baird, the Scotsman, was evolved in an attic."[57] Here Gernsback envisioned an order in which his readership could exploit the sloth he attributed to the manufacturers. By creative vision and hard work, readers might make a name and fortune for themselves. His technical populism sold a vision of individual success that was congruent with culturally powerful narratives of self-reliance and transformation. Significantly, this success would be enabled by the technical knowledge found in the magazine's articles and the equipment sold in its advertisements. While Gernsback's populism certainly seems sincere, it also was tightly aligned with his business interests.

In addition to furthering circulation and sales goals, the image of the inventor-hero worked to establish a course of progress for readers. The magazines and inventors regularly promoted the trope of the amateur or experimenter as squire and aspirant to the noble causes of developing electronic media and fighting corporate control. The trope also did significant cultural work by creating distinctions among electronics users that posed televisual enthusiasms as masculine activity, in contrast to the radio listener's supposed feminized passivity. Although enthusiast publications continued to celebrate radio amateurs' recent contributions to the growth of sound broadcasting in the 1910s and 1920s, the imagination of user activity changed in the mid-1920s as the bulk of radio practice shifted to an audience that was increasingly perceived as female and using largely mass-produced receivers for the purpose of one-way communication, the aspirations for an active group of users were briefly displaced onto television users.

The cause of transposing the active technical contributions of early radio amateurs onto television was taken up by inventor Charles Francis Jenkins, who particularly emphasized gender. By 1925 he was arguing for the collaborative development of television between inventors and amateurs, affirming his faith in "the American boy" in a letter to then Secretary of Commerce Herbert Hoover.[58] By the late 1920s, this imagining had taken on greater urgency for Jenkins, who desperately sought the right to advertise television receiver plans on his experimental broadcasts. In a piece for *Radio Digest* he claimed, "I am an enthusiastic believer in the cleverness of the amateur and the probabilities of surprising development when he takes up radiovision as an avocation after the day's work at a regular task."[59] In this same article Jenkins went on to castigate the major manufacturers for underestimating the "American boy" and putting their faith in hierarchical labs. He provided a litany of major US inventors who were not engineers but essentially amateurs. This was, of course, a canny public relations strategy for an inventor and entrepreneur attempting to buck the oligopolistic proclivities of American communications, but it also spoke to a residual logic of interactive invention. This older notion of invention stood in contrast to the relatively newly dominant system of research and engineering as disciplines in the service of rational management by institutions. Jenkins, like Gernsback, was espousing a different model of productive relations for technical innovation in mass communication. In these models the visionary was still privileged, in an enterprise conceived of as shared and working toward a common, rather than corporate, goal.[60]

A corollary effort in this push to defy the ongoing concentration of cultural authority in broadcasting was an assault by the independent inventors and their journalistic surrogates on the entire process of credentialing through education and professional societies. For example, *Radio Broadcast*'s Alfred Dinsdale derided the Royal Society's skepticism of John Logie Baird's work. Explaining their doubt as snobbery, he enthused, "[Baird] has no letters after his name, and belongs to no scientific societies and other highbrow institutions."[61] Likewise, Jenkins fought the established order, claiming, "Television, like radio broadcasting, will reach its ultimate development through a nation-wide pooling of resources and, if I may say so, the hearty and intelligent co-operation of the amateurs. Radio broadcasting owes its present status, in large measure, to the unsung efforts of thousands of plain people who do not share the dignity and distinction that comes with an 'E.E.'"[62] Both of these examples speak to the ways in which independent inventors challenged the coalescing order of scientific and engineering authority, especially as it was vested in professional societies and processes of academic certification. These attacks on authority, however, were not a radical, Rabelaisian leveling, not an attempt to remove hierarchy, even temporarily.[63] Rather, they were themselves attempts to establish positions of authority within a developing hierarchy.

These efforts to stake out contingent status were also evident in the imagination of the public by both the enthusiast press and inventors. One of the striking things in Gernsback's writing is the manner in which he rapidly shifts from condemning the big laboratories for their inertia and praising the individual inventor or home experimenter to fretting about the competencies of the domestic user. For example, he argued, "It may be said that the final television receiver must be as simple to operate as the present day radio receiver. As a matter of fact, it must be even simpler."[64] Similarly, Jenkins imagined an uninformed body of users: "Confusion is unquestionably the dominant note with regard to the present status of television."[65] Thus, two of the foremost populists in imagining a new electronic order placed strict limits on what constituted informed and engaged involvement on the part of users. Like regulators' and manufacturers' statements regarding the audience's lack of discipline, Jenkins's and Gernsback's declamations on television bespeak anxieties about the public's interest. Their populism notwithstanding, they spoke for order, in this case a hierarchy driven by invention.

Yet, then as now, authority opened up space for contestation with its display of power. The affirmative imagination of television as a technology and communication system, no matter how orderly, had the potential for provoking transgression instead of discipline.[66] Drawing a line—to some degree—invites its crossing. Not all enthusiasts would be content to simply sit still and read about the television to come. Some wanted to speculate and tinker in a reprise of earlier radio practice. Consequently, the technical populists, particularly through enthusiast magazines, attempted to channel such activity into the construction of proper knowledges and imaginings of television that provided a contingent authority in contrast to a presumably misinformed and docile public. The potential for rebellion against the broad ordering of television was primarily contained through rituals that rendered these power plays as sport. Throughout the late 1920s and early 1930s, inventors, publishers, and experimenters worked to establish the boundaries for televisual practice, in which a key means of containment was the cultivation of televisual insiders through the publication of humor, hoaxes, and technical mysteries.

Perhaps no greater device exists for separating inside from out than the joke. You get it, or you don't. You laugh with, and you laugh at. In early discourse on television there was regular recourse to the ridiculous, and these moments of ridicule worked to establish boundaries between television's insiders and outsiders, cultivating the aficionados and adepts who could contest television's future on behalf of the public in a manner that encouraged them to regard their fellow citizens as dupes. An early example comes from the May 1925 issue of *Radio Broadcast*, which facetiously compared the potential for visual and olfactory broadcasting: "The light waves are transformed into electrical fluctuations, and photographs are sent over the ocean. Anything that can be translated into electrical energy can be transmitted by radio. Hence why not smells?"[67] Humor pieces such as this worked to paint enthusiastic imaginings of communication technologies as silly, likening prospects for commercial success to the probability of "Trotsky voyaging to the United States to address Congress and to become a master of boy scouts," and going so far as to include a cartoon representing a man "smelling a civet cat [depicted as a skunk] across the world." With this article those who understood broadcasting's technological limits were clearly distinguished from those who did not.

Likewise, misprints and misstatements about radio technology were a regular feature in the "Radiotics" and "Broadcastatics" humor sections of *Radio News*, working both to entertain the audience and foster a sense of informed participation that depended on ridiculing those outside of technical knowledge. Thus, a simple misprint of "phonograph" as "photograph" was construed in cartoon and caption to imagine a successor to television that would allow family albums to bring access to the sounds of the past.[68] Throughout the magazine the point of the joke often was to call on readers to curb their enthusiasm and be sensible. For example, one piece embellished *Punch*'s punning assertion that "the linking of the British Empire by radio is a big step toward the circumlocution of the globe," with the wry rejoinder, "And television, it is to be hoped, will shortly lead to its greater circumspection."[69] Though Gernsback and Co. were likely poaching on *Punch* rather than misguidedly mocking something that was constructed as a piece of humor, the ultimate butt of the joke is the unrestrained enthusiast, the fan as fanatic. Other variants on misunderstanding the technology included jokes about the personification of technical difficulties, such as a cartoon in which a "Fan" regarded television as a means to "see . . . Old Man Static" and "get him good."[70] For *Radio News* in particular, the cultivation of an "other" in the form of a passive or underinformed audience—listeners rather than experimenters—worked to flatter its readership and distinguish the publication on the market.

These attempts to construct a proper knowledge of the underlying physical phenomena by marking certain conceptions as ridiculous existed alongside a coupling of anxiety and excitement over television's potential to disrupt the structures of everyday life by reordering processes of surveillance. For example, one cartoon from *Radio News* imagined the common trope of television allowing illicit glimpses into the domestic sphere on the model of dialing the wrong number or being mis-patched by the operator (figure 5).[71] In the punch line panel the reader, along with the subject of the cartoon, looks in on an old man in the tub. While this certainly suggests the potential for being watched in one's home, it more directly hails the reader as a frustrated looker whose private wooing of a young woman is interrupted, albeit with what for some readers would be the titillating prospect of slightly altered circumstances. More directly addressing anxieties about surveillance was a cartoon in which television was imagined to allow employers to catch truant "boy" workers at a baseball game, thereby undermining the anonymity of crowds.[72] But again, television was also imagined to provide new opportunities to look back, as in a sketch of a television contraption that would allow motorists to evade speed traps (figure 6).[73] These examples bespeak uncertainty and anxiety about television's restructuring of

The Humorists Begin Worrying for Us

"When the latest television invention is attached to our telephones, we shall be able to see the person we are speaking to—

—but no invention has yet been discovered that entirely eliminates the possibility of being suddenly switched on to a wrong number!"
—"London Opinion."

FIGURE 5. Pitching woo is interrupted by crossed wires in this imagination of video telephony, reprinted in *Radio News* in 1928. Articulating a familiar annoyance with the televisual future, this cartoon inverted notions of progress with the promise of more obtrusive invasions of privacy while also suggesting the pleasures of more serendipitous misconnections. Courtesy of West Campus Library, Washington University in St. Louis.

A Proposed Television Set—"The Motorist's Friend"

The Bystander.

FIGURE 6. Not quite a radar detector, this humorous rendering of distance vision reverses the process of surveillance to better enable individualist transgression. Reprinted in *Radio News* in 1928. Courtesy of Wendt Commons, University of Wisconsin–Madison.

the orders of looking, while offering the prospect of new knowledges to the possessors of technological aptitude. All three cartoons recognize that the reordering would likely work to magnify the importance of the power to look rather than to be looked at, and in the logic of *Radio News* under Gernsback, the technological adept would be equipped to look out for himself.

Congruent with these cartoons and jokes, the magazine tended to find entertainment in boosters and hucksters who exploited public enthusiasm about television. One notable example involved a movie theater manager who claimed he would show "pictures of the Dempsey-Sharkey fight . . . received by radio" but actually played the broadcast of the fight accompanied by film of an earlier "Dempsey-Gibbons encounter."[74] Here there was no condemnation of the fraud being perpetrated and probably some amount of pride that the exhibitor, described as "more than enterprising" and "wily," was applying a modified version of Gernsback's 1919 strategy for combining sight with live sound.[75] Instead, the 1927 report suggests that it was incumbent on the audience to be informed and to have "detected the trick" themselves. Yet the account also points to the ways in which television demonstrations were as much popular events as a means for making public the latest accomplishments of this or that laboratory. There was substantial overlap between these demonstrations and the presentational mode of magic, asking the audience for amazement rather than understanding. Like the amateur magician, however, the amateur experimenter or enthusiast was offered a type of pleasure in and relation to the art that differed from an audience's amazement because such hoaxes offered the opportunity to puzzle things out.

A similar form of hailing readers as contingent experts was through mystery stories that hinged on technical knowledge. For example, C. Sterling Gleason's short story for *Radio News* titled "Rays of Justice" told the tale of dashing film star, philanthropist, and amateur radio engineer Harold Dare, who used television to foil his archenemy Dandy Diavolo's plot to disrupt Los Angeles's electric supply by zapping the tower insulators with X-rays.[76] The story combines the juvenile adventure genre—complete with a Dare and a Dandy, who respectively stood for valued and derided versions of masculinity—with a puzzle set to reward the reader who can synthesize prior technical articles on Baird's experiments using infrared television or "noctovision" with other articles on the photovoltaic properties of various materials, including the video foundation story of the discovery of selenium's properties while it was being used as a telegraph insulator. As with the humor and hoaxes, readers were offered certain insider pleasures for being fully versed in technology and terminology, the satisfaction of knowing that they got the finer points, but this instance anchored those pleasures in tropes of masculine heroism and initiative that circulated in broader popular culture. *Radio News* would take this form of appeal further in contests that offered to reward reader knowledge with recognition, prizes, and a handy means of building a sense of distinction.

"What's Wrong with This Picture?"

Many of the attempts in magazine culture to define both television and its ideal constituency invited enthusiasts to participate for fun and profit. Readers who submitted jokes and misprints to *Radio News* "Broadcastatics" and "Radiotics" pages were rewarded with small payments, but larger-scale activity was encouraged through the staging of contests for cash and prizes. Notable among these was *Radio News'* 1927 "What's Wrong with This Picture?" contest.[77] The contest provides a glimpse into the divergent popular imaginings of future televisual norms, in this case by the magazine's readers, who were also asserting their own contingent expertise. The 1927 contest was based on an earlier successful promotion offering $300 in prizes to readers who could correctly identify thirty-four failings in a 1925 cover illustration of a man listening to a radio (figure 7).[78] The 1927 sequel asked readers to imagine television as a technology and practice in the near future, identify the cover's errors in realizing that future, and comment in twenty-five words or fewer (figure 8). Intriguingly, the contest worked both to

FIGURE 7. *Radio News*' 1925 cover contest invited readers to find thirty-four errors in the illustration. This imagination of current technology served mostly as a test of readers' ability to spot flaws in the design and set-up of the apparatus. Courtesy of Wendt Commons, University of Wisconsin–Madison.

FIGURE 8. In 1927 *Radio News* tasked contestants with finding sixteen errors in this image of a future television. More than the 1925 contest, the television version involved presumed norms of domesticity, program production, and audience attention. Courtesy of Wendt Commons, University of Wisconsin–Madison.

incite and contain reader interest in television, mapping out the impossibilities of television and the boundaries of proficiency in the enthusiast community. That is, the contest did substantial cultural work to demonstrate that enthusiasm must be directed into the appropriate channels to become expertise. This containment occurred at several junctures: the framing device and rules of the contest, the picture itself and the anticipated correct answers, and the publication and evaluation of actual reader entries. Each of these instances buttressed claims to expertise with appeals to gender hierarchy, but as the contestants' responses indicate, the meanings and identifications made by various enthusiasts were not straightforwardly products of the ways in which they were hailed.

The contest was introduced with a story that revolved around office boy Fips, a recurring fictional character in *Radio News*, who served as a regular example of problematic boyish enthusiasm. Given the opportunity to design the cover and a chance at a $5.77 per week raise, Fips decided "that people are mostly interested today in Television, so what better opportunity is there than to show what is going to happen when Television actually will be with us, which, as the Boss has informed us so often, is right around the corner?"[79] After commissioning the cover art, Fips presented the picture to Gernsback, "the Boss," who found "no less than 16 mistakes in this contraption that you have the temerity to show me," but Fips saved his job with the inventive idea of turning the mistaken drawing into a cover contest, though sadly his first year's raise would fund the prizes. The contest did significant work to delineate what was in and out of bounds for speculation. Thus, the wiring and tuning of the television receiver was marked out of bounds with statements such as, "Please do not try to find fault with the radio outfit itself, that is, the design of it. . . . The whole apparatus is supposed to work by the throwing of the center switch when the radio is put into operation." Speculation on the actual operation, frequency assignments, and linking of technologies would seem to be a key form of interest, but for the purposes of the contest, *Radio News* shut down these avenues for imagination and debate. The stated rules anticipated "many" entries that would correctly identify all sixteen "unmistakable mistakes" and thus stipulated, "The first prize will then go for, not only the correct list, but the best 25 words, accompanying the entry."[80] The readers' answers would confound these expectations, in part because the picture itself and the anticipated answers straddled a fault line of contradictions in popular conceptions of the medium, its place in the home, and the gendered uses of broadcasting.

A depiction of the future in intentional error opens up spaces for contesting meaning and identities. The illustration speaks to both contemporary "common sense" about television and domestic entertainment and the publication's sense of the strengths and weaknesses in the general public's understanding of television as technology and social practice. On newsstands and coffee tables, the cover was seen by readers and nonreaders alike. Consequently, it held the perverse promise of flattering a group of insiders who understood the future that *Radio News* envisioned and undermining the understanding of this future among those who were not sufficiently steeped in televisual lore to properly channel their enthusiasm, thereby furthering the processes of distinction.

The picture, however, also reveals the brewing gender conflicts surrounding the domestication of broadcasting. In historical hindsight the depiction of the television screen itself is striking in that it would take better than a half-century for large, flat, and thin television screens to become a plausible option, but this in itself was not considered an error for the contest and was in fact common in the magazine's renderings of television.[81] Indeed, the depicted television receiver attempts to integrate the technology with tastes in interior decor, as was the trend with radios by the mid-1920s. Just as later televisions would mimic cabinets, buffets, and armoires, this one domesticates the technology by imitating a dressing mirror atop a bureau. Here, television is a vanity, and the picture as a whole—intentionally or not—reproduced patriarchal pictorial codes for female conceit and frivolity that date at least to the Renaissance.[82] Given the similarity in hairstyle and dress, one possible interpretation of the picture is that the woman in the foreground is imagining herself as the star of a radio program; and, in fact, her dreamy demeanor was frequently commented upon by the contestants.

The woman's lack of attention to the televisual image was not only deemed an error by the magazine but also was sometimes read as an affront to enthusiast desire to see and play with television. The degree and nature of what was wrong and perhaps culturally threatening with this picture is evident in its differences from the earlier contest portraying a flawed radio hookup. In the earlier (1925) cover, in front of a blank background, a man sits behind a radio set with detailed dials, inputs, power supplies, and antenna wiring and blows smoke rings from his cigar, while pulling on his suspenders with his thumbs—notably, for the purposes of both the contest and the meaning of the image, he has doubled up with earphones and a loudspeaker. In contrast, on the television cover a woman sits as if in a swoon in a furnished parlor, with hand over heart and a book in her lap, before a television receiver featuring purposely ambiguous dials. Although some of the elements were identified as mistakes, when the pictures are considered together, they articulate quite divergent modes of interaction with broadcast technology.

These covers' iconic iterations of stereotypical assumptions about user behavior and technologically determined modes of engagement with the apparatus speak to powerful gender ideologies of the 1920s that were promulgated by the radio industry among others. Media historian William Boddy finds that the redefinition of radio in terms of household reception and a female audience produced an industrial assumption of "the distracted housewife-listener."[83] While this woman is not harried by housework, which was one key trope in the discourse of female inattention, it fits well with the "escapist daydreaming" that would come to be attributed particularly to women listening to soap operas.[84] The covers build on this and other stereotypes. The man is hyperattentive, with a surplus of listening devices and controls, while the woman looks away from a set presumed to operate at the flip of a single switch. The man's position behind the complex apparatus gives him access to the device's interior wiring. In contrast, the woman is not pictured as controlling the set. The abundance of knobs, dials, and power supplies in the radio cover is coupled with a blank background,[85] whereas the television cover devotes a significant portion of the picture to domestic decor. The man's cigar smoking (perhaps evocative of a proud new father) and suspender-thumbing pose connote self-satisfaction, or a sense of accomplishment, while the woman is pictured in passive repose.

Sometimes a cigar is just a cigar, but in this case, the gendered meanings encoded in the picture fall squarely within what were established binaries for most of the history of US broadcasting. Man is active, inventive, attentive, and in control regardless of location. Woman is passive, receptive, vain (and yet to be looked at), and properly contained within the home, largely anticipating the patterns of representation that media historian Lynn Spigel found with the introduction of electronically scanned television years later.[86] Notably, of the nine other *Radio News* covers featuring television between 1925 and 1930, two feature the "family circle" imagery that was so successfully used in the later television's launch and was already being used to envision radio as a domestic technology, and two others depict couples.[87] Of these, only one features the woman operating the device. The rest of the covers feature a man operating or working on televisual apparatus on his own, or in one case using a videophone to propose. Given the discourses of gender, media, and technology in circulation at the time, the manifest representation of the 1927 contest cover would have confounded a substantial subset of enthusiasts by projecting the domestication and consequent feminization of electronics into the future and onto television, and this aspect came under specific scrutiny in both the anticipated answers and contestants' responses.

Significantly, the magazine's sixteen anticipated answers for the 1927 contest were far more preoccupied with domestic furnishings and end use than the thirty-four errors from 1925, which focused on technical practice (see figure 9).[88] This is no doubt in part because it was easier to make normative assertions about furniture than a future technology, but it reinforced the focus on television's domestic installation. In addition, many of the supposed errors in the television cover presume quite narrow technical and aesthetic norms, presuming single-camera shooting and simultaneous broadcast.[89] That the "girl" not looking at the image is described as an error defines an entire mode of engagement as defective.

CORRECT ANSWERS TO
"WHAT'S WRONG?"

(1) No wire connection on microphone.

(2) Television machine in studio cannot possibly show, as it cannot transmit its own picture.

(3) Time of clock is wrong by 15 minutes. One hour's difference is possible, because the transmitter might be in New York and the receiver in Chicago.

(4) Radio set has no loud speaker.

(5) Radio set and television attachment has no projecting apparatus. Where could the television picture come from? (Description in RADIO NEWS said that the apparatus was *self-contained*, therefore transmitter could not be located elsewhere.)

(6) Girl in front of the apparatus would be looking at the television screen, not looking away.

(7) No colors can show on screen, because if one color shows and there were colored picture transmission, all colors would show, not just the green and the red. (Pointed out in May issue.)

(8) Microphone entirely too high.

(9) Picture behind screen could not show through it, as screens are not transparent.

(10) Radio set is minus one rear support. It would topple over in position shown.

(11) Table leg is apparently sawed off, and could not support table.

(12) Knob missing from left upright holding television screen.

(13) Pendulum of clock too high.

(14) Piano top has no supporting stay.

(15) Hinges on clock do not match.

(16) One leg on piano bench is missing.

FIGURE 9. The answers to the 1927 *Radio News* contest include a number of supposed errors that would turn out to be relatively commonplace in television as realized. Courtesy of Wendt Commons, University of Wisconsin–Madison.

What emerges from the combination of the picture and its answer key is a set of presumptions about television that draws more heavily on normative notions of gender, domesticity, and contemporary radio practice than specific knowledges of television as an emergent technology. These norms, however, would be renegotiated by contestant responses and their deviance from the anticipated answers.

To the magazine's purported surprise, no single contestant identified all sixteen errors. This did not spare poor fictional Fips from *Radio News* readers, who expressed sympathies, teasing, and derision in what seem to have been equal measure.[90] Fips himself, along with his misplaced exuberance and lack of technical skill and attention to detail, fostered a sense of in-group identification among those who could spot most of the errors and take either pity or delight in the situation.[91] Moreover, this mode of distinguishing differential claims to authority over broadcasting in general and television in particular worked to secure the rapidly cohering technical hierarchies, which were readily modeled on and mapped back on established cultural hierarchies tied to gender and middle-class domesticity.

In considering these responses, we cannot be sure of the identities of the contestants. *Radio News* emphasized self-reported markers of difference describing respondents as "a Chinese gentleman" or "a contestant from Barbados" and quoting their deprecatory disclaimers such as "I'm a woman—how can I say anything in twenty-five words?" and a supposed male sailor who similarly averred, "I couldn't say good-bye in such few words."[92] In examining identities as expressed through discourse and having an unprovable relation to both bodies and lived experience, however, we should be careful not to allow dominant habits of thought and expression to obscure the breadth of identifications and evaluations prompted by this invitation to imagine and judge future television. Of the thirteen prizewinners, three were identified with likely female first names, "Miss Andrea Duquet" (sixth), "Marad Serriov" (seventh), and "Alice Stevenson" (eighth).[93] Of the other identified prizewinners, only two, "Ovila C. Duquet" (an early twentieth-century male first name) and "Norris E. Wilson," were listed with a full first name. Everyone else was nominated by a first or first and second initial plus their surname, which seemed to be a commonplace for identifying men in the magazine. It is certainly significant that a quarter of the winners were nominally feminine and thus clearly defied the conceit that radio and television enthusiasm was decisively or intrinsically masculine, as well as the notion that gender identities were a simple dichotomous binary. These traces are better suited to demonstrate the variance of identities hailed and taken up than to evidence a robust pattern of dispersal of lived identities, not only because the data set is both thin and groomed according to the precepts of *Radio News* but also because the contest was always discursive and imaginative. Evaluating the portrayed medium in relation to imagined futures and identities was the game, and contestants worked sometimes to conform and sometimes to contend television's integration into a variety of existing frameworks in ways that complemented and confounded dominant values.

Among the follow-up article's reported replies, the depiction of the woman in the home drew a significant number of comments that worked to frame her within contemporary gender discourse. For example, one paragraph began, "'The lady is faultless,' said a gallant Englishman; and one of the feminine prize-winners noted that 'there seems something wrong with about every leg in the picture, except the lady's'" (206). Another respondent took issue with her lack of a "very fine diamond on the proper finger" (206). Other readers saw errors in the length of her hair and her "wearing [a] 'party dress' in [the] home" (279). Two of the prizewinners followed *Radio News'* logic and regarded the woman's distant gaze as worthy of poetic explanation invoking feminine desire. For instance, A. F. Helmkamp's thirteenth-place entry rhymed:

Thoughts afar, a distant stare;
She doesn't know what's on the air.
Screen's not worth a wasted minute,
Because a handsome 'Sheik's' not in it. (279)

Significantly, the woman is assumed to be more intrigued by programming than the technical marvel that is television. This ran counter to the fetishization of technology that was part of *Radio News'* appeal to a readership addressed as male. Moreover, the poem's allusion to Valentino's "Sheik" invoked the supposed hysteria and unruliness of his female fans, accentuating the contrast between the woman and the scientific, rational enthusiast. Yet the specter of Valentino also points to what film scholar Gaylyn Studlar deemed "the dreaded possibilities of [a] woman-made masculinity" invested with "erotic promise,"[94] along with anxieties about who gets to look and how.

For some respondents the figure of the woman in the foreground disrupted normative, gendered structures of looking relations. The image and its designation as error speaks to persistent cultural anxieties over the potential for a woman to direct or avert her gaze according to her own desires within the domestic sphere. To reconcile these emerging discontents, one possibly female prizewinner transposed the problematic system of looks into a key more harmonious with contemporary gender ideology with a sketch and poem (figure 10):

SO MANY

Nights I've battled with failure!
Now I've lost the decision
What chance has a 'radio widow'
With this picture-sque Television?
NOT ANY! —*Marad Serriov, Seventh Prize* (278)

FIGURE 10. One winner of the 1927 *Radio News* cover contest redrew the gendered processes of looking at television into a configuration more in keeping with patriarchal voyeurism. The "radio widow," however, has a gaze of her own, seen only by the reader. Courtesy of Wendt Commons, University of Wisconsin–Madison.

The "radio widow" was a common trope in 1920s accounts of radio's disruption of domesticity. An exemplary instance of this discourse is the *Radio News* cover from July 1926, captioned "Alone at Last," featuring a couple on their honeymoon with the bride sitting on the bed clutching a handkerchief to her tearing eyes while her headphone-clad groom adjusts his portable radio atop their unpacked bags. Tales of female dissatisfaction with rug-ruining batteries, cluttered garages, and sleep-deprived experimenter spouses made for reliable humor in *Radio News*, but such stories also portrayed both men and women as insiders in the practice of radio enthusiasm, albeit with dramatically different gendered relationships to the device and medium. As Serriov's sketch indicates, to some degree what was wrong with the picture was having a woman as television's user. For some readers the cover illustration served to place future television not in the realm of experimentation and fun but instead as the end point of the ongoing domestication of radio. Technological and commercial standardization had the potential to tame the unruliness that provided pleasure for enthusiasts hailed as adventurers, inventors, frontiersmen, pirates, and "hearties." Small wonder that some enthusiasts saw gender trouble in this future.

Spying on Television

Despite some trepidation over a domesticated future, amateurs and enthusiasts found substantial potential for adventure in this relatively unformed and mysterious thing called television. Several interrelated amateur practices of the lower resolution, mechanical television era answered Jenkins's call for participation while carving out subcultural space through alternative and unsanctioned use of licenced experimental television transmissions. Ranging from building home sets to spying on and even attempting to record secretive television tests, a subset of the public would not wait for the large manufacturing interests to perfect television as a consumer good. Significantly, the most ambitious of these practices were framed in terms of transgression and voyeurism. Enthusiasts wanted to use television immediately and, in some cases, went to great lengths to do so while asserting their ability to look in transgressively on private views.

The initial problem for the television enthusiast was the lack of a set. One strategy for confronting this problem was simply to listen-in by sending the demodulated signal to a loudspeaker. As early as 1926, journalists noted the potential for discerning pictures by sound. For example, in reporting on J. L. Baird's research, *Radio Broadcast* noted, "The face of an individual looking directly at the transmitter sends out a series of sounds something like 'brump, brump, brump' but, when turned sideways, the profile gives out a note like 'perahh, perahh, perahh.' A hand with fingers extended, if passed in front of the transmitter, will sound like the grating of a very coarse file, and an inanimate object, such as a box, gives a single steady note."[95] The *Living Age* enthusiastically opined, "In time it will be possible to recognize people merely by the sound of their faces."[96] Several early accounts of public reception of television broadcasts remark on the radio audience's interest in the "freak whistle" created by television transmissions in the sound broadcast band. For example, an article in the *New York Times* subtitled "Experimenters Are Striving to Interpret Peculiar Drones and Squeals That Indicate Television Images Are in the Air" noted, "The sounds are high-pitched, sometimes droning and sometimes squealing. To the uninitiated they mean nothing, but many will recognize them as the signals of television which become not speech or music, but pictures, when translated by suitable apparatus."[97] Indeed, the ability to decode the television signal strictly through its sonic qualities became a mark of expertise for engineer and enthusiast alike.[98] Still, listening to the signal was merely making do.

The most straightforward solution was to build sets and tune them in to transmissions produced for public consumption. In 1928, Experimenter Publishing, Gernsback's company, exhorted enthusiasts: "So, fans! Dig out the old soldering iron, the bus bar and the rest of your paraphernalia and get to work on the latest hobby. Build yourself a Television Receiver," and for twenty-five cents offered to send instructions.[99] Television's incompleteness, far from being a detriment, was part of Experimenter's pitch: "Of course, Television is far from perfected. It is still in a most elementary stage. There is little use in trying to gloss over the truth. But a start has been made and it remains for the 'fans' to do their share, as in radio, in developing the new art. . . . The old 'fan days' are here again. Don't miss the fun!" Here, again, we can see the developing enthusiast discourse of the closing of radio as field for exploration and the desire for television to provide new avenues for mediated adventure. Likewise, Jenkins invoked the collective ideal attributed to sound broadcasting's popularization through "cooperative development, with many taking part": "I have encouraged boys and grownups to participate in television reception, even going to the extent of supplying television kits at cost price, so that with an old electric motor, anyone could tune in my Radio signals at an investment of about $2.50!"[100] Beyond these specific opportunities to purchase instructions and kits, homemade-television enthusiasts had a number of suppliers looking to sell them "apparatus," ranging from complete kits from Insuline Corporation of America ($52.00) and Daven Corporation ($45.00) to scanning disks from the National Company ($15.00), neon lamps from Ratheon ($12.50), and variable speed motors from Interstate Electric Company ($23.00).[101] Moreover, information on homemade television began to be disseminated by publications targeting readerships beyond the radio enthusiast. For example, *Popular Mechanics* ran a series of articles starting in 1928 on homemade television including such early tips as how to build a multistandard scanning disk and a "Television Receiver Run by Fan Motor" (1929), and *Popular Science* ran a ten-part series on building a home set from 1931 to 1932.[102] By the time the latter series was published, an enthusiast could purchase a kit or an assembled set from Hollis Baird's Shortwave and Television Laboratory, which advertised universal compatibility regardless of scan rate or resolution.[103] The pre-1930 early adopters faced a common problem, however: a shortage of programming.

Simply put, despite more than a dozen licensed experimental stations in 1928 and 1929, their transmissions were inconsistent and often poorly publicized, provoking great frustration and commensurate compensatory strategies among the enthusiasts and their advocates to make television yield the pleasures it could. In 1928 *Radio News* lamented, "Television has arrived, but as yet only a few scattered stations are transmitting television images." The always inventive magazine had a plan, however, using a television receiver to turn music into light patterns.[104] This practice would ostensibly give the experimenter a better understanding of "some of the fundamental theoretical principles and practical operating difficulties . . . [to be] better able to make and use a real television receiver when regular television program service is available." At roughly the same time in late 1928, *Radio Broadcast* published a number of articles by noncommercial experimenters, who gave advice on such necessary considerations as the power supply for the lamp, how to control scanning-disk vibrations, and proper tuning, but flatly admitted that the pleasure was not in the programming. One of the experimenters explained: "The interest and pleasure associated with their reception is found in the novelty and fascination of the achievement with home-made apparatus rather than in esthetic considerations associated with the reproduction."[105] For most experimenters the pleasures seem to have been in taking what they could get from broadcasting and focusing on the articulation of gadgets and circuits in test runs for commercial television reception.

For at least a few experimenters, however, this was not enough. Boyd Phelps expressed another set of pleasures to be wrung from television, those of solving a mystery and defeating attempts at secrecy—in other words, spying on unpublicized television experiments. After recounting the ability of an adept to make sense of the sound of a television signal, Phelps noted, "The experimenter who intercepts a television program of unknown origin has before him the intensely interesting problem of deciphering these signals and determining the number of scanning holes and the speed of the disc, for this may be obtained through laboratory tests." The rest of the article used his efforts at "unscrambling mysterious television signals which were heard regularly on Long Island" to lay out a plan for enthusiast practice.[106]

Phelps explained the complex sound generated by a television signal, which includes the thumps caused by the signal's frame rate (for mechanical television often 10, 15, or 20 Hz); a higher, louder, and more consistent tone called the "scan frequency" created by the frame rate multiplied by the number of scan lines (ranging between 360 and 720 Hz with mechanical television of the era); and various frequencies particular to the image itself. He then outlined a methodology for listening and then looking in on secretive signals. In essence, the method consisted of first comparing the sound of the scan frequency to the notes generated by a piano, on which "the keys now look like a log of Who's Who in Television." Then he matched the piano pitch with a table of sound frequencies. Finally, using a slide rule and the process of elimination to determine the probable frame rate and number of scan lines, Phelps attempted to tune in the picture. Reporting on his success and expressly invoking voyeuristic transgression, he noted, "It was the morning of the third day when the disc was tried out and the interesting pictures watched with a thrill of one eavesdropping in on something unusual—like watching the antics of a comedian practicing in supposed solitude. This key-holing being absolutely a one-way affair added to the charm, due to security from detection" (158). In the next issue Phelps would argue for and explain strategies for amateur transmission, but in the main, amateur television experimentation in the late 1920s was limited to reception, with Phelps himself admitting that amateur "transmission seems to be considered out of the question."[107] And so it remained, despite his efforts to the contrary.

The machinations of various amateurs and their advocates notwithstanding, the regulatory picture was fairly consistently bleak in terms of the near future of television broadcasting. At the close of the 1920s, inventors like Jenkins continued to argue that still and moving pictures might "ultimately have real service value in the broadcast band,"[108] but by the early 1930s, television in the broadcast band was a dead letter as most experimental stations, requiring greater bandwidth for greater resolution, moved to the four FRC-approved shortwave channels. The four channels and the FRC's licensing policy imposed a scarcity of access that would not accommodate, much less cultivate, amateur involvement as several notable amateurs including Phelps were denied licenses.[109] Moreover, the four channels came with their own problems of interference and dead spots caused by the shortwave's propagation characteristics.

As television moved into the 1930s, however, the far greater problem for the television enthusiast and smaller-scale entrepreneurs was the commission's firm refusal to allow commercialization. As a result, Jenkins was prohibited from publicizing his television kits, which he claimed to be selling below cost, on his experimental broadcasts.[110] This was a telling contrast with the early 1920s, when Westinghouse and the other sound broadcasting technology manufacturers had been able to subsidize their productions with equipment sales from almost the beginning of their consolidation of the intellectual and actual property of US radio and their concomitant co-optation of amateur practice. Moreover, as I noted in chapter 1, while lower resolution television innovators worked to develop interest, they were forbidden from broadcasting images of sponsored sound programs. Consider this conundrum: would-be television broadcasters had to simulcast their images with sound broadcasts, but they were strictly forbidden from exploiting any commercial opportunity that might arise on the sound side and were likewise prohibited from promoting television by linking it with preestablished popular programs. Thus, lower-resolution television was cut off by the FRC from its most likely users and its most likely synergy until it could meet the FRC's engineering department's undefined standard of providing "real entertainment value."[111] Experimental broadcast television became a proving ground for a few organized interests rather than a relatively open field in which televisual practice would be tested by many, in which users and nonusers might have greater agency in technological and cultural change.[112] Consequently, hierarchical systems of authority and institutionally defined expectations trumped the actual practice of television's early users, prescribing a relatively closed architecture in the interest of consistent quality for the new medium.

Allocating Authority, Judging Quality

In 1926 RCA engineer and *Radio Broadcast* columnist Carl Dreher asked, "Who Shall Judge the Quality of Our Broadcasting Stations?"[113] Dreher imagined radio's philosopher-king as a "first-rate engineer who is also a first-rate musician." Dreher conceded that such a beast was hard to come by, if not mythical: "When we poor devils who, for our sins, have been set to running broadcast stations— when finally we have completed our penance, and the last milliampere has quivered through our nerves, then, operating the broadcast stations of heaven, we shall have paragons like that working with us. Oh for those celestial studios and control rooms. . . . But here on earth we must take men and materials as we find them, and there is no use looking for such engineer-musical genius combinations as those we have been dreaming about. Their very qualities are antipathetic." Among other things, Dreher imagined artists to be "more nervous than the average engineer" and asserted that "there is not much room for nervousness in broadcasting." Moreover, he and his illustrator, Franklyn F. Stratford, imagined the "radio man" as a figure of hermetic devotion to signal quality (figure 11).

Nevertheless, Dreher argued that the radio man must cooperate with artistic authorities and foresaw with television "a similar incursion of radio men into the field of pictorial art. But inherently such invasions are self-limiting in their nature. Invariably the investigators and research men improve the equipment to such an extent that the most artistic interpretations become possible, and the aid of men with an artistic background becomes essential for the best possible result." As the next two chapters discuss in greater detail, when questions of evaluation turned to content, systems of exclusionary authority were harnessed to arguments about the nature of the audience, the nation, and the aesthetics and ethics of television programming that spoke *for* rather than *to* radio and television's users and ultimate owners. The logics of priority as linked to invention cum ownership, the framing of expertise in terms of education and institutional credentials, and the paedocratic imaginings of the citizenry in regulatory thought all worked together to establish positions of authority. These processes complemented the laudatory but ultimately marginalizing cultivation

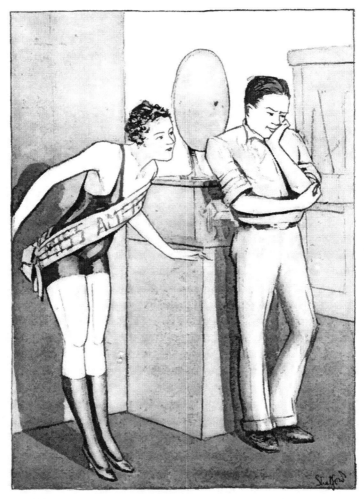

"IF MISS AMERICA ARRIVED, HE WOULD NOT STOP
LISTENING"

FIGURE 11. In this illustration for *Radio Broadcast* in 1926, the dedicated engineer cares more for sound than the live beauty in his studio. For author and sound engineer Carl Dreher, focus, knowledge, and dispassion were seen as key traits in those who would evaluate and regulate broadcasting. Courtesy of Memorial Library, University of Wisconsin–Madison.

of the amateur's, experimenter's, and enthusiast's place in the public conversation about the realization of television. Consequently, the engineers, artists, executives, and critics refined their envisioning of sight broadcasting in a largely closed conversation.

Early decisions favoring experts in the regulation and realization of television should caution us against an overreliance on exclusionary constructions of authority today, but this history should also warn us that the foreclosure of television's possibilities did not simply happen as a result of regulatory, industrial, and technical choices. Instead, the power to articulate television was enmeshed in cultural hierarchies, systems for ordering our homes, hobbies, and habits of mind. The grand maneuvers of industry and law occur on a field shaped by culture. The identities constructed—not just for television but its various users—narrowed the imagination and realization of possibilities, perpetuating a self-sustaining circuit of identity and authority. Media have consistently been defined as commerce and then measured in terms of assets and profit, as technology and then assessed in terms of utility and elegance, as art and then evaluated in terms of content and style. Users have been defined as viewers and then judged for their attentiveness and fluency, as consumers and then graded for their buying habits and purchasing power, as denizens of the mediated public sphere and then castigated (without irony) for solipsism and voyeurism. Although none of these processes can be distilled to a singular purpose, the point remains that in the affirmative imagination of television—and in calling the modern, electronically mediated public sphere to order—one of the primary products was silence, at least from the majority of potential users. In particular, the determination of who should be seen and not heard mobilized discourses of gender and age to erect a hierarchy that shut out both audiences and amateurs, consequently disciplining televisual enthusiasms.

It is worth remembering, however, that the amateur was flattered and hailed into a set of hierarchical identities before being marginalized—or more precisely, those acts of interpellation began the process of marginalization through exclusions along established lines of cultural power such as gender, sexuality, race, and class. Although television was ultimately framed as a mass rather than individualized medium, distinguishing among users and audiences consistently contributed to both the profitability of broadcasting and its hospitable regulatory sanction. The example of early television points to ways in which the promise of greater individual involvement could ultimately contribute to a sharply stratified pattern of use and authority. The available evidence indicates that early enthusiasts and their advocates largely accepted the language of exceptionalism and distinction undergirding regulatory and cultural authority. Rationalized roles took precedence over consideration of either the spectrum or culture as something shared by the public, and vestiges of this conception continue to this day.

Questions of evaluation and authority regarding broadcast content as a somewhat self-determining commodity in circuits of economic and cultural exchange would take on increasing salience as the values and institutional precepts of sound broadcasting were mapped onto television. This was especially true as evaluations of and authoritative pronouncements about content were configured around conceptions of quality. Discourses of quality mostly staked out a supply-side model in which audiences would congregate around recognizably good programs. In this conception users or audiences did not make good broadcasting through effort or demand, but instead, their use or interest legitimated the prior decisions of experts. The actual choices of listeners and enthusiasts—as well as radio broadcasters' attempts to court them by means of direct address and audience participation—demonstrate a more complex set of interactions between the culture industries and audiences during this era than is represented through these acts of evaluation and exercises of authority.[114] But, as amateur television participation was stymied in the United States, conceptions of a television system were increasingly organized around centralized production and distributed reception of content rather than more expansive forms of interactivity as had been the case during the heyday of the radio amateur. The next two chapters will examine the ways in which such constrained chances for participation worked in combination with the forestalled regularization of broadcasts to amplify arguments from the 1920s for concentrated and commercial radio broadcasting in the name of quality. In doing so, they will show how processes of evaluation not only directly rework matters of cultural power into questions of taste and assertions of essence but also facilitate a stabilization of practice in the interests of industry and institutionalized authority.

3

Programming the System for Quality

As television's supposed technical nature came to be defined along increasingly narrow lines by the mid-1930s and hierarchies of authority concretized into a few sites of institutional power, the evaluation of television's content—particularly as organized around notions of quality—became a key area of struggle in debating the US television system. Continuing a tradition from sound broadcasting, public discussions of quality programming were most often inverted arguments about the identities and capacities of audiences and the methods for funding and regulating broadcasting without the direct involvement of the audience. Rather than lay out the boundaries of what constituted quality, commentators tended to presume agreement on the term and proceed directly to the means for achieving quality and its presumed manifold benefits. Early on in broadcasting, the chief means advocated was commercialization. Although sponsorship would quickly provoke a series of regulatory, public, and activist discontents that produced counterdiscourses of quality, the prevailing logic in American broadcasting tied program quality to production values as a function of economics and consumer choice. Consequently, commercial rather than public, communal, or philanthropic funding won out at least in part because it provided the imprimatur of public consent. Eventually, the quality of programming would be presumed to do something to or say something about American audiences.

Questions of quality have borne considerable evaluative weight throughout the history of broadcasting, but they tend to be a way of talking about cultural power and its allocation without clearly defining the stakes for individuals, communities, institutions, and the culture at large. Appeals to quality have not been simple acts of deceptions—at least not consistently so. Rather, as with the other evaluative discourses examined in the previous chapters, quality has been a means of anchoring broadcast content and practice in broader cultural values while also articulating affirmative norms necessary for coordinating human activity into a seemingly coherent system of cultural and economic exchange. The discourse of quality has a productive nebulousness that has enabled disparate parties to negotiate rough consensuses, hashing out a functioning, or at least plausible, sense of agreement about what broadcasting should be and the various purposes it should serve. In this respect quality has functioned in a manner somewhat similar to "the public interest" in Thomas Streeter's critical analysis of broadcast regulation;[1] it serves as a label that can contingently unite not necessarily congruent, and perhaps irreconcilable, aims in the name of a certain type of order. Although there are, at any given moment, various parties and logics vying for discursive dominance in the accepted meanings of quality, the notion that quality is recognizable and desirable is crucial to its cultural utility. Consequently, those who would talk of and use quality have found built-in incentives to work at framing any particular version of quality as a deep-seated and widely shared form of common sense about not only broadcasting but the institutions and people who made it and made use of it.[2]

Although the incentives to assert a unitary and coherent notion of quality have been strong, the discourse's gravitational pull on other propositions and cultural values in its orbit was never so potent as to collapse them into a cohesive amalgam or even bring them into stable alignment. Instead, each competing articulation has been inflected not only by the overarching logics of quality and conceptions of broadcasting but also the many tidal forces of alternate notions of quality and the cultural, economic, and institutional imperatives that underwrote them. Consequently, while appeals to quality facilitated both the rise of the commercial sponsor system as analyzed by the historian Susan Smulyan and the privatized nationalism examined by the media scholar Michele Hilmes, the articulations of quality ranged far beyond these two precepts.[3] To some degree, commercial and national quality would become foundational in US broadcasting, but the examples that follow demonstrate that the discursive uses of quality were considerably more variegated and subject to dispute. This is how discourse works. Significant disagreements erupt about influential terms, and those struggles are played out through a series of definitional skirmishes. In keeping with Antonio Gramsci's model of hegemony, the dominance of one particular version of quality is never entirely secured.[4] However, as much as the competing articulations could not be decisively reconciled, they have been hashed out into several relatively stable orbits, such that the dynamics of quality's uses can be assayed and participants in the discourse can both abide by and contest its rules of formation.

The prevailing wisdom began to coalesce in the debates over quality in sound broadcasting in the decade prior to the Communication Act of 1934 and was refined in the discussion of quality in public pronouncements about television programming as it tarried at the corner until 1939. What emerged from the debates was an unruly set of discourses that required regular efforts to corral quality television in the pen of commercial broadcasting, while quality was simultaneously being used as a justification for the commercial system.[5] In part this was a result of the contradictory impulses bound up in quality's fostering of cultural and economic hierarchies—the sometimes competing demands of cultural and economic capital. Yet the logics of quality also have, if not relative autonomy, a complex set of relationships with the imperatives of institutions, the practices of professions, and the idiosyncrasies of individuals. For example, while much of the history of American television has been characterized by a confluence of the interests of networks and regulators in a manner that often smacked of protectionism, NBC, CBS, ABC, and the FCC never had an absolute congruence of opinions or agendas.[6] At times quality can seem to be merely a device for producing regulatory disapproval or the semblance of competition in the public interest while not making demands that would provoke significant change. When considered in terms of the contention over quality along and across professional lines, however, the role of quality as a compromise and compromised term in the aspirational language of television suggests something more multifaceted than simply a self-serving feint by the dominant bloc.

Instead, what emerged from popular accounts and imaginations of broadcasting and television was a set of discourses about the quality of broadcast content that were far more concerned with institutional form, practice, and structure than with conventional conceptions of content. That the distinction between form and content is artificial is something of a poststructuralist commonplace, but that distinction was regularly transgressed in the criticism and commentary of the 1920s and 1930s. The era's pragmatics of quality presumed a certain fuzziness in recognition of individual taste and specific context while still seeking to delimit the possible claimants to cultural authority. Indeed, judgments of content quality independent of arguments advocating larger mechanisms for achieving or ensuring quality were relatively rare and largely dependent on notions of generic legitimacy or pure critical authority. In the case of sound broadcasting these were concentrated on endorsements of classical music programs, primarily by classical music critics. In the case of television, with its extended experimental era, criticism of actual content—and the concomitant policing of public tastes—did not gather steam until after World War II, and then only slowly. More commonly, competing notions of quality content were employed in debates about how radio and television should be organized as economic and cultural systems.

The fault lines in the discursive formation of quality content powerfully impacted the shape of broadcasting. The ways in which these seams were managed with the rise of commercial sound broadcasting in the 1920s set the stage for the articulations made of television in the 1930s. In particular, the discontents over commercialism, centralization, competition, and popularity with regard to entertainment programming and the structural regulation of radio created institutions and expectations for television. Later in the 1930s, questions about television programming provoked cultural concern in the absence of commercial broadcasts or even much in the way of public demonstration. A series of speculations about television's content and the function of programming within the imagined television industry worked to assuage anxieties over television programming's lack of publicity in the United States. These speculations were abetted by apologies and explanations made for the American commercial system in the face of public television broadcasting in London in the mid to late 1930s. The work performed to maintain discursive coherence and justify broadcasting's institutions and practices was considerable, and here quality's nebulousness was instrumental to its ability to negotiate among the tensions that threatened rupture among parties with incongruent goals for electronically mediated culture.

Debating and Paying for Quality in Sound Broadcasting

Questions of program quality during the early years of sound broadcasting were debated along several axes, each of which reduces into opposing propositions: quality is undermined by commercialization versus quality demands commercialization for high production values; quality can only be guaranteed by monopoly or centralization versus quality can only be guaranteed by competition; quality is the diversity brought by quantity versus quality is the opposite of quantity; and the audience is the sole appropriate judge of quality versus the audience eschews quality, and thus experts and authorities need to ensure quality. While two or more of these propositions were often allied in the regulatory and cultural debates of the time, the alliances were not necessarily stable and the espousal of a specific position on the quality of broadcast programs was driven by the contingent interests of institutions, creative professionals, activists, and audience members. These oppositions gave shape to the discursive terrain on which television's programs would be planned and evaluated, and although they would undergo dramatic reemphasis as television technology cohered into what would be a very costly means of mass communication, these early articulations echo in debates over the quality of television programs to this day.

By the mid-1920s, debates over commercialization tended to take as their starting point the agreement that in order to have quality, someone had to pay for it, give it away, or—as alleged by the American Society of Composers, Authors and Publishers (ASCAP)—steal it. Quality was intimately tied to economics through questions of capital, investment, labor, and intellectual property. For example, in a 1924 article with the headline "Continuance of Broadcasting Depends on Paying Talent," the *New York Times* reported on a controversy brewing in radio over music royalties and the larger questions of funding broadcasting and warned, "The broadcast listener has never been cautioned that a condition might develop where broadcast service might fall far short of the quality the buyer expected, and might even be discontinued altogether."[7] While E. C. Mills, chairman of the Administrative Committee of ASCAP, provided reassurances that continued profitability of set sales would ensure the continuation of program service, he also contended that broadcasting had been freeloading and must stop: "The purchase of apparatus will be in direct ratio in volume to the quality and merit of the programs. . . . Radio is a niggardly buyer, as now organized. It expects free service from its talent and proposes that the advertising it gives will compensate the entertainer. Radio must pay its way."[8] The key issue for Mills was payment for music, which he considered "the foundation" for popular radio. Although ASCAP would have to seek remedy through the courts, where it won handily, the fundamental question was not *whether* broadcasters would pay but *how* they would finance it all since the model based on set sales was unsustainable with higher operating expenses.

RCA's David Sarnoff agreed that radio must pay for talent and used this premise to advance his argument for organizing broadcasting around a "chain" of a few high-power stations funded by radio manufacturers. Sarnoff averred, "Broadcasting can be made commercially practicable without any means being found for collecting from the consumer. Just as soon as the freedom and universality of radio is destroyed and it is confined to only those who pay for it the fundamentals of the whole situation will be destroyed." He acclaimed a transformative power in radio and sought to maintain "that element of the broadcast situation which makes it possible for opera to go into the districts of the poor as well as the rich, everywhere in the world without charge." He argued that economies of scale could be achieved by nationalizing broadcasts: "If we have a national broadcast station and we have to pay for the talent, we will do it. An industry of half a billion dollars could support it if it were equally and equitably well distributed even if it became necessary to spend two million to five million dollars a year for talent."[9] Sarnoff's argument served RCA's interests in articulating a loosely regulated and hardware-driven future for broadcasting, but it also laid out some clear ambitions for broadcast programming and suggested a set of relations and convergent interests among the audience, the industry, and the cultural imperatives of the nation. Thus, in Sarnoff's early imaginings, such supposed quality programs as opera would bring the nation together, effecting both democracy and uplift.

Other figures in the culture industries disagreed with Sarnoff about the means for achieving quality and pursued a model rooted in transaction rather than transformation in imagining the relationship between broadcasting and the audience. For example, ASCAP's Mills argued, "The radio audience will never permit monopoly to limit the stations to three. If properly approached, a practical plan can be devised whereby broadcasting stations may render superior service for payment instead of inferior service free."[10] Within a month one such alternative method of financing was launched in New York, where the Radio Music Fund Committee sought to gather contributions for music programming on AT&T's station WEAF. The *Times* reported, "It has been apparent during the past year that the novelty of broadcasting was wearing out. Performers became reluctant to actuate the microphone free of charge. If the Music Fund plan is successful it will increase the quality of radio programs because the services of popular and highly talented artists can be obtained."[11] Anticipating in some ways the funding of public television, this scheme would have relied on donations of private citizens and local businesses to ensure that programming to their liking would continue to be broadcast. Using donations to fund public culture was not new, but the *Times* viewed this plan with considerable skepticism on both practical and philosophical grounds. Comparing this model to the emerging public service and license fee model most commonly associated with the BBC, the *Times* emphasized the potential for freeloading in both systems, which presented an obstacle for the plan's gathering sufficient funds.

Significantly, if freeloading was a practical problem, the supposed freeness of content for the private listener was considered part of broadcasting's essence. Here, the article gave considerable weight to Sarnoff's rebuttal, which built on his earlier implication that broadcasting's indirect economics fostered democracy and uplift: "I believe the greatest advantage of broadcasting lies in its universality, in its ability to reach everybody, everywhere, anywhere, in giving free entertainment, culture, instruction and all the items which no other agency has yet been able to do, and it is up to us, with intelligence and technique and broadness of spirit and vision as to the future, to preserve that most delightful element in the whole situation—the freedom of radio." Sarnoff painted the Music Fund as the first step on the road to a subscription system and inveighed, "Just so soon as we destroy that freedom and universality of radio and confine it to only those who pay for it—those who pay for service, in other words—just so soon as we make of broadcasting 'narrowcasting,' we destroy the fundamentals of the whole situation."[12] Sarnoff's invocation of the breadth of broadcasting advanced RCA's corporate interests in maintaining a strong market for equipment sales, but it also represented broadcasting as a national institution with a duty to freedom—and both of these imaginings would complicate commercial broadcasting's negotiation of its economic mission and civic duty.

Because broadcasting could not continue to infringe on copyrighted material and failed to continue to lure talented performers to the microphone with only the hard-to-measure benefit of publicity, it was generally agreed that broadcasting must find a way to pay for itself. AT&T's innovation of toll broadcasting—in essence charging commercial interests for airtime in the same manner as charging for a telephone call—was a key development in sustaining the growth of broadcasting as a commercial venture in the United States.[13] Forecasting developments in broadcasting for 1926, Orrin Dunlap specifically linked commercial sponsorship to quality programming: "One of the big problems which faced 1925 at the beginning was 'Who will pay for broadcasting?' The trend of events and the recognition by advertisers that the ether is a good advertising medium has apparently solved that problem."[14] Crediting AT&T and anticipating the expansion of its chain, Dunlap further noted that "no steps were taken at the 1925 radio conference, called by Secretary [Herbert] Hoover, to prevent advertising over the air; in fact most of the delegates voiced the opinion that it was beneficial to broadcasting because it improved the quality of the programs."[15] Likewise, broadcaster Charles Burke of station WHT hailed the "recognition by leading national advertisers of the value of good-will radio publicity" as improving program quality in a survey of "radio impresarios" at the beginning of the winter 1925–1926 season.[16] Thus quality programming was linked simultaneously to professionalism of the artists, the status of material as intellectual property, the broadcast facilities, and—somewhat counterintuitively—unfettered audience access through the indirect funding mechanisms of sponsorship.

Advertising also drew immediate ire, however, and persistent anticommercial discourses developed alongside the formalization of sponsorship practices. One such critique held that paid radio work placed performers in a position where they could not effectively advocate quality programs while undermining artists' value in their original format. For example, an anonymous singer writing as "The Voice" lamented, "I am seriously wondering if it is worth while [sic] to risk damaging a slow and laboriously built-up reputation for well-chosen, balanced programs in personal appearances by continued paid appearances before the microphone when the studio manager insists that I do the cheap, hackneyed stuff done by every other person with pretensions to a voice in the same classifications as mine." The Voice hypothesized that managers of live entertainment venues would hesitate to hire performers who undercut their reputations for quality by submitting to the demands of radio, and he further advised, "Do not always blame the artist for a poor program in which he may not take much pride of accomplishment; lay it to the studio manager and the dear public and apportion the fault as you see fit."[17] Alongside ASCAP's campaign for compensation, the growing skepticism of radio performance's promotional value worked to shift the financial structures of broadcasting, and significantly, some of these discontents were framed in terms of the intersection of creative control and economic interest.

Taking a different approach, others asserted that artists should perform for art's sake and that concerns with the business side of performance would distract from if not debase the true purpose of art. One listener's letter published alongside that of The Voice opined, "Some of the most prominent musicians in the country have entered into a controversy on the question 'Is broadcasting killing the concert business?' It seems to me that the artists in discussing the subject intrude themselves into a sphere of sounds that is distinctly nonmusical: it is the chink of dollars and cents." This listener idealized the artist: "The musician, the prophet of the world of harmonies, feels the impulse to express himself and brings a message to the soul of man; and as he rises above the common clay, as he reaches a greater number of listeners, he never finds his satisfaction until he embraces the whole world."[18] While such a view worked to silence artistic workers' legitimate interests in their economic well-being, it also articulated the contradictions inherent in broadcasting's oscillations between public and private, intimately touching the soul while promiscuously embracing the whole world. Thus could radio be hoped to provide public betterment through private uplift. Talk of money or soap threatened to spoil those ambitions. Nevertheless, advertising became a foundational element of American broadcasting and with a few notable exceptions, complaints about the nature of broadcast advertising and "idealistic" appeals to art for art's sake predominated over and distracted from calls for a structural reform of American broadcasting.

Centralization, Competition, and Diversity

Complementing the emergent system of sponsorship as a key structure in American broadcasting was the rise of the system of regulated scarcity of broadcast stations. As broadcast historians such as Michele Hilmes have noted, the Radio Conferences and the initial reallocation schemes of the Federal Radio Commission took as a central concern the taming of "chaos" in American broadcasting, and by the late 1920s the preferred tactic was a reduction in the number of stations, which effectively marginalized noncommercial alternatives such as amateur users, unions, churches, and educational institutions.[19] The historian Hugh Slotten finds that the rationale offered for this thinning of the airwaves tended to be couched in technical terms allowing officials to avoid claims of censorship.[20]

Arguments for order, however, were also often intimately linked to the quality of radio signals and programs. Hilmes sees these questions of quality in the distinction between Class A and B stations in the early 1920s,[21] and express invocations of quality in this context appeared in my sample by the mid-1920s. For example, the articulation of quality to centralization could be seen in Sarnoff's call for a few superpower stations or H. P. Davis of Westinghouse's endorsement of radio repeaters: "The primary broadcasting stations need be but a few in number, but will be located where the best of program material is available. This system will materially strengthen the quality of programs, heighten the interest of radio broadcasting and increase its value to the public by enormously increasing the scope of the program and the availability of simple receiving sets."[22] Sound historian Steve J. Wurtzler finds that the national interests in the radio industry "equated *quality* with *standardization*," "extolling . . . chain broadcasts" and ridiculing "local programming for its uneven, indeed amateurish qualities," all while local affiliates were expected to perform nationality by integrating nationally distributed information, formats, and advertisements into local performances and practices.[23] On the government side of the circuit of authority, Secretary of Commerce Herbert Hoover, in a 1925 address calling for regulation, commercialization, and "unobtrusive" advertising, generally advocated a relative scarcity of stations and specifically condemned time-division schemes: "It is quality of program, location and efficiency of transmission that count. None of these will be improved and in most cases they will be ruined by introducing more stations to traverse the same channels. A half dozen good stations in any community, operating full time, will give as much service in quantity and a far better service in quality than eighteen, each on one-third time."[24] Although this signaled a departure from Hoover's earlier assertion that "any attempt to give preference among stations on the basis of quality of programs raises questions of censorship, the implications of which I cannot at present accept," the emergent elite consensus on broadcast regulation used the vehicle of commercial competition to justify the move toward scarcity and centralization of program supply.[25]

As formalized in the Radio Act of 1927, regulated scarcity was quickly articulated in popularized Darwinian discourses of competition, as in the following self-congratulatory statement from the Federal Radio Commission: "The metropolitan listener, with a wide choice of local programs . . . has already had his day in court with the commission. The necessary separation between programs and the stimulation to produce quality programs brought about by the 'survival of the fittest' policy—the commission's interpretation of the public necessity clause of the Radio act—has provided these urban dwellers with first-calls [sic] service."[26] The commission presented its policy of clear-channel allocations as a service to rural listeners who lacked access to local stations and warned that although it was neither inclined nor authorized to censor content, it would consider redundancy in content in future allocation and renewal decisions. As media historian Clifford Doerksen observed, however, the stations failed to live up to those expectations, "making only desultory efforts to discover and meet the particular desires of the rural audience, they put greater energy into simulating grassroots support by wooing the top leadership of agricultural groups."[27]

Despite the FRC's attempts to encourage a variety of programs for remote listeners, public and legislative discontent with allocation policies led to the Davis amendment to the renewal of the Radio Act in 1928. The amendment sought to protect the interests of rural listeners by dividing the country into zones in which equality of service was to be guaranteed.

This plan met with almost immediate criticism on the grounds of quality. The *New York Times* opined, "Programs are the backbone of the radio industry. . . . Radio fans will probably ask why a station sending out high calibre programs from New York or Chicago should have no more power and no better a wave length than a rural station, which does not have the same high-class talent available."[28] Arguing for frequency and power allocation on the basis of program quality, the *Times* held that the law's new standard of geographic equality in terms of licenses and reception misjudged how to provide listeners with the best service. This was echoed by *Times* reader Saxe H. Hanford, who argued in a letter to the editor, "The radio-listening public really expects the commission to do what ought to be done in the public's interest, regardless of fine phrases about State or regional equality. . . . Consideration should be given to the point of the actual listeners they [the stations] have and the quality of programs they can furnish, rather than merely to the population."[29] In these examples some of the underlying contradictions papered over by the label *quality* are brought to the fore, with quality defined in terms of production values or the aesthetic codes of adjacent cultural forms such as vaudeville, legitimate theater, and opera, while competing definitions rooted in equality of access or diversity were silenced in the name of urban cultural hegemony and the interests of industry.

Quality was specifically tied to centralization, and if that resulted in cultural or economic monopoly, then so be it. Indeed, *Radio Broadcast* magazine argued, "It has been established quite definitely as a general principle that communications systems are most efficient as monopolies but, as such, should conduct their operations strictly in the public interest without discrimination and at a carefully regulated rate of profit."[30] This line of argument reached its apogee in 1931 with RCA's assertion, quoted in the *New York Times*, that it should not be held responsible for antitrust violations through nonrenewal of its licenses because, among other things, the public should not lose RCA's subsidiaries' provision of "broadcast programs of exceptional quality."[31] Thus, program quality was both a product and a guarantor of centralized control according to one set of logics.

But countervailing conceptions of competition breeding innovation and quality preexisted broadcasting. The celebration of competition increasingly found advocates within the broadcasting industry as radio regulation raised the possibility of a public service model. Here, the American radio powers were fortunate to have a foil in the British Broadcasting Company/Corporation. The most persistent critique of the commercial system's impact on program quality took shape with the effective counterexample of the BBC, yet the transatlantic critical dyad proved to be more a source of mutual self-definition—indeed self-defense—than self-doubt. Still, the threat of public service broadcast models to the emerging commercial system should not be underestimated. Both Australia and Canada moved in the direction of public service systems during this period, and in both cases the specific question of quality without commercials was an issue in press accounts.[32] Hilmes details the ways in which the two models were deployed in opposition to one another, even as the institutional leadership at NBC and the BBC engaged in diplomacy or cooperation.[33] In the discursive struggle over the relationship between funding and program quality, NBC and the BBC had two points of agreement and several points of contention. The first point of agreement was the aforementioned assumption that quality programming had a value and therefore had a cost (notably, the corollary proposition that cost indicated value and quality was and is a typical marketing strategy that will become significant to our examination). The second point of agreement was that there should not be a direct economic mechanism between program and audiences. In the emerging American model sponsors would fund programs in their own interest and pay for them through surcharges on products sold to consumers. In the British model a license fee would be collected from all set owners, and that fee would fund programs designed by the BBC, ostensibly for the benefit of the public. This agreement on programming being situated within specific dynamics of ownership and labor and the abstraction of the audience—often couched as a technical necessity but just as significantly a choice that favored radio sales and the cultivation of a national audience—cast questions of quality programming in terms sufficiently similar that British and American broadcasting could mutually serve as defining others.[34] The BBC's salience to American debates on quality programming was accentuated in the early 1930s after the Federal Radio Commission's reorganization of American broadcasting through substantial reallocation of frequencies that effectively favored commercial broadcasters.

In the period between the reallocation schemes stemming from the Radio Act of 1927 and the cementing of the commercial system in the Communications Act of 1934—or rather the failure of the later act to reconsider, much less reform, the pre-Depression, corporate-friendly thinking that had long made communications the purview of commerce—there was a brief moment when other possibilities were put forth. Media historian and activist Robert McChesney argues that this period should be conceived in terms of "conflict, not consensus," and emphasizes the political and economic interests that underwrote this foreclosure of more diverse access to the public's airwaves.[35] Michele Hilmes looks at the same moment and emphasizes the cultural struggle to define broadcasting, finding that proponents of the commercial system pointed to the BBC as an example of inadequate program diversity and proposed that highbrow broadcasters such as educational institutions would demonstrate similar limitations in the United States.[36] Meanwhile, these advocates simultaneously silenced the multitude of voices derided as propaganda programming of one stripe or another through such acts as the FRC's favoring "general public service" stations, defined as those stations that sold airtime, over "special interests" such as trade unions, religious broadcasters, and educational institutions. Here questions of quality were wracked by contradictions over commerce, competition, and centralization.

Commercials remained a key dispute in questions of quality. The chairman of the British Radio Manufacturers' Association, R. Milward Ellis, asserted, "There is, however, a uniform high quality to the British programs not to be found in America. This is likewise due in large measure to the economic system in the United States which permits advertising to destroy the otherwise splendid quality of many American programs."[37] While Ellis conceded the considerably greater economic resources provided by the sponsor system and greater quantity of programming, he argued that the American system was hampered by hucksterism and too great a dispersal of investment. Others saw the BBC as illuminating additional shortcomings in the American system, such as an incorrect professionalization of broadcasting. Felix Orman, a frequent correspondent to the editor of the *New York Times*, wrote, "The difference between the English and the American system of purveying radio entertainment is not merely that in England they have no advertising and in America we have: it is in the very important fact that in England radio entertainment is regarded as professional work, just as much of the theater is, and is in [the] charge of experienced professional people selected for their skill in devising and presenting effective entertainment."[38] Orman asserted that "the tragedy of American radio" stemmed not only from its being captive to "the dragon of shrieking commercialism" but also because the admen in control lacked both knowledge of and skill at entertainment and "radio technique."[39] Through these and other pronouncements about professionalization, reliability of both content and the system was framed as a key concern in achieving acceptable quality.

The standard rebuttal of this position depicted sponsorship as the fountainhead of higher production values. This was expressly articulated in terms of quality in a letter to the editor by Orman's fellow reader Edward F. Thomas, who noted that in 1931 American broadcasters spent more than thirty times as much as the BBC, which consequently allowed American radio to regularly air talent whose fees would be prohibitively expensive for British broadcasting. While Thomas believed much could be done to improve American broadcasting, he argued that "the adoption of a non-advertiser system as in England in place of our advertiser system would so reduce the income of broadcasting that the high quality programs now on the air would be impossible. As to the complaint, it is unfortunate that many advertisers and station operators are misusing the medium, but there is nothing to prevent the listener from turning his dial."[40] Notably, Thomas and others perpetuated a version of the either/or fallacy in their assertion that American broadcasting's relative diversity of service was incompatible with a public service system. While the United States and the United Kingdom may have shared a common language, the technical, geographic, and diplomatic conditions in which their broadcast institutions emerged limited the latter's options for diverse and competing broadcasters. In contrast, while internal political and cultural concerns militated against a BBC-style public service broadcaster in the United States, having such a broadcaster would not have precluded having a number of other broadcasters or their use of advertising. Still, the ability of the American system to finance higher-cost programming worked to articulate a causal link between the commercial system and program quality.

Others would continue to question this system and argue that bigger did not mean better. Stanley Rayfield, another *Times* reader, rejoined, "Above all, we need to distinguish between the qualitative and the quantitative in entertainment. Seventy-five million dollars may buy bigger programs, but are they better ones?" After lauding several BBC programs as "sustained entertainment of the highest quality," he lamented, "American broadcasting, with all its floods of money, is not giving us a standard of entertainment—let alone education—that is reasonably intelligent. Its most glaring weakness, of course, is that it has precious little to offer Mr. Menken's [*sic*] 'civilized minority.' So long as most of the major programs are in the hands of advertisers, radio standards are bound to remain on the lowest level of intelligence and esthetic appreciation." In particular, Rayfield held that American programs were insufficiently attentive to the needs of the listener, holding that English programs, free of the influence of advertising and "big business," were more attuned to the "intimate" nature of radio.[41] In this string of exchanges, the writers traversed the discursive terrain shaped by the emerging systemic dichotomy typified and largely defined by Britain and the United States. Here quality is structured in ambiguity, agreed upon as an ideal but left undefined in substance and the subject of contradiction in terms of broadcasting practice.

Condemnatory accounts of the BBC also often emphasized its monopoly structure and the paternalistic emphasis on needs rather than wants. For example, a 1930 article, subtitled "3,160,000 Set Owners in British Isles Get What the Broadcasters Think They Need Rather Than What They Want," reported: "The attempt to carry out an ideal in regard to music is particularly pronounced and complaints from angry listeners as to some of the high-brow nature of some of the programs do not deter the broadcasters from devoting an extraordinary amount of work to what they believe are the best."[42] This account ran adjacent to a report of Lee De Forest's call for increased regulatory scarcity combined with higher power stations, which was justified in part in terms of quality. His scheme was similar to the one advocated by Sarnoff in the mid-1920s. He advocated cutting the number of stations from five hundred to fifty, increasing their power, and networking them in order to provide everyone in the United States access to ten stations, providing "programs of the highest quality" with the stations differentiated by musical genres such as classical or dance.[43] De Forest's vision of quality in diversity or a diversity of quality appears to have been more a function of his belief in technical and institutional fixes than of his belief in the salutary effects of commerce. The argument, however, "that under commercial sponsorship of programs there is more competition and therefore greater liveliness and diversity" was sufficiently widespread that *New York Times* radio journalist Orrin Dunlap reported it was a stock line of argumentation among "thousands of high school students throughout the country . . . debating the merits of the American broadcasting system vs. the British plan."[44] Thus, the American system produced quality through the mechanism of quantity while being simultaneously underwritten by scarcity, or so the arguments went.

Audience Quality

Complicating the uses of quality further was the contradictory set of propositions about the relationship between the audience and the quality of the program. According to these, the audience either could not be trusted to appreciate quality—gravitating toward the basest programs and possibly being actively repelled by good programming—or it was quality's sole measure, with the ability to draw and keep the audience proof of high quality. Neither of these propositions would result in giving the audience much control over programming.

Since the 1920s, one line of argument about broadcasting and its audience has sought to oppose quality and popularity, ranging from station WHN's policy of "masses rather than classes" to Sarnoff's opposition to subscription plans as elitist incursions on radio's universality.[45] To some degree this view drew on the conceptions of quality steeped in paternalism and the Arnoldian/Reithian vision of cultural uplift—the quality of the BBC. It also had a domestic dimension, however, in which regional discontents and an emergent popular culture provoked a cultural struggle that sought to deny hegemony to various high cultures.[46] For advocates of cultural uplift these populist and rural resisters became the presumed target of ennobling programming, while their varying forms of otherness served as the proof that popularity was problematic.[47] The position presuming popularity to be a function of mass audience approval and thus a marker of low quality is captured in a letter espousing "uplift" and disparaging

"the poor quality of the programs being broadcast," where *New York Times* reader
and atheist activist Freeman Hopwood opined that the people might want "jazz
and junk," but broadcasting should also cater to "enlightened folks, people of
culture."[48] He asked, "Can we not have a few programs free from the taint of
commercialism, free from the whinings of the mammy-shouters, free from the
hoarse bleatings of the politicians, free from the inanities of the preachers, free
from the bunk of the Kiwanians and the Rotarians, free from the clanging of jazz
bands, free from the silly and really detrimental bedtime stories, or what not?"[49]
Again obtrusive commercials and commercialism are presumed to taint radio's
programs and subvert the true purpose of broadcasting, whether serving the
enlightened or enlightening the servants. Hopwood's chief concern was that
the emerging commercial structure of broadcasting was giving too much power
to the masses.

In contrast, other early voices, particularly those within the regulatory and
industrial communities, saw a convergence of audience interest with quality.
In 1927, for example, FRC commissioner Bellows regarded the anonymity of the
audience as a barrier to quality. He argued that unlike the indices for "quality
and quantity of services rendered" that might be found in newspaper circula-
tions, church attendance, or a store's gross receipts, "by no system of math-
ematics yet devised can you find out how many people listen to a radio station,
and still less can you find out what they really think when they listen to it."
Bellows, however, stated his certainty that the audience was not yet satisfied
with programming, asserting that radio's novelty had worn off and that "the
listener of today has been educated to demand quality in entertainment; he
is fast learning to demand, in addition to entertainment, a varied and complex service of education and enlightenment." Bellows foresaw "two dangers"
confronting broadcasting: "The first is that the public demand for quality and
service will progress more rapidly than the ability of the stations to keep pace
with it, while the second is that the listeners will become bored and surfeited
with the programs they are receiving before the broadcasters are aware of it."[50]
In this imagining, the audience demands quality, but the necessary feedback
mechanisms are lacking. This position resounds to this day in claims that better audience measurement through demographics or active feedback or a more
direct economics will finally bring broadcasting in line with the conceptions of
quality of various elites. In a similar vein Bellows advocated a second solution
that came to characterize optimistic visions of the multichannel world: "offering more programs."[51] Thus, quantity was posed as a solution to the conundrum
of the unknowable audience's desire for quality.

While we can hear echoes of both in the debates of today, neither Hopwood's nor Bellows's early articulations of the relationship between quality and
the audience called the tune in the near-term orchestrations of the politics of

quality in American broadcasting. Both were undermined by one of the key iro-
nies of broadcasting—the uncertain reception of radio makes the audience a
convenient screen onto which critics, producers, and advertisers project their
hopes and fears, yet to honestly confront the audience's being in quite a significant way an imaginary group would not only gut American broadcasting's
emergent economic model but also call the political justifications for licensing
and other regulation into question. Instead, the positions that would come
to speak for quality over the next fifty years worked to disavow or exploit the
disconnect with the audience in order to fit particular institutional needs. The
industry relied on flimsy audience measurement schemes that were probably
inaccurate in terms of the size and composition of the audience and could not
possibly have met Bellows's standard of revealing what the audience thought
of programs.[52]

This is not to say that the audience was actually silent. While the measurement systems that sought to reify audiences as a medium of exchange may
have found it convenient to render listeners in the abstract, listeners regularly
provided feedback through a number of mechanisms. They wrote letters to the
fan magazines that had supplanted enthusiast publications like *Radio News* as
the sites for popular reflections on broadcasting. Historian Elena Razlogova's
analysis of listener letters reveals that these writers, the measurable majority of
them women, reflected not just on individual programs but their perceptions of
radio's impact on its listener and the political economy of broadcasting.[53] Crucially, Razlogova finds that listeners' mediated "debate" about the structure of
broadcasting and its institutions "started out from an assumption that listeners
have the power to control broadcasting," and in the early network era listeners
were able to exercise that power, at least with regard to programs if less so in
the case of the larger structures of broadcasting.[54] By the early 1930s, broadcasters, producers, and agencies made use of fan letters and responses to contests
to measure popularity, plan program development, and argue with one another
about how to attract and please the largest group.[55] Members of the listening
public even made their voices heard over the radio through audience participation shows ranging from contest and quiz formats to forum and debate shows to
documentaries about daily life. Media historian Jason Loviglio argues that such
formats "made this new national audience an important part of radio entertainment" and facilitated that audience's "stand[ing] in for the nation in general and
'the people' in particular."[56] In this last instance, in particular, there is an attempt
to fuse popularity and the national vision of quality in a manner that served both
the political and economic interests of the developing broadcast order.

Meanwhile, advocates of high-culture programming came to rely on already
hoary notions of education and art as bulwarks against the depredations of the
masses and simultaneously claim a significant audience of cultured listeners,

and later viewers, who were not being measured and were not writing in to make their opinions heard. An example of the latter can be seen in a 1932 article arguing, "People are—or ought to be—pleased with the improved quality of musical programs. They are better, even in their jazziest moments, than they used to be because more varied by excellent selections. But listeners-in do not write much when they are pleased. It is when they dislike a program that they take pen in hand and say so."[57] This example shows the beginnings of a discourse that held the critically ascribed quality of a program to predominate over the various measures of audiences.

Moreover, high-culture skepticism of audience taste ran sufficiently high during broadcasting's formative years that popularity was more likely to be considered suspect than was quality. For example, classical music critic Olin Downes condemned musical programs of the early 1930s as "hav[ing] been of an exceedingly cheap and inferior quality," and he equated popularity with pandering. Downes hailed new "ambitious radio programs" in which "the 'best music' will include a number of well-known and popular masterpieces, but in no case are the programs supposed to go beneath the level of the best, or make compromises or concessions for the purpose of 'popularity.'"[58] That *popularity* should wear the punctuation marks of contingency reveals two facets of the emerging definition of *quality* as claimed by broadly construed high culture. On the one hand, quality was removed from systems of measurement, while on the other it was placed within regimes of institutional authority that claim a direct correlation between ascribed quality and an audience appeal that is unmeasurable yet essential. The historian Bruce Lenthall observes that public intellectuals in the 1930s conceived of the masses, in both condemnations and celebrations of popularity, as the guiding principle for producing not just programs but the systems of communication and consumption that stemmed from broadcasting.[59] Attempts to standardize programming and institutional structure and legitimate those processes in terms of audience demand certainly effected a more centralized and commercialized system of broadcasting, but as Lenthall argues, the ability of broadcasting to create a mass culture or a mass audience is complicated by the local and personal uses of that culture and reception of particular programs. As much as the personalization of radio may have afforded listeners ways to make broadcasting their own and make a way in modernity, in the specific logics of quality as they ran a critical-industrial-regulatory circuit, the imagination of audiences as a collective mass predominated.

Nevertheless, some participants in the discourse on radio's quality sought to add particularity to conceptions of listening and listeners, even as they argued that quality was proven by popularity. The clearest articulation of this position was put forth by Marian S. Carter, assistant program director for CBS, in 1932. When asked what women wanted out of broadcasting, Carter first decried the inherent sexism of a question that sought to reduce the tastes of half the population into a single stereotype and then argued, "In my radio experience I have discovered no program structure in which quality does not determine the program's popularity. Who can say, for example, that programs specifically designed to obtain the maximum of feminine appeal exert a more effective influence than *Amos 'n' Andy*, *Myrt and Marge*, Jessica Dragonette, Kate Smith, or the glorious music of Leopold Stokowski? I feel that each of these in its time and place awakens a response which may be called universal. Quality will invariably dominate, irrespective of the guise in which it appears."[60] Carter follows this claim by pinning quality to "entertainment," a concept she sees as fraught with the potential for dispute but nevertheless the *sine qua non* of a program's ability to be "effective," in attracting and influencing an audience.[61]

In a follow-up article Carter expanded on these principles. The crux of her second article was that entertainment might be idiosyncratic, but quality was first in an industrial hierarchy of values: "First—quality; second—competition; and third—universality of appeal." Carter saw quality as subsuming the other two: "But in the last analysis, it invariably resolves itself to the question of quality, irrespective of type. The beauty expert, salon, jazz or symphony orchestra, the exponent of domestic science, the personality singer, the comedy and dramatic sketches, the opera stars and favorites of screen and theatre, each and everyone, thru the quality of their performance, and quality alone find their rightful places in the minds of the radio audience."[62] In this scheme quality is the guarantor of the proper execution of broadcasting's commercial and social obligations yet is also still mysterious, vaguely defined, and the province of professional expertise. The audience could be conjured to verify the authority of network executives and advertisers, but to some degree the audience was a formality needed for the practices of mass marketing and the claim that new nationalizing chains still cared about local or individual consumers.

At this juncture, with the consolidation of American broadcasting into the commercial structures that would persist with intermittent challenges throughout the twentieth century, the high-culture and industrial arguments for quality draw their respective sides of the curtain on other possible models. Systems in which quality was defined as a diversity of access and voices or a paradigm that relied on actual audience responses to programming and its social effects or a wholehearted embrace of commercials and commercialism were not to be. Instead, the diverse and contradictory strands of quality, present in this early period, were snipped off to cleanly tailor American broadcasting to the dimensions of oligopoly capitalism as wed to the vestigial elements of the progressive movement that permeated the Roosevelt administrations. The progressive-corporate bloc that emerged through fierce struggle over the NRA and other elements of the early New Deal would disarticulate industrial structure and program form and content in such a fashion that skirmishes at the margins would provide cover for a thoroughly captive system of regulation. The presumed duties of broadcasters came to be defined in terms of economic performance rather than specific metrics of social or cultural obligation. Here, notions of quality—especially as superficially opposed to commercials yet reliant on commerce and competition, as a function of consolidation yet dependent on diversity, as opposed to the basest impulses of the audience yet bound up in an odd dichotomy cum symbiosis with popularity—served to distract from contentious policy questions about the emerging industrial-cultural order.

Quality and Television's Anticipated Audience

In the early 1930s, despite mechanical television's suppression and the continued assessment of electronic television as commercially unviable, the emergent radio order had trouble accommodating television in general and articulating a coherent place for television programming in particular. Television programming posed challenges for broadcasting in terms of imagining the audience in the home, imagining the national audience as the product of networked broadcasts, and imagining the superiority of the American system to competing public service models. The following sections explore each of these problems in detail. In each instance television threatened to disrupt a seemingly sturdy but ultimately vulnerable construct. For example, the conception of national programming as the cultural dominant was a wish on the part of certain parties rather than a fact. As both Clifford Doerksen and Alexander Russo have demonstrated, rural, rogue, and regional broadcasters and audiences complicated and contested the nationalization of broadcasting and the dissemination of cosmopolitan culture.[63] Television's technical and economic barriers to networking—particularly the lack of suitable infrastructure—would exacerbate these complications. Consequently, in each instance quality had to be subtly rearticulated to contain potentially disruptive contradictions. In none of these cases was success total. Among other obstacles, the absence of American television programming for public consumption deprived the discourse of quality of two of its most powerful tools, the affirmative and negative referents. A large part of quality's power with regard to programming is in naming, and the programs labeled quality or dreck serve as trim to hide the seams. The absence of programming also allowed, however, for speculation on the part of institutional authorities, who ably exploited the situation to frame questions of quality in their own interests.

A chief concern for the broadcasters starting in the late 1920s was the process of adapting the audience to television. Early on, the audience and its competencies were thought to pose problems for television. As I noted in the preceding chapter, H. Davis of Westinghouse saw the audience's habituation to quality radio programming as a significant barrier to the early introduction of "gawkish" television.[64] In contrast, Orrin Dunlap regarded the breadth of broadcasting and its indirect economics as a specific threat to television. In a tribute to John Hays Hammond, Dunlap first hailed Hammond's early schemes for charging listeners tolls or subscription fees as the proper solution to paying for programming and then portrayed the sponsor system as a serendipitous solution that staved off broadcasting's collapse.[65] Yet television threatened to upset the delicate balance by costing more while attracting more freeloaders and thus was considered to necessitate a further technical and economic fix. For this Dunlap praised Hammond's invention of a device that would encrypt radio signals and thereby allow for a process "called 'narrowcasting'" of events such as high-profile football and baseball games.[66] Here, in 1930, we see the beginnings of the line of thought that seeks to distinguish premium television from mass communication through technical means of distribution. Attempts to pin broadly construed notions of quality programming to a rarified audience through technical and economic discrimination have formed a recurrent theme in the history of television, spanning from Hammond's narrowcasting to Pay TV of the 1950s to Home Box Office to Video On Demand, and spawned substantial ambivalence on the part of critics and industry insiders about the nature of television's audience.

Two additional questions of audiences, quality, and the aspirant commercial structure of television came into play in the early to mid-1930s. First, the relationship between quality and novelty was complicated by the emergence of television, and second, the tacitly assumed identity between quality and morality was both openly articulated and called increasingly into question. In both cases there is an underlying presumption about the industrial imperative to titillate the audience with the new, the illicit, or better both. In the case of the former, the ideal audience was presumed to be a savvy consumer with contemporary and cultivated tastes. In the case of the latter, the audience was presumed to be heterogeneous, and an argument was made to favor supposed tasteful adults rather than children. If the imperative to excite underwrote both strands, its corollary was the assertion of an ability to edify.

In a 1935 article William S. Paley, head of CBS, argued that broadcasting could serve as an effective and democratic countermeasure to the notion that culture was the birthright of an elite few. Although Paley's argument and position of authority rested on a bedrock of capitalist privilege, he clearly advocated a specific obligation on the part of the government and private enterprise (in the American tradition of pragmatically enlightened self-interest) to educate the individual: "In a society which the masses govern, order can be preserved and social progress assured only if the masses receive the necessary education to bear their heavy responsibility."[67] In developing an informed citizenry, Paley

saw a specific challenge: "A very brief experience with broadcasting is quite sufficient to prove that if radio is to teach at all, it must first master the problem
of attracting and holding its audience—an audience not confined to the classroom, not deferential to an instructor's authority, and not indisposed to ram-
ble all over the air waves if one turn of the dial provides a voice that bores."[68]
Paramount among the virtues that would attract an audience for education was
"quality." In a section titled "Novelty versus Quality," Paley argued that whether
for commerce or public service the audience would no longer stand for gimmicks such as a broadcast of music via transoceanic hookup: "It also has to be
a very good quartet, playing very good music. If on another wave length, there
is available better music from a trio in a nearby town, most listeners will today
choose the trio."[69] This praise of quality over novelty fit within a push to lock
broadcasting, particularly network broadcasting, into a stable set of practices
alongside the regulatory surety of the 1934 Communications Act.

Significantly, the issue of quality versus novelty was also identified as a significant challenge to the popularization and commercialization of television.
For example, *Business Week* reported that the production values and consequent
costs needed to maintain an audience and foster their investment in relatively
expensive receivers made regular live television broadcasts impractical in 1935:
"Now an advertiser might be willing to splurge on an occasional broadcast of
this kind, but he could scarcely be expected to meet the costs of sponsoring
a live talent show over the local television station in each major market. And
he would be faced with that necessity if he wanted to do the job on any sort of
national basis, for to date the problem of transmitting television by a hookup
comparable to a national radio network is far from licked."[70] For this reason
Business Week held that filmed programming was most likely to predominate in
television. In these circumstances television was to be held to a more stringent
standard than either sound broadcasting or early cinema. It could not be merely
entertaining; it had to endure. By these measures television was bound to fail as
it could not live up to its unreasonable, prepopular positioning, nor were there
adequate technical means to preserve experimental or even early commercial
television broadcasts to later assess its staying power.

These built-in failings were exacerbated by a pessimistic streak in the
pragmatic posture of the great defender of the popular or lively arts, critic
Gilbert Seldes, who would eventually become CBS's chief of experimental programming. Paley's future employee argued that radio was a particular failure
in terms of education because the educational broadcasters had presumed a
captive audience, as in the disciplinary classroom.[71] His intermingled valorization of entertainment and castigation of other cultural authorities continued:
"The high-minded do not like to face the actual situation in radio, which is that
all of its desirable effects are based on the habit of listening which was created

largely by programmes trivial and banal in themselves. In countries with highly centralized authority it is possible that people listen to the radio because what they hear is important; and the extreme form is obligatory listening as it is practised in Germany." In contrast, Seldes asserted that for democracies "radio is important because people listen to it, even when it is trivial; the audience which listened to the radio debate on the Supreme Court was created in the first place by Ed Wynn, Rudy Vallee, Amos 'n' Andy, and Kate Smith." Seldes argued that this phenomenon would likely be accelerated by television, claiming, "The unforeseen result, the creation of an audience which can be influenced to political action, is the thing that makes radio programmes important and justifies all our speculations about television. For the audience which television will create will be more attentive and, if properly handled, more suggestible even than the audience of radio."[72] Notably, he regarded audience attention with ambivalence, seeing it as a necessary precondition for aesthetic uplift but also social control.[73] Here and elsewhere, Seldes was perhaps the 1930s' foremost advocate for what contemporary critics have termed "popular quality,"[74] a form of the argument put forth in the 1930s by Marian Carter, in which the audience is the court of final appeal in judgments of quality, yet he was not shy about criticizing successful cultural products as he viewed the culture industries as fundamentally skewed by economic and institutional biases. Among the many tenets of Seldes's critical philosophy were an emphasis on maturity on the part of both cultural products and the audience and a corollary dismay over what he saw as the counterproductive US preoccupation with courting youth both in marketing and attempting to make all of culture safe for children.[75]

Based on present-day uses of quality, one might expect to find a robust body of discourses advocating quality in terms that were either expressly moralistic or preoccupied with the negative effects low-quality broadcast content would have on children or a more broadly paedocratized audience. But the record in the popular press was considerably more complicated. Certainly there were persistent discourses positioning the audience as children or justifying regulation in the name of children as with the Payne Fund studies of the 1930s, but most of the language about protecting audiences in terms of quality involved the questions of technical obsolescence that I addressed in the first and second chapters. Although quality was invoked as part of broadcasting's mission of education and uplift, the specific language of quality as a bulwark against immoral incursions on the home was relatively rare in the 1930s.

Instead, quality was at least as commonly portrayed as under threat from would-be arbiters of the nation's taste. In a letter to the *New York Times*, for example, Roy L. Albertson complained, "The question of what is good and what is bad in radio seems to be agitating the minds of many professional busybodies these days." He decried "these super-patriots [who] would have you believe that they have a direct command from heaven to protect little Willie from the daring exploits of a hero who develops stamina from eating a bowlful of cereal each morning. Now that everything else has been thoroughly reformed through the noble experiment of prohibition, they must now turn their attention to the field of broadcasting." With derision for the paedocratic justification for regulation, Albertson argued, "the uniformly excellent quality of the network programs" obviated the need for "self-appointed vigilantes" and "the meddling and censorship of noisy minorities." He advocated a pluralistic, if stereotypical, vision in which "a good hillbilly program from a station in Dallas is just as uplifting to the plain, homespun people of the Southwest as is the WJZ or WEAF symphony hour in the ultra-metropolitan atmosphere of New York." In the end, quality was the result of choice and with choice "the mere twisting of the dial on the individual receiving set will serve as the finest kind of censorship for a good many years to come."[76] Thus, moral evaluation of broadcasting beyond the individual was framed in opposition to quality.

Nevertheless, broadcasting's domestic reception was regularly put forward as a justification for content regulation. For instance, an opinion piece in the *New York Times* complained of "brazen broadcasts," arguing, "Furthermore, radio flashes directly into the family circle. There are countless children in the audience. Good taste is in order at all times. In 'public interest, convenience and necessity' which the law specifies, there is no place in the American air for what a listener might term 'a brazen or raw broadcast.' With every broadcast station license goes a heavy public responsibility."[77] Quality came up in the rebuttal, where a recent speech by the vice chairman of the FCC, Dr. Irvin Stewart, was quoted:

> Good taste cannot be legislated and I suspect it cannot even be administratively required. . . . Good taste, a sense of public responsibility and elementary decency on the part of the broadcast licensees should make it unnecessary for the commission ever to explore the possibilities of its power effectively to regulate advertising. Can the commission set up minimum standards of program quality which all licensees would have to meet? Standards of engineering efficiency are fairly easy of formulation and of application. Standards of program quality would be difficult both of formulation and of application. . . . I for one, however, am not prepared at this time to state that standards of program quality are impossible either of formulation or of application. The field is one in which the commission has done nothing—it may possibly remain one in which the commission will do nothing. The answer must depend on the broadcaster.[78]

Three things are of note in these comments by Stewart. First, the governance of content was considered to be the regulation of advertising. The system of commercial sponsorship in which advertisers bought time from the networks and stations and then produced programs held particular appeal for regulators and legislators uncomfortable with governing content in that it purported to reproduce the marketplace of ideas and thereby allow them to focus on supposedly technical regulation. This is not the absence of regulation but instead the privatization of regulation. Second, though couched in terms of the difficulty and questionable desirability of regulating content quality, Stewart is clearly making a threat. This is part of a long tradition of warnings, of which Newton Minow's "Vast Wasteland" speech to the National Association of Broadcasters [NAB] is the most famous, where broadcasting authorities assert the power to govern content as a means of steering industry behavior without exercising direct control. Third, in this instance the combination of quality's nebulousness and uninterrogated desirability provided a mechanism for both the justification of privatized regulation and the surveillance of the commercial guardians of the public's airwaves.

For television the contradictions between quality as maturity and quality as morality would play out on the figure of the child in the late 1940s and 1950s,[79] but in the 1930s quality for broadcasting, and particularly for television, rested on uncertainties about the audience that stemmed not only from the technological underpinnings of radiating a signal but also from the decisions to keep higher-definition television programs largely out of the public eye. A different set of decisions had been made across the Atlantic in Great Britain, and the fact of television broadcasts for public consumption opened up another site of ambivalences about quality programming.

National, Quality Television

In the 1930s television provoked two sets of disruptions for American conceptions of broadcasting as a national institution, and questions of quality would play a role in both. First, higher-definition television technology was unworkable for conventional national networking with either high-power transmission or use of standard phone lines, which were unsuitable for television's bandwidth demands. As I noted in my first chapter, this problem posed a specific threat to the economic interests of RCA and its subsidiary NBC, but it was more broadly disruptive of the established definitions of broadcasting and the foundational precepts for radio regulation. Quality would be deployed by broadcasters and regulators to shore up the boundaries of national broadcasting and consequently that construct of the American "nation," itself an ongoing project of formation through the rituals of national imagination such as gathering around radio's communal hearth for a fireside chat with the president. The second source of disruptions was the publication of reports of television broadcasts by other nations, including Germany and other European nations but principally the broadcasting activities of the BBC. These broadcasts raised difficult questions, in particular for the FCC and RCA, and launched an armada of American explanations drawing on quality to explain how the United States was not falling behind in television and why the BBC's move into sight broadcasting did not reflect favorably on the British system of regulation, financing, and production. In both cases quality came to the rescue of broadcasting as a national institution, yet quality stood in adjacency to nation as a defining term for broadcasting, occupying the liminal space that gave it access to notions of cosmopolitan sophistication and aesthetic transcendence.

Broadcasting as a national enterprise, rather than a primarily local, regional, or transnational set of institutions and practices, emerged in the period between the beginning of World War I in Europe and the Radio Act of 1927. Prior to the First World War, radio was characterized by transnational commercial structures such as the Marconi companies, a nationally enforced yet internationally applicable system of intellectual property, and a technology subject to the limitations of distance rather than borders. Nations claimed regulatory power and the right to negotiate use of the spectrum with other nations, but many of the early uses of radio either exceeded the bounds of the strictly national in their most basic application—as with colonial administration, imperialist military command and control, or transnational shipping and transport—or emphasized locality, as with municipal uses for police and fire communications or amateur practices such as dx-ing, where nationality was a marker of distance first and distinction second.[80] Radio's organization along national lines was a product of assertions of power through legislation, coercion, and organization. Measures such as the formation of nationally organized amateur groups like the American Radio Relay League (established 1914) were certainly significant in the assertion of radio as a national enterprise,[81] but foremost were the actions of governments, such as the United States' expropriation of the American Marconi company and its holdings, the formation of a wartime patent pool, the banning of amateur transmission during the war, and the enlistment of many of those amateurs in the armed forces.[82] Coming out of the war, American radio had been reconfigured with a concentration of assets along national lines, formalized with the creation of the Radio Corporation of America in 1919.[83]

By the early 1920s, Westinghouse's KDKA and AT&T's WEAF were developing business models for the profitable exploitation of *broadcasting*—a term adapted from agriculture into publishing and finally coming to mean the transmission of a signal from a single point to multiple recipients.[84] With the rise of commercial broadcasting, radio's role in the imagining of American national identity and culture was accelerated. Broadcast historian Michele Hilmes argues that radio was a significant factor in the creation of a national identity, promising to span the physical vastness of the landscape and cultural divisions of a heterogeneous society.[85] Broadcast programming was crucial to the national imagining of "who we are and who we are not," conceived by Hilmes as interconnected processes of identification and othering encouraged by programs such as *Amos 'n' Andy*. These programs along with what Steve Wurtzler identifies as "the notion that such broadcasts simultaneously addressed and could thereby (re)constitute a geographically dispersed national public" aimed—or at least claimed—to shore up the cultural bounds of a nation wracked with the tensions provoked by internal and external immigration, industrialization, urbanization, persistent discrimination against women and racial and ethnic minorities, and the rise of mass culture.[86] At the same time, as the historian Susan Smulyan details, those tensions were real and persistent as was resistance to monopoly and northeastern cultural hegemony over broadcasting.[87] Nevertheless, a national stamp was placed on broadcasting through a series of regulations culminating in the Radio Act of 1927, which firmly entrenched federal control over broadcasting, and through the establishment of networks, notably the formation of RCA's subsidiary, the National Broadcasting Company, in 1926.

For NBC, quality programming was articulated as an adjunct of the network's national mission. In one of the advertisements announcing the formation of NBC, RCA framed the relationship among nation, quantity, and quality:

> The market for receiving sets in the future will be determined largely by the quantity and quality of the programs broadcast.
>
> We say quantity because they must be diversified enough so that some of them will appeal to all possible listeners.
>
> We say quality because each program must be the best of its kind. If that ideal were to be reached, no home in the United States could afford to be without a radio receiving set.
>
> The purpose of the new company will be to provide the best program available for broadcasting in the United States. . . .
>
> It is hoped that arrangements may be made so that every event of national importance may be broadcast widely throughout the United States. . . .
>
> The Radio Corporation of America is not in any sense seeking a monopoly of the air. This would be a liability rather than an asset. It is seeking, however, to provide machinery which will insure national distribution of national programs, and a wider distribution of programs of the highest quality.[88]

The distinctions between quantity and quality at the beginning and national programs and programs of the highest quality at the end point to the complex linkages among these structuring concepts in the consolidating system of

broadcasting. The relationship between quality and quantity was one of ambivalence; similarly, the national and quality missions of NBC were conceived in
distinction—a cooperative distinction in this instance, but a distinction nonetheless. The creation of NBC threaded both cultural and regulatory needles.[89] In
the name of nation and quality NBC would be America's BBC but without the
troublesome government oversight and supposedly stodgy "programmes."

NBC was an argument and institution that would serve RCA well. Even so, the
nationality of the network was sometimes more a product of rhetoric than a fact
of practice or infrastructure. As radio historian Alexander Russo demonstrates,
networks had to negotiate coverage gaps, stations and sponsors opting in and out
of programs and markets respectively, and the development of local and regional
markets, among other challenges to a "uniformly connected and fully integrated"
national network.[90] By the mid-1930s, television promised to amplify those challenges to the parent and subsidiary with problems of corporate identity and strategy, threatening the degree to which the National Broadcasting Company could
remain both *national* and *broadcast* oriented. Early concerns focused on the ability of wire systems to adequately relay signals without entirely supplanting the
broadcast system. In a report to stockholders in 1935, David Sarnoff noted the
first half of the problem: "existing and available wire systems are not suitable for
interconnecting television stations."[91] Even earlier, NBC's employees had devised
elaborate schemes for nationwide distribution of both entertainment and news
programming via film, but filmed distribution was unsatisfactory for RCA and
NBC because it would have opened up opportunities for competition with NBC's
network operations.[92] NBC's rhetoric of live national programming was already
undercut in radio by electrical transcription for local and regional broadcasting.
As Russo notes, NBC itself capitulated to affiliate and sponsor demand and sought
to fend off the incursions of competitors by offering transcription services beginning in 1934. Russo also found, however, that the business of transcription was a
topic of considerable dispute inside NBC and its parent as the norms of liveness
as quality they had espoused in the 1920s were disrupted by their competitors'
alternative rearticulation of quality in terms of "perceptual fidelity," in which
listeners could not tell the difference between electrically transcribed and live
programs.[93] The growing acceptance of transcribed radio content suggested that
an acceptance of filmed content (rather than a fully electrical system) at the out-
set might grievously hobble NBC's and RCA's ambitions to replicate NBC's radio
networks and maintain broadcasting on a nationwide scale. For RCA this would
mean a national market for television receivers and, for NBC, a national market
for advertisers, who had themselves begun the transition to national brands and
national chains in the preceding half century. It was also clearly in their interests
because RCA's patent position was strengthened by an emphasis on live broadcasting to the nation.

This valuation of live broadcasting came to shape perspectives on television's essential programming as well. In early 1934 an NBC executive lamented that with (then) current television technology, "General views, parades, outdoor scenes, crowds, choruses, stage spectacles, grand opera, etc. will be reproduced with insufficient detail and will probably not prove attractive to the viewer, so that they probably will be avoided in the early stages of the art."[94] Sarnoff also framed the ability to broadcast live programs as a public service in the national interest: "Important as it is from the standard of public policy to develop a system of television communication whereby a single event, program or pronouncement of national interest may be broadcast to the country as a whole, premature standards would freeze the art."[95] The emphasis on live programming was an important concern for NBC throughout the 1930s, as shown by the company's investment in mobile broadcasting and remote broadcasts of such events as the 1939 World's Fair and the World Series.

But why was live broadcasting in the public or national interest? Liveness was linked to the national interest for several reasons. In part it stemmed from the early ban on recorded entertainments in radio, which as Hilmes notes was intimately tied to an attempt to squelch the popularity of so-called race-records and consequently established an enduring cultural hierarchy in American broadcasting.[96] In addition, the favoring of liveness stemmed in part from FRC rulings valuing as public service the presentation of "events or entertainment unavailable to the public in any other form," such as recorded music.[97] Hilmes argues that the networks conflated liveness and public service such that "any type of entertainment, whether manufactured specifically for the medium or not, would count as public service if it were transmitted live—a neat twist of logic most beneficial to major network market position."[98] Additionally, Russo details how early on in radio NBC and CBS strove to celebrate liveness and derogate recordings, often eliding electrical transcription with the noisier technology of the phonograph.[99] The discursive deck was stacked differently by the mid-1930s, however, and questions of quality programming were more ambivalently positioned in relation to liveness on television.

Notions of technological quality had been used to forestall lower-resolution television, and at least some advocates of mechanical television tied lack of quality programming to the regulatory ban on commercialization.[100] Yet these early programs epitomized live broadcasting, and they suffered for it, even by friendly critics, as their adaptations of vaudeville dumb acts, puppet shows, cross-dressing performances, and gimmicks for presenting live sports served to mark their inadequacy in comparison to sound broadcasting and cinema.[101]

Instead, quality stemmed increasingly from a bifurcated notion of network distribution. As expressed by former president of NBC Merlin Aylesworth upon his assumption of the chairmanship of RCA subsidiary Radio-Keith-Orpheum in anticipation of the coming of television, "the quality of programs coming over the air" rested on two pillars. The first was programs and performers that were recognizably excellent, "the ones we never worry about." The second was of greater concern: "It is the other group, however, which reaches the broad general audience, that presents problems. And that problem is how to reach and maintain a consistently higher level. Entertainers and entertainment go in cycles. At the present it is now apparent that a fresher quality, a newer and more original quality in certain types of programs, would be highly desirable. But, of course, that is an ancient cry in every type of show business."[102] Thus, definitions of quality broadcast programming were tied as much to generic legitimacy and the ineffable criteria of creativity as to a strict appeal to live transmission. Indeed, in the same interview, Aylesworth argued that in television actual liveness was secondary to national habits, opining, "The equation of time presents another vital problem: How to broadcast through television, through sight and sound simultaneously, the important news events of the day. The television public will want to see these events when it can conveniently view them at home—not necessarily when those events happen during the work-day hours. The hour that marks waking in one country signalizes sleeping in another."[103] Aylesworth was no doubt mindful that in a nation spanning four time zones it was not simply a matter of what was happening in other countries but of creating a functional simulation of simultaneity in which communal experience fit with the rhythms of local and domestic life. Yet it was a set of events occurring simultaneously in another country that would provoke an equally vexing dilemma for the RCA/NBC model of television broadcasting—a dilemma inspired by the television broadcasts of the BBC.

The Problematic Fact of BBC TV

In 1935 Benn Hall, writing in the *Review of Reviews*, remarked on the BBC's decision to move "ahead with commercial television on a wholesale scale," announcing that "England is about to embark on the most startling entertainment-engineering program since the first radio set emitted tinnish music amid the static."[104] In a section titled "Fine for Dictators," Hall noted Hitler's plans "to strengthen his grip on Germany by popular television," and later asked, "Why is Europe moving ahead of us? When will we have regular television?"[105] Hall and others made note of the challenges to national broadcasting posed by the size of the United States and lower technical thresholds for Great Britain, which he compared in size to New York State. But Hall was also explaining the British advances in television by rearticulating the discourse of BBC autocracy: "In other words, televisionally speaking, Britain is a tight little isle, ideal for television *pioneering.* This is true of most of the continental countries. Areas are small, populations are concentrated and governments can decide at will when to introduce television."[106] Arguing against calls for US governmental control, Hall posed the barriers to television as a business issue in which the costs of television sets, but more significantly those of program production, would stymie market-driven expansion. Hall cited calculations by himself and esteemed radio engineer Dr. Alfred Goldsmith that found an hour of film costs forty-eight times an hour of radio. Hall concluded, "Television will use either film or stage entertainment or both. Obviously it will be impractical to produce radio quantity at film costs. While a theatre film may be shown thousands of times all over the world, once a film is televised generally, it is quite dead."[107] Though inaccurate, Hall's claim of the limited prospects for televised films as fact captures the prevailing wisdom of the time. This wisdom would only be overturned by actual television broadcasting in the 1950s, when reruns of filmed shows proved popular and profitable.[108] Similarly prescriptive, Hall's implicit contrast between radio quantity and film quality placed television programming in a familiar aesthetic bind, judged in advance for not being film, while also using the questions of financing quality programming to explain the delays in American television.

The dilemma provoked by the BBC broadcasts persisted in press accounts throughout the second half of the 1930s. For example, on the same page that complained of brazen broadcasts and offered FCC vice chairman Stewart's equivocations on the regulation of program quality in 1937, the New York Times ran Dunlap's account of how British television broadcasts were both not up to American programming standards and yet simultaneously spurring televisual competition between CBS and NBC. First came the praise for Darwinian rivalry: "Competition having always been the greatest spur for all radio developments in both the scientific and artistic fields, it is believed in broadcasting circles that with Columbia in the race with a 7,500-watt experimental transmitter developed by RCA at Camden, N.J., the pace is surely to be quickened." Dunlap noted that CBS had spent half a million dollars to install its studio in the Chrysler Building (mimicking NBC's operations in the Empire State) and asserted, "Television, it can be seen by this figure, is no toy in the attic or 'shoe string' experimenter. Seeing by wireless is a costly science, compared to the beginning of broadcasting, which was a free-for-all. Only the fittest, however, survived." This was followed by a defense of American television strategy on pragmatic grounds: "American television engineers have kept a watchful eye on foreign developments, especially on London's ultra-short wave telecasts from Alexandra Palace. Up to now the experts on this edge of the ocean seem to have been content to let the British pioneer in this new science and art, just as the Americans did in broadcasting. They reasoned that since the English use practically the same apparatus as the experimental television stations in the United States, whatever is learned in London might be applied here."[109]

Dunlap defended the American system by asserting that US companies were focused on the technology required to achieve better television rather than production technique.

But British television was a potent threat to the American system's claims to superiority. It provided a vivid counterexample of what broadcasting could be if subjected to different methods of funding and schemes for evaluation. As noted above, for technical and spatial reasons, the BBC had the ability to pursue lower- or higher-resolution broadcasts on a national scale without the long stretches of coaxial cable that bedeviled RCA and NBC. Although the BBC actually concentrated its efforts on London, much to the chagrin of the rest of the country, whose radio license fees underwrote the broadcasts, US accounts generally emphasized the lower technical threshold for national programming, at least partly explaining away British successes as a matter of geography.[110]

Nevertheless, British television broadcasts challenged the American commercial system in general, and RCA/NBC's model of broadcasting in particular, at an existential level. The key institutions of US commercial broadcasting had failed to deliver the goods while Great Britain and Germany began to offer television to their citizens. In the public discourse, the BBC had more traction than German television as a counterexample to the US system for a number of reasons beyond simply sharing the English language. First, the high-profile contests between the Baird and EMI systems had begun a year prior to the corollary competition between Fernseh and Telefunken. In both cases electronic systems licensed from RCA won out over mechanical systems, so Telefunken's triumph was to some degree old news, albeit garnished with the 1936 Olympics. Second, as media historian William Uricchio demonstrates, German television of the 1930s manifested a greater degree of variation in concept and practice than the centralized broadcast model being prophesied in the United States and deployed in Britain: "Thanks to a series of often-bitter struggles among political factions, governmental ministries, and interested corporations, television found itself pulled in at least four different directions."[111] Television in Germany would be conceived of and used for home viewing of broadcasting, communal viewing of events in "television halls," two-way communication, and military "reconnaissance . . . and telepresence (visual guidance systems for bombs, rockets, and torpedoes in the form of mini-television cameras and remote controls)."[112] Consequently, the narrower conception and practice of television on display in Britain made for a more defined foil for speculation on and evaluation of television in the United States, where, from the late mechanical era onward, broadcast had become the dominant articulation in imagining television.[113] Finally, while the German system of broadcasting was consistently portrayed as authoritarian and as a result was less plausible as a viable alternative, the British public service monopoly put its advantages on display. As opposed to the system in the United States, the BBC was in a secure position to run television tests to be viewed by all who could, as a result of the different mix of commercial and government involvement.

Advocates for US broadcasting publicly called the prospects for British television into question.[114] For example, Henry E. Stebbins, assistant trade commissioner for the Department of Commerce, remarked, "The size of the market will depend on the price of receivers, quality of programs and the number of people brought within receiving-distance of stations."[115] Stebbins anticipated that it would take years for British television to achieve the appropriate intersection of price and quality for popularization. The same article equivocated: "The quality of the program is said to depend entirely on the future policy of the British Broadcasting Corporation and the amount of money made available for program material. Improvement has been noticeable recently, according to London observers, and it is obvious that the BBC producers at Alexandra Palace are benefiting by experience and criticism, despite the fact that they are laboring under severe handicaps of lack of sufficient money and limitations of stage."[116] As Benn Hall had reported in 1935, cost and other business issues were key concerns for television's planners, and the British experience would be used in the United States to reemphasize the notion that quality came at a cost that someone had to pay. Yet, as this article suggests, the development of television aesthetics could also be considered to benefit from feedback and practice. With the regular framing of program quality in terms divorced from reception by actual viewers, instead relying on proclamations about hypothetical audiences, the stage was set for dominant uses of quality that reified the audience and traded in its representation.[117]

The audience has another function, however, in addition to being the target of advertising or uplift. Viewers are the primary investors in television's technical infrastructure.[118] Neither the commercial nor the public service model would work without set sales. The British experience suggested that program quality would be a key concern. Reporting in the *New York Times* on lagging set sales, L. Marsland Gander reported from London that the BBC was starting over with television and claimed, "In fact, the question is being asked, Was America right, after all, to defer the beginning of a public service until the prospects were more certain?"[119] In Gander's estimation the "bitter disappoint[ment]" of manufacturers stemmed from both the size of the image and "the fact that television, though good, is not quite perfect by comparison with the cinema; most blame the quality of the programs." In a second report, Gander expanded on this claim, contrasting the choice of "most countries" to keep television in the laboratory with Britain's public experimentation with both technology and technique. He held that "the most important lesson concerns the quality and type of programs. When the BBC first began to televise they imagined that people would be so overwhelmed by the miracle that almost anything would do for programs."[120] In Gander's evaluation the BBC had believed too heavily in television's appeal as a technical wonder and therefore skimped on the dramatic and other entertainment content that might help build an audience. He found "the result of all this was that the public came, saw and were unconquered. They said 'Marvelous! Amazing!' But they did not buy sets."[121] Maintaining the distinction between quality and novelty, these reports put forth the argument that program quality was essential to convince the public to buy sets but sufficiently costly that television could not compete with cinematic expectations.

These reports also testified to a second belief about the structural barriers beyond mere expense that might preclude television from replicating radio broadcasting's forms and cultural role. For example, later in the second article, Gander posed the problematic relationship between quality and quantity partly in terms of cinema, finding that "broadcasting is a prodigal consumer of entertainment material; television is infinitely more voracious, infinitely more expensive. British experience seems to show that television can never be a running tap like radio. The BBC is attempting to pump out a minimum of thirteen hours of entertainment weekly and the strain on material and resources is terrific." He argued that "every bad program is a liability showing television as far inferior to the [sic] film. Though by comparison with sound standards two hours of televising a day seems little enough, there is no possibility of an increase for a very long time. All the tendency is toward improving quality."[122] Variations on this theme would reprise with RCA's rollout of television at the 1939 World's Fair. As television historian Ron Becker has noted, RCA's initial plans to provide programming live from Radio City to its television exhibition at the fair were substantially revised to rely much more heavily on filmed content, particularly newsreels.[123] Although this had as much to do with uncertainty over signal reception amidst the electromagnetic noise generated by the fair's other exhibits as it did with NBC's capacity to provide programming, the result was a repetitive demonstration that suggested some of the challenges US television would face with program supply. Despite RCA's much-publicized television launch and the similar efforts of other manufacturers, particularly General Electric and Westinghouse, which also had television exhibits at the fair, the FCC used lack of program quality and quantity as an explanation for low interest in television as part of its easing without lifting restrictions on commercialization.[124] The quality of television's programming became an oft-cited explanation on this side of the Atlantic for sluggish set sales and continued vacillation over regulatory and industrial sanction of television broadcasting.

Keeping the Rust Off the Towers: Cultivating Oligopoly

In July 1940 the *New Yorker* published a satiric short story by Russell Maloney that looked back on "The Age of Television" from some point in the distant future.[125] Recalling 1945 as the year "television passed from the experimental stage to the status of important industry," Maloney's fictional historian argued that "the moment commercial sponsorship entered the picture, the future of television was, of course, assured."[126] Yet the demands of reaching a national audience began to warp first the broadcast and then national economies. Starting with the technical demands of national broadcasts, which were in this future-past achieved through relay towers "as high as the Empire State Building" and proceeding to the increased surcharges on consumer products that trickled down from distribution costs, it is a story of inflation followed by full employment in a bubble economy, where "small communities grew up around towers erected in desert or mountainous regions, each with its cocktail lounges, restaurants, apartment buildings, shops, garages, Turkish baths, and Yale club."[127] Those not supporting distribution became ensnared in production as "by 1958, the membership of Actors Equity reached 34,789,008 with an additional 334,917 under temporary suspension for non-payment of dues or other infringements of rules," with a similar number represented by the technical unions. This led to suspension of child-labor laws for work in television and eventually a labor shortage in which Ford Motor Company "successfully petitioned the State Department for permission to import coolie laborers."[128] The voracious maw of television would similarly devour "the European war" by outbidding the munitions plants for raw materials. In sum, Maloney painted a Swiftian vision of society formed and deformed around television.

The dangers imagined were in unrestrained growth—a too-free market coupled with inadequate planning—rather than oligopoly or mass manipulation of either the political or commercial variety. The curtain was drawn on television's metastasis throughout society and the economy by moral scolds outraged by a known mischief-maker:

> The now-famous occurrence of May 16, 1960, precipitated the downfall of the Television Age. It will be remembered that an actor named Orson Wills or Orton Welles, somehow misread his script, or got carried away by the tenseness of an emotional scene he was playing over a coast-to-coast hookup, and instead of saying (as the author had, of course, written), "Gosh darn it, you're lying!" cried, "God damn, it you're lying!" The next day the Watch and Ward Society of Boston, the D.A.R., and the Friendly Sons of St. Patrick all lodged protests with the Federal Communications Commission, which, after a fair trial, acceded to their request to have television discontinued, as detrimental to the morals of the nation. A hundred and ten million people were immediately thrown out of employment, and all of their worldly possessions were taken over by mortgage-&-loan companies. The towers rusted, and the screens of the receiving sets were blank. The starving Americans were easy prey at

the first uprising of the coolies, who had been counting on something like that all along.[129]

Nativist nightmares notwithstanding, the story anticipated the discontents that would be expressed about the vulnerability of the postwar consumer economy and its dependence on television as a means of selling not only products but a way of life. Moreover, with its burlesque of television boosterism, it crystallized the justifications that had been made throughout the 1930s for a rationalized, regulated, and closely held system of television. Although Maloney certainly made sport of the outrage over Orson Welles's adaptation of *War of the Worlds*, that panic also stood as a potent reminder of why broadcasting would not be governed by the precepts of art but rather its supposed effects on audiences.[130] Likewise, while television was imagined as a means of further knitting the nation together, the medium might be for the people or of the people, but television by the people was the stuff of comic dystopia, warning of a weakened national fiber. Instead, the television system and the quality of its programming were planned and evaluated in the terms most suitable to networks, advertisers, and the protectionist FCC.

Some of this was a result of design—as with RCA's obstructionism in the early 1930s—but much was a result of enabling happenstance—as when television was further delayed by the Second World War. Nevertheless, the consequences remain salient. As the next chapter will further explore, televisual aesthetics were designed not in open experimentation but in imitation and as a self-conscious hybridization of other media. This worked to erect a cultural hierarchy in which television has had trouble claiming the artistic status accorded cinema or the theater, while having demonstrably higher barriers to access than sound broadcasting. Television would top its sibling media and become the dominant communication and cultural form of the second half of the twentieth century, continuing to negotiate its aesthetic and cultural hierarchies partially through the nebulous concept of quality. But this mode of legitimation would come with considerable costs to both the medium's imagined expressive capacity and the relationships among viewers, audiences, broadcasters, and the wider commercial and cultural order.

4

Seeing Around Corners

Throughout the 1930s, television programming in the United States was largely an adjunct to experimental work. We saw some of the consequences of this situation in the prior chapter, which investigated the ways in which arguments about program quality were used to support the consolidating regulatory and economic regimes of American broadcasting. This chapter examines another facet of television's slow unveiling. As television programming was imagined and realized largely outside public view, early television practitioners and critics founded their evaluative frameworks on essentialist claims on human nature and the nature of television and its programs.[1] Although such appeals to essentialism are fairly typical in the development of new media, television's extended and not particularly public experimental period amplified this tendency. During the period prior to 1939, this imagination occurred in trade press accounts of experimental broadcasts, speculative essays about the nature of television programming and its impact on the anticipated audience, and the practices of aspirant broadcasters such as CBS in the early 1930s and NBC's Television Programming department in the middle of the decade. After RCA's decision to press the case for television in 1939 and the eventual accord on standards reached by the NTSC and endorsed by the FCC, several additional major manufacturers such as General Electric and Philco increased their production of experimental programs, and this experimental programming was broadcast to small audiences of early adopters and employees throughout the Second World War. During this later period, earlier imaginings of television programming and its qualities were tied to some of the practices and precepts that would shape national television broadcasting in the late 1940s and early 1950s.[2]

Spanning these periods was also the continued interpenetration of theory and practice, and emblematic of this was the critical and practical influence of

Gilbert Seldes. In a process complementing that discussed in the prior chapters, in which executives like David Sarnoff and inventors like Charles Francis Jenkins and Ernst Alexanderson had been drawn into express articulations of theories of history and culture, Seldes, the cultural critic, was swept up in practice, becoming director of CBS's experimental television production unit in the late 1930s. Seldes served as a vital—though certainly not singular—figure straddling criticism and execution, inspiring rivals and disciples to invoke television within a matrix of pragmatism and analogy, whereby television would be realized in managed and justifiable difference from precedent media.[3] As a consequence of this growing confluence of principle and pragmatics, evaluative schemes were actively discussed among those who would make and speak for television. In these debates the ellipsis lurking in the contemporary invocations of "quality television"—the missing "high" or "good" or "professional"—collided with questions of the medium's intrinsic nature, resulting in meditations on television's true purpose. Popular critical discourses of this era asked what compromises among art, communication, and economics were necessary to make it, in Rod Serling's words, "the happy medium."[4] That is, conceptions of quality served both to negotiate competing aesthetic and economic aspirations and to articulate visions of television's ontology and sociological significance.

For American television, first under experimental wraps and then wartime limitations, the consequences of these emergent evaluative frameworks were significant. Regulatory resistance to both commercialization and audience-oriented experimentation on a wide scale combined with the effective obstructionist lobbying of various manufacturers to place American television in a position where it would be asked to work out its aesthetics prior to its introduction to a mass audience. This is a significant contrast with the development of sound broadcasting, the motion picture, and television in Great Britain. At the same time, public prognostication about the tastes and habits of the television audience set expectations for the medium's programming in something of a paradox, presuming an attentive and demanding audience but one nonetheless obsessed with the supposed superficiality of the image. Thus, the frameworks for evaluating television's programs were erected in the name of the audience but largely absent its participation. Likewise, the debates over techniques and formats that would shape the aspirational language of television production occurred mostly in conference and control rather than living rooms. Consequently, notions of quality would be imported from sound broadcasting along with a more ambivalent adoption of notions of proper technique from Hollywood cinema. Theorizing about television's aesthetics and effects presumed a reciprocity between the two as notions of the televisual good were posed in answer to anxieties about the cultural and commercial changes anticipated in the wake of a break with sound-only broadcasting.

Of Hierarchies, Hybrids, and Human Habitats

Beginning in the 1920s, the cultural critic and future television programmer and producer Gilbert Seldes developed a theory that media forms evolved in a somewhat predictable pattern in relation to adjacent arts and technologies. Cultural historian Michael Kammen finds that even before he moved into media practice, Seldes was already distinct from most of his critical peers in his relative enthusiasm for the "democratization of culture," and Kammen attributes Seldes's perspicacity on the relations among the arts to his prolific work across a number of fields as critic and practitioner.[5] Comparative media evolution was not just a theory for Seldes but at various times an experience, practice, and plan. He articulated his view in terms of television in 1931:

> The catch in assuming that television does for radio what the sound mechanism did for the silent movies is this: the results are parallel, but the processes are reversed. In the silent picture you had movement and physical beauty, the gratification of the eye and a minimum of intellectual content; and while I have listened too long to the radio to say without blushing that its intellectual content was high, it remains perfectly true that the addition to it of the moving picture adds chiefly a sensual, and not a rational, pleasure. In other words, the sound mechanism could, and actually did, raise the intellectual level of the movie; and television can, and I fear will, lower the intellectual level of radio.
>
> This, if it happens, will be quite logical and will probably continue for ten years. Each new form of entertainment drains off the cheap and accidental elements of its predecessor.[6]

In the early 1930s Seldes tied his theory to a hierarchy of cognitive processes in which perception is shackled by the limits of representation. That is, words hit the "rational" centers of the brain, whereas images impacted the "sensual" and presumably appealed to more base elements of human nature. This is a thematic consistency in Seldes's arguments about media, where abstraction, impression, and interpretation mark the path to creative breaks with convention, yet his prioritization of the spoken word is somewhat surprising given the trajectories of film and television criticism that have generally ascribed greater value to the image.

Seldes's theory of media emergence was strained by the circumstances of the Great Depression. As we now know, television did not follow the path he predicted, and its development as a full-fledged commercial broadcasting enterprise was forestalled for more than a decade; so in 1937 he argued, "As television will be, in effect, a combination of the radio and the moving picture, it has an exceptional importance; and since the early programmes of television will be based on the experiments now being made, the citizen may well begin to think about television now instead of neglecting it for twenty years as he neglected radio and the movies. Twenty years from now will be much too late for complaints."[7] It was to some extent already too late for complaints, and perhaps for meaningful participation as citizens. As we saw in the last chapter, the institutional fix was in, and television programming would mostly be developed out of sight and consequently with perhaps even less regard for public wants than shown by the BBC. Yet the audience's identities, capacities, viewing environments, and behaviors were a source of profound ambivalence among television's advocates and practitioners.

Foremost among the ambivalences about the audience was the presumption that the television audience would be simultaneously more enthralled and more demanding. Envisioning television as a hybrid of radio and cinema, many commentators asserted the audience would no longer perform the set of negotiations between household and programming flow that were settling into a somewhat stable cultural practice by the early 1930s, though how stable was a matter of cultural and industrial contestation throughout the broadcast era. Particularly as distraction was mapped onto representations of the female audience, media scholar William Boddy finds a developing industrial common sense that radio programming need not be designed "to elicit or repay full attention."[8] This presumption informed early thought about television reception. In a 1930 memo arguing the need for enhanced programming in television, NBC executive C. W. Horn invoked cinema and argued, "While we are quite content to sit at home reading or otherwise engaged, and incidentally listen to music from the radio, this will never do in connection with television as that will require fixed and undivided attention on the part of the 'viewer.'"[9] The degree to which listeners were content to be "otherwise engaged" and the satisfaction of broadcasters and sponsors with distracted listening provoked a series of renegotiations for both radio and television. As radio historian Alexander Russo documents, the phenomena of daytime radio for women working in the home, multiple-radio homes, and car radios all complicated anticipated dynamics of reception, engendering ambivalences on the part of industry and listeners alike and inspiring new program forms and habits.[10]

Nevertheless, radio's ongoing engagement with distraction structured thinking, wishful and otherwise, about television. Horn's boss and president of RCA, David Sarnoff, remarked to a reporter for *Collier's* in 1935, "Television reception is not, cannot be, like sound reception. Today radio is used as background for other entertainment, or by the housewife who turns the button and listens to the music while she goes on with her work. Television can never be like that, because not only will it require close attention on the part of the onlooker, but also it will be necessary for the room to be somewhat darkened." In Sarnoff's estimation, television would "naturally . . . require a considerable change in the habits of listeners who, instead of roaming around as they now do while enjoying a program, will have to sit tight and pay close attention to whatever is being thrown on their screen." He went on to opine that impulses to distraction notwithstanding, it might do the body and soul good to have "something in our homes that would cause us to sit quietly in our chairs for an hour or two a day."[11] This mix of uncertainty about the audience of the present and the desire for a pacified audience of the future is striking not only for the straightforward though delicately put ambitions of social control but also for the technological determinism that presumed television would be driven by the image and thus radically disrupt broadcasting's relationship with its audience.

Seldes's 1937 article similarly stated the threat in commercial terms. First noting that sponsors of sound broadcasting had become adept at fitting advertisements to the divided attentions of the audience, he then argued, "The image on the television receiver makes no such compromise. The thing moves; it demands complete attention. You cannot walk away from it, you cannot turn your back on it, and you cannot do anything else except listen while you are looking. At first guess the sponsor who goes before the scanner will imagine that this is the long-desired ideal, the conquest at last of indifference or casual interest."[12] Seldes thought otherwise. Hypothesizing a viewing mode distinct from the purported absorption of the cinema, he speculated, "The physical conditions of the moving picture house will not be duplicated. At home we shall not be compelled to sit through a dull episode in silence, hoping for an exciting one to follow. We will, in short, look into the mirror of television only so long as the movement upon it is of surpassing interest."[13] To a certain degree these statements of ambivalence mask fantasies of powerful media effects that were seductive for television's planners, but they also point to the practical uses of adjacent media in the planning for television in the context of regulatory and industrial choices to keep television out of the public eye. As media historian Rick Altman has argued, contrary to these predictions, television's textual and commercial forms would be adapted to the household flow largely through the continued emphasis on and manipulation of television sound, which for much of the television era gave clarity and musical or laughter cues for significant program segments and demanded attention for advertisements through increased volume (among other strategies).[14] Throughout the rest of this chapter we will explore how these elements of television sound became linked to key distinctions in program quality and assertions of television's fundamental qualities, but at present it is worth noting that the notion of television's demanding a different degree and kind of attention structured early thought on programming and commercial form.

Planning Programming, Debating Aesthetics

The previous chapter recounted the ways in which notions of quality programming were developed in the United States in advance of television having a broadcast audience and consequently were built to suit institutional interests—whether in the service of coercion or consensus. Yet it is not precisely correct to claim that American television did not have an audience in the 1930s. In addition to the amateurs and enthusiasts from the first boom, the critics, regulators, and reporters cited above, as well as the engineers and production staff of would-be-broadcasters who were engaged in television research and planning, not only made predictions about the audience but also acted as an audience themselves.[15] Throughout the 1930s, as lower-resolution television was stymied and higher-resolution systems were tested, the quality of television programs was debated inside broadcasting organizations and by critics who sought to shape it prior to its release for general viewing. These debates laid a groundwork of aesthetic assumptions about content, form, and production organization that helped to shape evaluative norms well into the broadcast era.

From early on, speculation about television content presumed that the addition of sight to broadcasting would work to buttress cultural hierarchies threatened by radio's disembodied voices and sought to pin down more firmly the identities of who would, could, and should be televised.[16] For example, in 1930 Bertha Brainard, NBC's programming director, was asked to consider the "pictorial quality" of NBC talent as television drew nearer.[17] Her response was telling: "I find, unfortunately, a question of who is and who is not good looking, arising in the men's minds." Although Brainard's observation of the sexism inherent in the request drew a response proffering the supposedly more neutral term *salable*, [18] the notion that television performers must look a certain way appears to have been persistent. In 1937 *Variety* claimed that "pretty girls are the easiest television test because imagination fills in the gaps," and in 1945 the *New York Times* reported in an article on television's impact on opera, titled "Video Bars Hefty Singers," that "television calls for a special type of singer. Fat and ugly tenors and sopranos are debarred. Good looks are essential. The facial contortions that accompany much singing will never do for the television screen."[19] Although *Variety*, in 1931, reported viewer complaints about popular Chicago radio personalities, televised in low resolution, having such imperfections as spectacles and a preference for bowties,[20] there is not a robust body of evidence in support of this anticipation. Regardless of its accuracy, once the notion of radio faces became operationalized at roughly the same time visual broadcasting was withdrawn from the public eye, the common sense among television's planners and critics was that a beauty standard much like Hollywood's should guide who would be televised.

In addition to standards of beauty, racial determinacy was a chief concern. Whether complaining about early television's inability to capture blackface or the necessity of makeup to keep white men from looking like "Uncle Tom," these concerns were often expressed as technological problems.[21] The use of whiteface—or often greenface—in early television highlights the technological construction of whiteness that film scholar Richard Dyer has argued shores up the foundations of white normativity and its consequent cultural power.[22] Although these questions of who would be televised were relatively sporadic and generally made at moments when television seemed imminent, they speak to fundamental questions of access to representation—and particularly self-representation—that continue to complicate notions of quality programming to this day.

Another form of translating established cultural hierarchies into speculation on programming came in discussions of genres and modes. Vaudeville, talk, and novelty acts were consistently marked as low. For example, *Variety* described the Western Television Corporation's programming's use of vaudevillians as "freak ether entertainment" and a "daily peekshow."[23] High culture would be tweaked from radio notions of opera and "serious music" to opera and drama.[24] Indeed, one very early account, titled "Television Makes the Radio Drama Possible," implied that only through the addition of sight can broadcasting be truly dramatic.[25] Radio historian Shawn VanCour finds a common pattern of derogation of radio's dramatic potential even as radio producers, performers, and critics were developing an aesthetics and practice of realism that both drew on and broke with the adjacent dramatic traditions of the stage and screen.[26] The swipe at sound drama in a report on television continued this belittlement while also seeking to define television as greater and having drama as its proper territory. And drama was desirable for a medium seeking an audience. American inventor Hollis Baird was quoted in *Literary Digest*: "Simple variety or vaudeville acts lend themselves most easily to television, but there is a far richer field than this, particularly in the dramatic field. That the public favors drama is shown by the great popularity of dramatic skits on the air to-day despite the very definite limitations of drama which might come to the ear only."[27] Baird prophesied the potential of broadcast visual drama: "Television will have a technique different from motion pictures, altho allied to them, and once this has been worked out along with the normal progress television is making, the ultimate result will be home entertainment which, if mentioned even ten years ago, would have labeled the prophet as at least some one with badly wandering fancies."[28] Baird's comments worked to raise television's cultural profile by allying it with entertainment forms higher in the cultural pecking order and eschewing the ease of translating vaudeville for the home screen.

In addition to the seemingly ever-present issue of television's definition in terms of cinema, the matter of developing television technique also raised persistent questions involved in television's problematic negotiation of realism and reality. Radio realism was developing systems of narrative and technological conventions that television threatened to upset. The problems of costuming, sets, and even having performers without scripts—or "continuities" in the parlance of 1930s radio—were the subject of regular and public fretting by broadcasters contemplating television.[29] Simultaneously, television programming was being imagined as having special duties of accuracy, authenticity, and able reproduction of the real. For example, Bill Schudt Jr., television program director at CBS during its early 1930s lower-resolution broadcasts, posed one of the questions to be solved by experimental programming: "How shall plays be dramatized to accurately portray the author's work?"[30] In addition, Sarnoff's pronouncements about television's duty to capture events as they occurred, to represent real life with at least the pretense of being unmediated, were key components in defining television programming as having a special relationship with the real.

Nevertheless, as the first boom ended, internal debates over program quality at NBC turned to questions of technique and institutional organization. The former were dominated by the matter of adapting cinematic continuity style to television and the latter by bringing definition to the blurry line dividing programming from engineering. In his "Treatise on Television Planning" Julius Weinberger noted, "The size, detail, and brilliancy limitations of the picture will make it necessary to confine the entertainment material largely to 'medium shots' . . . and close-ups."[31] Although spectacles such as parades and sporting events were thought of as the sort of live events that would allow the current broadcasting model to continue in television, Weinberger speculated that image quality would be insufficient to broadcast such events. He noted that holding television programming to Hollywood standards of lighting, shot selection, editing, and even costuming while maintaining the live broadcast model from radio would introduce significant expense and complications to television programming. Instead, Weinberger recommended using prefilmed programming, which he stated would allow for better quality and ease in transcripted distribution.[32] Filmed content, however, posed two significant drawbacks for RCA and NBC. First, as I noted in chapter 3, filmed content obviated the need for a wired network, thereby taking one of NBC's putative institutional strengths out of play. Second, filmed content opened the door for direct competition in entertainment distribution from the Hollywood studios, which at the time were hampered by Depression-era bankruptcies and reorganizations but were not yet legally enjoined from moving into broadcasting as they would be as a result of the government antitrust cases that would culminate with *U.S. v. Paramount et al.* RCA and its subsidiaries were not about to surrender an advantage while simultaneously throwing the doors open to formidable competition if they did not have to. Thus, it was likely with pleasure that William Fairbanks reported to Brainard in 1935 that "recent BBC 30 line broadcasts give hope that reliance on 'Hollywood' type won't be essential."[33] In this case Fairbanks was not merely engaged in an assessment of the large-scale business interests of NBC

and parent RCA but also in an internecine struggle within NBC. Even as technological concerns such as resolution and business questions such as distribution
remained salient issues in planning for television's eventual programming, the
nonengineering staff at NBC was beginning to claim programming as its own.

Although the radio programming staff, particularly Brainard, had been
participating in the planning for television within NBC in the early 1930s, they
began to take a more active role in the second half of the decade, beginning
with the formation of the Television Program Committee in June of 1935.[34]
Among the causes for this shift were the programming activities of the British
Broadcasting Company, with which NBC maintained close contact for the purposes of both televisual diplomacy and industrial espionage. Although the BBC
model of broadcasting was and is quite different from the American model (as
noted in chapter 3), the BBC's television broadcasts certainly provided another
key term in the discursive construction of quality television. In the memo to
Brainard, Fairbanks used the example of the BBC's more public and active production schedule to advocate a shift in corporate emphasis from technology
to programming.[35] Indeed, although the BBC's television broadcasts may have
complicated RCA's strategies for rolling out television ready-made, NBC employees were eager to benefit from the British experience. For example, in a 1937
report on European television, C. W. Farrier characterized the BBC's programs as
"technically . . . more pleasing than ours" and attributed their "boldness" to the
centralized authority and concomitant authorial vision of the producer, whose
"orders can be questioned but not argued."[36]

Moving in this direction, NBC formed its Television Program Division in
late 1937.[37] Once established, the Television Program Division sought to reorient
the institutional hierarchies surrounding television and articulate a vision of
aesthetic production independent of engineering and technology. In particular,
division members thought that the programming department, as opposed to
engineering, should have control over such aspects as camera work, editing,
lighting, titles, and miniatures.[38] In a reversal of the electronic aesthetic, they
advocated the relegation of engineering to the "electrical content of the picture only." This was the latest iteration of a dispute between programming and
engineering dating back to the 1920s and persisting to this day. Wracked by class
divisions, competing hierarchical notions of gender, and odd steps in the daily
dance of business and boredom that is work, the institutions of broadcasting saw
regular skirmishes over the nature of creativity and professionalism. Professional
codes of quality required not only aspiration but also the exclusions that create
specialization and notions of distinction, and not everyone can be in the club.

Thus, in contrast to the events recounted in chapter 1, where the electronic
aesthetic was embraced by the engineers as part of the core values of their discipline, here the programming personnel used it to squeeze the engineers out

of key creative areas. That is, because the electronic aesthetic worked to paper over the numerous articulations of crafts and practices by presenting a coherent, integrated system, it also worked to present a thin, bright line that could be drawn between programming and technology. Engineering, of course, did not want to concede control, while programming accused engineers of claiming responsibility only for the things they found enjoyable. The entire debate demonstrates the ways in which the distinctions among form, content, technology, and programming are historically and even institutionally specific. Yet, as it had been with sound broadcasting, the growing distinction between technology and programming was becoming conventionalized and ingrained in institutional hierarchies, and it would manifest itself in the FCC's regulatory schemes of the 1940s and NBC's growing emphasis on programming with the field tests of 1938 and introduction of RCA receivers in 1939.

Practice Television: Adventures in Medium Specificity

At the end of the 1930s, and throughout the war years, the poetics of television were renegotiated as small but symbolically significant audiences were targeted with programming that focused increasingly on commercial broadcasting's aims of entertaining, engaging, and managing the time and attention of audiences for the eventual purpose of advertising. With the unveiling of television at the 1939 World's Fair, the conversation about programming shifted in degree and kind. Even in the largely controlled circumstances of the exhibit hall, television programming proved problematic, requiring redundant transmission systems and more reliance on filmed programming than RCA initially planned.[39] RCA's attempt to launch television was considerably less decisive than the communications giant anticipated,[40] and disputes over standards and the massive social and industrial disruptions of the Second World War would delay the wide-scale distribution of televisions and programming. Throughout the 1940s, however, various broadcasters and would-be authorities set about the difficult task of reconciling notions of television's perfection with the demands of making television work as a business by engaging and selling audiences. This period saw a profusion of discourse about television programming across multiple print genres, from how-to manuals to formal reports by the networks and manufacturers to juvenilia to satirical short stories to scholarly essays to newspaper reportage and editorials. Several consistent tropes emerged from the engineers, showpeople, executives, reporters, and critics who claimed the expertise to speak for television: the continuing argumentation about the essential nature of television in relation to other media and human nature; anticipation and evaluation of the proper techniques that would lead to television being uniquely itself, rather than cinema or theater seen through a glass dimly; proclamations of the phenomenological and sociological significance of television; and negotiations seeking to reconcile the body of knowledges built up around constructions of the audience with the feedback from actual viewers.

Across all of these tropes we can see attempts to define the quality of television programs primarily in terms of theory—be it aesthetic, psychological, sociological, or technical—and consequent tendencies to monopolize meanings of television that are deeply enmeshed with the industrial, regulatory, and cultural sanction of concentrated control of television in this country. To a significant extent these discourses prefigured the critical hierarchies established around liveness, realism, and writing that were later transmogrified in the wake of the quiz show scandals into the cultural underpinnings of the classic network system.[41] Nevertheless, these parties' competing aspirations for television, when combined with a small but responsive audience, created an imaginative landscape far broader than would be seen in the era of consolidated network control.

In 1941 the *Annals of the American Academy of Political and Social Science* published a series of essays on television and broadcasting, in which "The Nature of Television Programs," an article by Seldes, then head of television programming at CBS, ran alongside "The Possible Social Effects of Television," by Sarnoff.[42] Both articles evidenced a teleological faith in the essence of not only television but also human nature and in history as a narrative of progress. The authors, however, took dramatically different paths to tackle the subject of television programming. Sarnoff saw programming as one of many dimensions in the overall social significance of television. Largely embracing technological determinism, he argued that television was a "Power Invention," with the potential for social transformation on par with the steam engine, that would likely reestablish the home as the center of human activity by allowing for social participation at a distance. He argued that the immediacy of broadcasting produced a more "intense . . . sensation" than recorded sound or images and asserted, "With the advent of television, the combined emotional results of both seeing and hearing an event or a performance at the instant of its occurrence become new forces of great significance, and under the influence of the quiet and intimate background of one's own home these are much greater forces than anything we have yet known."[43] Sarnoff's initial example of television's power to foster a communal yet individuated and domesticated experience was NBC's broadcast of the Republican National Convention in Philadelphia in 1940, calling it a "major milestone in the long struggle of humanity to triumph over its physical limitations." Anticipating Marshall McLuhan by two decades, Sarnoff briefly laid out an aggrandizing history of communications: "Ever since the beginning of time man has sought to extend the power of his senses and to enlarge his capacity to perceive and to respond to the world around him"; now mankind had broken "the last shackle" as "through television his eyesight promises to become all-embracing and world-wide."[44] Sarnoff continued by predicting the contribution of television to the growth of suburban America and, while claiming a substantively different set of relationships between consequences and intention, described television's contributions to an emerging way of life that Raymond Williams would later call "mobile privatisation."[45]

While the medium held perhaps unprecedented social significance for Sarnoff, in this article his vision of dramatic programming was a cavalcade of vagaries testifying to his faith in aesthetic progress and his thorough articulation of television as a direct outgrowth of sound broadcasting. Asserting that radio had raised "the general level of musical taste in this country" through exposure to "grand opera and symphonic music," he claimed that "with television, a similar widening cultural development in appreciation of the best in drama, the dance, painting, and sculpture may be expected. Through television, coupled with the universal increase in schooling, Americans may attain the highest general cultural level of any people in the history of the world."[46] Remarking on NBC's experimental broadcasts thus far, Sarnoff claimed that the programming was based on audience-response cards and offered a table of NBC's programming broken down by genre as evidence of "audience preference," with news (33.4 percent), drama (29.1 percent), and educational programs (17.0 percent) as the most significant program types.[47] Yet behind the quantitative report and the claims made on behalf of the audience, Sarnoff offered enthusiasms that served RCA's promotional interests but little in the way of commentary about what television's entertainment programming would look like, instead providing vague assertions such as, "It is quite likely that television drama will develop in novel directions, using the best of the theater and motion pictures, and building a new art-form based upon these." The problems here are twofold. First, despite the promises that television drama will develop into its own art form, preexisting institutional interests and cultural hierarchies had already channeled the medium into a relatively narrow group of genres and modes as evidenced by the very categories Sarnoff used to describe the programming. Second, a significant philosophical contradiction is evident in the conception of the medium as both "guided" by the audience and raising that audience's "dramatic taste." Behind that contradiction lurks the invisible hand not of the market but of the master narratives of broadcasting's ultimate claims to cultural legitimacy resting upon the promise to create a better person and a stronger nation, as we saw in chapter 3.

This vision for television was brought to the fore in Sarnoff's enthusiastic discussion of television as a medium for persuasion in the form of advertising, political appeals, and the presentation of reality that was followed by a call for the maintenance of existing economic and regulatory frameworks of sound broadcasting into television to ensure against "propaganda" as was seen in the

"European countries which [had] succumbed to dictatorships."[48] In the end, for all of Sarnoff's invocations of art and his discussion of drama as disarticulated from broadcasting's political economy, programming was at best secondary to what he saw as the transformational capacity of broadcasting to bridge the public and the private and thereby ennoble American society. He predicted, "The ultimate contribution of television will be its service towards unification of the life of the nation, and, at the same time, the greater development of the life of the individual. We who have labored in the creation of this promising new instrumentality are proud to have this opportunity to aid in the progress of mankind. It is our earnest hope that television will help to strengthen the United States as a nation of free people and high ideals."[49] Thus, Sarnoff worked to establish evaluative hierarchies that judged television in terms of *intent* rather than *content* and justified concentration in the name of responsibility, uplift, and quality. That this paradigm was congruent with the interests of his corporation and his long-articulated positions on broadcasting is as consequential as it is unsurprising. This theorization of television provided a solid base of institutional authority coupled with a well-established discursive repertoire that would help the established broadcasting system to call the tune in television.

In contrast, Seldes pursued a new variation on his theme of the relationship between the arts in his account of television programming and directly articulated hybridization across media forms to the political economy of the arts. Seldes argued that television had "two functions, as many of the other arts have two functions," potentially working as "art or a form of entertainment," perhaps even simultaneously. The first function was the creation of works unique to the medium—here he invoked *The Cabinet of Dr. Caligari*, the Keystone comedies, and Walt Disney's Silly Symphonies as examples from cinema—and the second was the adaptation or derivation of works from other arts. Of these two functions, Seldes was content to regard the former as "more significant than the other. So long as man values his creative spirit, this is natural and good." Nevertheless, he went on to argue against treating adaptations as illegitimate, asserting that "we must recognize the brutal practical circumstance that the arts live by daily bread, and only occasionally bring us honeydew and the milk of Paradise. This is important because it breaks down one of his most highly regarded 'laws' of the arts, that each art should use for its material only that which it can do best."[50] Seldes saw the processes of adaptation and hybridization as a necessary outgrowth of the everyday practice of artistic production and as having the salutary effect of opening up new creative avenues.

This move was a refinement of Seldes's earlier positions on the arts in which he chastised emergent media for their susceptibility to foolishly adopt or aspire to standards from other media. Exemplifying this earlier line of argumentation, Seldes's 1924 treatise *The Seven Lively Arts* asserted that cinema's greatest failure was "in taking over realistic theatre," pursuing an aesthetic of "verification," and disavowing "that in the end the camera was as legitimately an instrument of distortion as of reproduction."[51] This position was an argument against the ossification of aesthetic forms and a celebration of liveliness and interplay. By the time of "The Nature of Television Programs," Seldes had translated these values into a celebration of experimentation and artistic discovery. Chiding an earlier proclamation of his "that, since television transmitted images in motion, one should never use it to transmit a still picture," and pronouncing himself happily surprised by the BBC's use of stills in tests he had observed, he went on to explain that the nature of television was yet to be discovered: "It is easier to name the fields in which television will transpose and reproduce than those in which it will create its own material; it is easier to say where it will mix genres than where it will be pure. The reason is that we do not as yet actually know the true nature of television."[52] Here, the unknown nature of television is not its technical workings or limitations but rather the nature of its relation to its audience as Seldes argued: "We know what it does physically. We do not know how it affects its spectators; we do not know whether it is better as a medium for fantasy or for fact; we cannot tell whether drama has persuasion in television, whether fact seems exaggerated, or fancy foolish." Consequently, Seldes advocated an approach of "trial and error" to discover this nature and develop "a new Poetics": "Ten years from now we shall be more certain of our ground, but by that time our imaginations may be haltered by fact. . . . At the moment we are fulfilling the great Aristotelian function of trying to ask the proper questions."[53] Trial and error was a common theme in Seldes's work, and as Kammen details, Seldes's ventures into practice themselves often ended in failure, such as when CBS eventually fired him.[54] But playing it safe was not the point. Seldes's extended brief on the value of experimentation was also a testament to his belief in the immanence of a true artistic nature waiting to bloom from the technical apparatus. Taking a winding path, he would ultimately argue, like Sarnoff, that television was to be an immediate medium—not just live but in some sense real.

Indeed, following his plea for flexibility, complexity, and contingency, Seldes reversed field and proceeded to stake out his assumptions about the types of material best suited for borrowing from other media in the service of arguing for television's true calling, and his conclusions pointed away from fictional programming. Seldes first considered the problems in distinguishing fiction from other types of programming with an example: "Thinking of fiction as material, not as method, we find that a reading of 'The Rime of the Ancient Mariner' ought to be included, regardless of the picture which accompanied this imaginative text. Actually such a reading would be considered by many people 'educational'; they would ask for dramatization of the poem if we announced it as part of our program of entertainment."[55] He hypothesized several strategies for dramatizing the poem, ranging from accompanying a recitation with collages of still or moving images or with pantomime to a performance with actors speaking lines instead of the recitation. He concluded that "the last of these only would be considered wholly 'fiction.' (It would, incidentally, run the risk of being the world's worst program.)" Following this thought-experiment knowingly leavened with characteristic digs at misspent pretense, Seldes argued that only drama could be considered pure fiction and that it was unclear if and how drama would work in television.

Indeed, he forecast an uncertain future for television drama: "Let us say that, on the surface, the dramatic material offers us the most abundant material, hedged in by the most bristling questions of aesthetics, finance, and presentation." The biggest question for Seldes was whether the economics of television could support the considerable promise of dramatic fiction. He argued, "To say that 'the sponsors will pay' is mere evasion. Sponsors have paid a great deal and received a great deal in radio, but the conditions of production have been logical; the radio production has cost what it should, not what a comparable movie production would cost." He noted it was "immaterial" who specifically paid, arguing, "A system of economy must be discovered so that highly polished, expert seeming programs can be produced within the natural limits of cost, or, say at a cost comparable to the return, whether the return be in prestige or purchases." Based on this assessment, Seldes speculated, "Perhaps the economy will dictate other sources of material," and concluded the more likely and lively contributors to television's true form were those drawing on codes that are currently termed reality.

Anticipating industrial demands very much like those that have given rise to the prevalence of reality and "docu-real" genres on contemporary television, Seldes put this content under the rubric of "actuality."[56] His prescience, however, speaks as much to his refusal to give free reign to experimentation for experimentation's sake as to his insight into the nature and future of the medium. Given his prior antipathy toward a monopoly of realism in cinema, coupled with his straightforward praise of contrived yet actual forms such as quiz shows, audience participation programs, and vaudevillian revues in "The Nature of Television Programs," his ultimate praise of actuality as the essence of television played out more as the conclusion of a proof than a leap of imagination. He argued from philosophical authority, quoting Sir Francis Bacon: "The contemplation of things as they are . . . without substitution or imposture, without error or confusion, is in itself a nobler thing than a whole harvest of inventions." For Seldes, television held the potential to make "the contemplations of things as they are" not only noble but "pleasurable." Here it is the conjuncture of what Seldes regards as the height of human experience and the capacity of television as a medium to convey actuality that harnesses the form to its purported purpose.

Yet Seldes carried the argument further and, not coincidentally, supported the arguments for CBS and its color system cum countermeasure to RCA's attempts to standardize the medium. Echoing Sarnoff's tendency to celebrate television with pronouncements about what it was not, Seldes declared, "Television is not the transmission of a photograph. It is the instantaneous and complete transmission of actuality. Sometimes that actuality is studied and arranged in a studio; sometimes it is an event, such as a parade, a fire, or a ball game. . . . In these events, the material is whatever the life of the community provides: its planned ceremonies and contests, its common life, its accidents." Here again television is seen as providing access to community, and Seldes argued that this connection was hampered by black-and-white standards. Contrasting it with the newsreel, he proposed that television "is the transmission of the image of an event while the event is taking place. This supreme illusion of reality demands completeness, and since it is not photography the color of actual life is required." Noting John Logie Baird's early experiments in color, Seldes claimed, "Without color, television was incomplete, reduced to being a picture. With color it arrives, in a spectacular way, at the threshold of its true destiny." Again we see television imagined as an extension of human perception and the fruit of this ontological argument is a particular subordination of content to form and mode that allows for a priori speculation that can enhance institutional authority and render the public a rubber stamp on decisions already made.

For all of Seldes's recognition of contingency, he was still working from a framework that held that television had a date with destiny. Despite the fact that it had been stood-up several times and was likely to be asked to split the check, the implication is that it was imperative that television be wedded to a construction of human perception that presumed the primacy of epistemophilia.[57] This vision begins to look very much like apparatus theory stripped of its critique of capitalist domination and reoriented to justify television's integration into existing economic and cultural hierarchies, while setting a standard that would guarantee dissatisfaction with television and its programs.[58] Left out are the possibilities that television should not be *one* thing; that it has no inherent purpose; that being domestic and mundane could be virtues rather than faults; that in making television one's own, many of the pleasures might stem from waste or defiance or deviance; and that experimentation might be an end and not a means.

Video Theory and the CBS School

The Sarnoff and Seldes think pieces were published in January of 1941 and anticipated a continuing boom in set sales and program service, yet by the end of the year, in broadcast historian Erik Barnouw's words, "the boom was being put in storage. . . . Television, in modest fashion, had gone to war."[59] As the nation's resources were marshaled, the production of television sets gave way to the manufacture of radar equipment. The major works in broadcast history tend to cover wartime production of television programs in a few sentences, which is a fair index of the significance accorded these years in the commonly told story of broadcasting.[60] But in terms of the imagination and planning of television programming, this period was far from fallow. CBS continued to broadcast television programs until November 26, 1942, and was back on the air May 4, 1944.[61] NBC dramatically curtailed broadcasting from October 1942 through all of 1943 but never went fully off the air.[62] Dumont's broadcasts went off the air in the summer of 1943 for retooling but resumed with the interesting twist of offering sponsors free studio time for program experiments.[63] Programming continued with some interruptions in Chicago and Los Angeles. And General Electric produced programs for and studied the responses of its audience of employees and enthusiasts in Schenectady. Out of these activities emerged a significant body of discourse and technique that had a material impact on the practices and expectations of American television that followed in the late 1940s and 1950s.

The newspaper articles, corporate publicity materials, and books targeting enthusiasts continued to articulate television (and television history) in teleological terms that harnessed authority to speak for television to essentialist understandings of the medium. Despite modestly expanded measurement and evaluation of audience responses that accompanied the incremental broadening of telecasting in the early 1940s, many of the attempts to define good television programming were founded on the abstract conception of television's essential nature. Consequently, when audiences were considered, they were often posited as an abstract set of viewing processes and conditions. While this was conducive to imagining television in the interests of broadcasting's dominant institutions, the actual practice appears to have had as much to do with the microprocesses of designing television programs in the constraining circumstances of repeated interruption, halting popularization, restrained and relatively homogeneous competition, and established professional habits of self-criticism and goal setting. This convergence of factors accentuated the tendency to think television in terms of essential and coherent qualities that pointed to a clear set of highest uses and could thereby serve as a guide to the development of television texts and techniques in the absence of a more robust relationship with the audience.

In late 1944 and continuing into 1945, a series of newspaper articles, anthologies, and manuals touted wartime broadcasts and anticipated the coming television boom. Seldes promoted CBS's experimental efforts in the *New York Times* on Christmas Eve 1944, arguing again for television's need for unique forms of expression: "Television will certainly live in part by the transmission of events or entertainments which are created by others; television will also live in part by imitating other entertainments; but television will not live very long if it fails to develop its own creative powers independently." Seldes held that television could not afford a protracted public experimental period because "television is entering upon a world already occupied by two great mass entertainments, the movies being the most spendthrift entertainment ever invented, and radio the most popular. We have to be creative—or die."[64] He went on to argue that as a practical matter many of the strategies employed in the two preceding media could serve both as a guide and a distraction. Noting that their adaptation of *The Missus Goes a-Shopping*, a radio audience-participation show, fared better than his translation of William Faulkner's "Two Soldiers," Seldes continued to lay out what he saw as the problems of television drama.[65] In particular, their attempts to adapt filmic techniques such as superimposition to the television switcher's ability to perform electronic dissolves were deemed "awkward." He then defended them: "So were the first process shots."[66] Likewise, the emerging consensus that television technology's limited image size and resolution mandated close-ups provoked new concerns of rendering scenes in the depth established by cinema.[67]

Nevertheless, Seldes was sanguine about the possibilities for television art and artistry. Lacking video recording capability, the pressures of live production placed particular emphasis on planning and timing, and the pragmatic accommodations made in adopting cinematic and radio storytelling techniques were articulated as providing glimpses of television's unique character. For example, he enthused, "We used radio sound effects to reinforce pictures; and in turn, when war played a part in the story, we not only used a radio bulletin but backed it up with visual animation, just as we do on our regular news programs. Finally, we found that in flashes we had created something new—it wasn't in essence theatre, or radio, or movie; it had a special quality of its own."[68] For Seldes "this special quality [was] the biggest kick in television," and he asserted, "Your audience gets it, too." In particular, Seldes saw "visual animation," rudimentary video graphics, as being a realization of this special quality. If this anticipates John Caldwell's contrast between the "televisual" and the cinematic,[69] it also worked to reinscribe Seldes's ideal of actuality into the results of the CBS experiments, and he saw it as particularly useful in the presentation of news: "The war, with its concentration on maps, made television news successful as far back as 1942; but when we resumed in 1944 we took time for experiments. . . . A big story today may begin with the newscaster speaking; the next series of pictures will be on a map; then a close-up of part of the front will be shown, perhaps in a terrain model; this will dissolve into an animation, which in turn will dissolve into and out of pictures from the actual scene of battle. For the first time, a news report had been completely visualized."[70] Fact haltered by but also harnessed to emergent televisual form and convention was to some degree

Seldes's vision of liveliness, with the unruliness of reality animating the new medium and rousting it from the comforting temptation to cleave to prior arts.

Nevertheless, for all the supposed thrill of discovery, a consolidating valorization of professionalism and specialization was gaining currency in the criticism of experimental television. In the second issue of *Television: The Magazine of Video Fact*, former CBS Television Program Department member Richard Hubbell opined that television programming was improving: "Prominent have been improvements in the quality of CBS productions, commercial development of the Lever Brothers stanzas at Du Mont as noted in a previous issue, experimentation with special effects by Bud Gamble in his sustaining series of fantasies over the latter outlet, and a growing realization among advertising agencies that television is a new art requiring specially trained producers and artists." Hubbell went on to argue that much of "program quality depends to a great extent on the conditions existing at each station, conditions which cannot be changed until new studios, new cameras, new lighting equipment can be built," but he also advocated that producers could overcome "wartime handicaps" to come up with inventive and creative paths to good and innovative programming.[71]

Among the programs Hubbell went on to praise was *Opinions on Trial*, an unscripted show in which matters of public controversy were debated in a courtroom setting with some participation by the studio audience and the broadcast audience positioned as the jury. Hubbell argued that while the program was "primarily aural in appeal," it was a mistake to call it "an illustrated radio show and not real television at all," asserting, "The slant given the program by its producer and director as well as an ingenious method of visualization [the camera as eyes of the jury], makes it a natural for television. It is an example of how television programmers can create visual-aural entertainment, which does not imitate the movies or theater and does not require uninterrupted viewing." Hubbell saw value in a form that allowed for variable levels of attention "without breaking continuity, as long as you have remained within earshot."[72] Here again are the recurrent questions of television's true nature in distinction from adjacent media, as well as the crucial issue of managing audience attention and harmonizing household and program flow.

Hubbell's article also points up the tensions between "technical" and "artistic" production values. Remarking on "The Favor," which was produced, directed, and adapted for television by CBS's Worthington Miner, Hubbell enthused, "Standout was its professional quality, its polish, the feeling of assurance that everything was proceeding on schedule. This was particularly true of the camera handling, the cutting, or editing, all of which were done with the finesse equal to any motion picture."[73] However, he saw one particular shot sequence as exemplifying both the program's potential and the challenges of adapting television to technical standards rooted in cinema. In Hubbell's description of this sequence involving a soldier and "his girl," there is a cut from a "medium close-up of girl at table, as she turns to look at phone booth," where the soldier has gone to make a call, to a shot from inside the phone booth showing that the soldier has disappeared. There was a focus shift from the empty phone booth to the girl some twenty feet away, who had been a white blur in the frame. Hubbell commented: "This momentary confusion as to the nature of the white shape detracted from the effect of the shot. It did not completely spoil it, but it hurt. On the other hand it was the best angle for that shot, from an artistic point of view—if not from a technical one."[74] Although television has greater depth of field than most motion picture film, the sort of deep focus sought by Hubbell in this scene was more easily created for film at the time through either process shots or changes in lighting (increased) and camera aperture size (decreased) that were impractical given live production. This instance exemplified the tensions that arose from the competing impulses to let television develop as an independent medium and simultaneously hold it accountable to professional standards, most conveniently imported from cinema, radio, and the stage. Thus, on the cusp of its final turn of the corner, television was steeped in incongruity, asked to both conform to the standards of adjacent media and decisively stake out its own aesthetics. This became a structuring absurdity in planning for television production, commercialization, and regulation, as well as a generic convention in writing on the emergent medium.

Authority continued to vest itself in essentialist conclusions rather than experimentalist contingencies. For example, Hubbell's book *Television Programming and Production*, published in 1945, again took up the argument of the medium's essential aesthetic characteristics. He first reiterated the distinction between programs "which involve *transmission only* and those which involve *creative* or interpretive effort."[75] Explicitly drawing on Lev Kuleshov's experiments and hypothesis, as articulated by Hubbell, "that *in every art there is (1) a raw material, and (2) a method of composing that material which is best suited to its essential nature*," Hubbell saw cinema realizing its true calling with the recognition of the image on film—rather than the event being filmed—as the raw material to be shaped by montage.[76] Hubbell was wary of the prospects for directly importing cinematic montage into television, "a subject about which considerable controversy will undoubtedly arise" (15). Invoking Aristotle, Kuleshov, and Seldes, he argued for letting television find its essence. Hubbell saw not only a lineage of critical practice but also an imperative in protecting television's nature and liberating it from the threat of becoming a subsidiary art. He asserted "that the characteristics inherent in television give it powers far beyond being just a substitute for celluloid, a new way to distribute motion pictures—or, for that matter, stage plays, picture magazines, and audience-attended radio shows. Television is a new art of the first magnitude, waiting for us to develop it. Let's not cripple that development by confining television within arbitrary boundaries, by failing to recognize and exploit all its potentialities" (15–16). Indeed, he worried that a host of motion picture, radio, theater, and most especially advertising people looking for a "better way to sell laxatives and soap" were, along with educators and manufacturers, crowding the "tele-woods" and foreclosing the medium's opportunity to reach its full potential (16). His remedy was to theorize television in limited distinction from the ends sought by these constituencies and yet wholly within the terms set by the commercial, social, and governmental institutions that had channeled film and radio into tightly controlled commercial systems that limited diversity of aesthetic and political perspectives.

Even when considering the hazards of premature theorization, Hubbell assented to both industrial assumptions about the commercial and social role of television and what had become generic conventions of print postulations of the new medium's nature. Tackling the problem of theory directly, he argued, "Theorizing is at best an uncertain business. With proper eloquence one can make out a convincing theory for almost anything, and it may or may not prove true. Theorizing about the nature of an art form before it exists is doubly dangerous since it is largely speculation" (133). Yet he argued that some theorization was necessary because "certain fundamental points of technique must be investigated, and the sooner the better. By calling attention to these problems we may arrive at a solution much sooner than if we leave things to chance—and then not recognize the correct solution when it does appear" (133). By positing the medium in terms of problems and solutions, Hubbell was inscribing it in a particular type of progress narrative—one that had been productive in the common imagination and realization of television as a technological system and had offered a coherent ethos of professionalism with the growth of production and programming. Missing from Hubbell's nod to theoretical modesty and his subsequent calls for "extensive exploration and demonstration" whereby theory would be "tried and proven" was the possibility that productivity and repression are two sides of the same coin, that in solving television's problems, there was the very real potential—perhaps, even a necessity—for ruling out alternatives.

This potential was exacerbated when the need for theory was framed in terms of commercial success. The strands of thought and discourse about television generated by those involved in the CBS prewar and wartime experiments were characterized by a resistance to hold television to the ideals of high art from other media and an assertion that popularity and commercialism did not automatically equal the debasement of an artistic form. The ethos of professionalism that grew alongside and informed the development of television aesthetics at CBS, however, also worked to shape this emergent theory in the interests of commerce. Hubbell argued, "If it seems academic to theorize about television and seek the answer to such questions, if you feel like saying, 'The success of television depends on pleasing the public, which is not interested in aesthetics, so let's find a couple of good tricks and formulas and forget about basic theories'—then it might be pointed out that the techniques and artistry by which a director creates an effect on his audience act unconsciously" (134). Asserting that "the vast majority of the television audience" would remain unconcerned with how programs were assembled even as they were influenced by them, Hubbell contended, "For this reason it follows that the most successful television programmers will be those who understand the fundamental nature of the medium. A producer, with no understanding of television, may happen to stumble on a successful program out of sheer luck. He may even do it twice, but the law of averages asserts itself sooner or later and he runs into trouble" (134). Like Seldes's vision, Hubbell's dance on the edge of exploration was safely tethered by concessions to the commercial structures of mass media. Moreover, we can again see an imagination of the audience as a conveniently docile and manipulable mass jarringly combined with the acclamation of that same audience as the final judge of television programs. If neither of these was or is entirely correct, the question of their accuracy is overshadowed by the articulation made, the work of discourse in unifying a contradiction of entrusting television to an "unconscious" audience. Verities about the medium served to solve the problem of the public for producers and programmers trying to work out television's aesthetics but much less so for advertising agencies and sponsors who had to be assuaged with demonstrations, data, and a respun discourse about broadcast audiences.[77]

Nevertheless, the CBS school as typified by Seldes and Hubbell regularly argued for complexity and, if caught up in essentialisms, also advocated—often passionately—the imagination of television outside of other media. Thus, while the recourse to essentialisms worked to forestall other television possibilities, they were also quite clearly defensive moves by practitioners cum theorists, who were seeking to stave off the colonization of television by prior media. Hubbell was less ecumenical than Seldes and far less enthusiastic about both radio as a medium and actuality as an artistic mode. Arguing that "art is neither nature nor truth but a pattern or rhythm imposed upon nature," Hubbell stopped short of a constructivist position, clinging tightly to his distinction between creation and transmission and implying a hierarchy in which transmission is at best a lesser art with this derision of radio: "In other words, radio is primarily a method of transmission and secondarily an art form. The reason for this seems to be the basic limitation of the medium itself. It appeals only to a minor sense, and it has no characteristics which can be developed beyond a certain point."[78] Hubbell saw television as problematically hybrid and predicted on the one hand that "most 'real television' programs will be visual first, aural second. On the other hand many 'acceptable' programs of future television schedules will probably be primarily aural with a visual accompaniment. They will not be 'pure television' but they will constitute a sizable portion of the daily fare and will be commercially profitable."[79] This "pure television" was to be "sports, news—as it happens and also visualized completely in summaries—programs involving demonstration, and maybe half of the dramatic programs and variety shows," and in Hubbell's estimation these program types were the key not only to television's success as "a mass entertainment medium" but also to the question of television's nature. Thus, he concluded that television's fundamental process will be "control-room editing" but with the caveat that "camera handling," by which he means "the fluidity of [camera] movement," would be far more important than in the motion picture and require the careful development of video technique. He argued this technique should be developed through specialization in television (as opposed to other media), coordination of crew and cast that bordered on choreography, "more leisurely cutting," greater camera mobility, smart use of subjective camera work, color, and high-key lighting.[80] These would enhance the immediacy and "sense of intimacy and transference of personality" that accompanied "the feeling that you are present at the scene of the action 'in two places at one time'" attributed to television and celebrated by the group Hubbell deemed "the *avant-garde* of American television" and the CBS "brain trusters."[81]

But Will It Play in Schenectady?

Hubbell's distillation of lessons learned and principles preached at CBS in the late 1930s and early 1940s was accompanied to the nation's bookshelves in 1945 by Judy Dupuy's *Television Show Business* and William Eddy's *Television: The Eyes of Tomorrow*, similarly coupling general pronouncements of television theory with the emerging programming and production practices at General Electric's station WRGB in Schenectady and Balaban and Katz's WBKB in Chicago, respectively.[82] Both pieces address a general audience, the former in the mode of public relations and the latter as a basic introduction, but in their elaboration of control, organization, and theorizing and measuring the audience they also speak to advertising agencies and sponsors' concerns over how to translate the radio model into television, with its presumed different demands on attention.[83] Historian James Schwoch found that throughout the late war years broadcasters had endeavored to persuade their customers that television would be a viable advertising medium.[84] The GE broadcasts Dupuy describes were part of that push, as was the experimental work at WBKB that informs Eddy's book. Eddy offered a brief overview of television history and the contributions to television programming and production by the nine entities broadcasting at the time: Philco Radio and Television Corporation (W3XE/WPTZ, Philadelphia); the

Don Lee Company (W6XAO, Los Angeles); General Electric; Dumont Laboratories (WABD, New York); Paramount Affiliates (WBKB, Chicago, and W6XYZ, Hollywood); CBS (WCBW, New York); Zenith (W9XZV/WTZR, Chicago); Farnsworth (W2XPF, Indiana); and RCA and its subsidiaries, including NBC (WNBT, New York).[85] In particular, Eddy credited Dumont with having spurred New York production during the middle of the war and RCA/NBC with "the establishment of a continued program service through which the first consistent television audience was attracted" and having "created the pattern for at least the opening phase of postwar television" (28). Notably Seldes, whom Hubbell compared to Aristotle and Kuleshov in his influence, did not warrant a mention in the discussion of CBS, which was treated much as a gadfly for its intervention in color as an important contributor to the development of television programming. Perhaps more intriguing was Eddy's suggestion to shift historical attention away from Manhattan: "Although our present perspective may point to New York as the focal point of pre-war development, we can more truthfully picture the growth of the art as being the result of a series of local endeavors. These suburban projects may have lacked the glamour and publicity of the more elaborate metropolitan field tests, but they did contribute to the formation of a pattern of television that is national in character. This pioneering became increasingly important in the light of network operation" (16). Stations in Philadelphia, Los Angeles, Chicago, and Schenectady were credited as equals in experimentation to New York and celebrated as "prospectors in the hinterlands . . . who produced the nuggets that have been fused into today's television" (16). The label *suburban* says more about cultural hierarchies at the time than it does the degree of urban development in Chicago or Philadelphia, but unfortunately Eddy only sporadically supported his claims to the significance of the hinterlands in developing distinct televisual practices and techniques and for the most part stuck to broad explanations of technology and its proper use, peppered with examples primarily from NBC and Balaban and Katz.

Complementing the technical emphasis, the book laid out a vision of television built on utility. For example, for Eddy the question of film versus live programming was "an economic rather than an engineering problem" (157) and had no other dimensions. Despite his emphasis on technology and engineering, Eddy most consistently invoked the producer as the key agent in television and implicitly described television programming as the rationalized planning and execution of tasks tightly controlled by the producer to transmit an individual vision onto the airwaves. Thus, he concluded his discussion of lighting by explaining what the producer must know to manage the lighting department (128). Eddy's focus on command and control of production's technical aspects was borne out in well-developed chapters on control-room operation, studio design, and visual effects and switching that were founded on basic assumptions of live production, seamless integration of image and audio sources, and a continuous flow of programming as the interlocking goals of television. Consequently, he argued the artful use of title cards and miniatures were most significant for their fostering a sense of program integrity: "Regardless of the quality of the separate sequences that make up a complete television program, the necessity for logical 'tie-ins' between acts is of the greatest importance in producing a television show."[86] Similarly, Eddy reprinted WBKB's primer for new producers, which would have included but not been limited to advertisers: "One of the outstanding problems in producing a good television show is the maintenance of continuous action—a problem that requires forethought by the producer as to his use of lighting, cameras, and microphones from the time the show first hits the air until the closing sequence. Remember, *there can be no pauses or blanks for the resetting or cuing of lines.* It is necessary, then, that the producer first establish in his mind a complete picture of what he wants to accomplish."[87] This warning against dead air is also an aesthetic philosophy. The program may be segmented into a flow of disparate elements, but it must also be whole in both conception and temporal execution.

This paradigm was directly articulated to a panoptic production hierarchy headed by the director and the supervising engineer at the master control station. Working in concert with the director, the engineer ran the switcher and should be positioned to "oversee the switching setup being used on the consoles as well as the panorama on the studio floor below" and "at the elbow of the director, thereby permitting the maximum intercommunication of ideas and orders during the broadcast" (95). With a trusty technical lieutenant at his side, the director "should be above and behind the desks of the operators at the window. The director, above all people, must have good visibility of the studio floor if he is properly to predict the camera shots required by the story" (95). Here is the continuation of the line of thinking about the separation between aesthetics and engineering—art and technology—that stretched back to the 1920s. Engineering may have been formally answerable to the director, but the emergent convention of production organization established it as a relatively autonomous realm. This channeling of knowledges and authority accentuated the tendency to think television in terms of limitations or problems and solutions, which in turn reinforced the veneration of hierarchical supervision and planning. Television production was being disciplined, and the panopticism of the control room was in many ways simply the practical application of a mundane technology of power. Nevertheless, it is instructive to note that Eddy conceived of the program as produced through directorial "predict" rather than edict. The director and crew were to some degree, like the audience, conceived of as witnesses to an unfolding reality, even if it was a reality of their own design. Here the program was imagined as an act of both vision and supervision.

In contrast to Eddy and Hubbell, Judy Dupuy, who had worked as a producer, writer, engineer, and newscaster with WRGB, WNEW, and WBNX and became the radio editor for *PM*, made far more extensive direct reference to WRGB's experiments and the responses of audiences.[88] Hers was straightforwardly a publicity and marketing piece for General Electric: "Out of these five years of experimentation and the telecasting of over 950 shows at WRGB have evolved the basic techniques of good television. It is with these basic techniques that this book deals."[89] Dupuy made the obligatory comparisons to adjacent media and made sure to assert the familiar verities about and stake claims to "television's very nature, 'seeing events take place at a distance,'" which meant "instantaneous shooting and telecasting of live action with no re-takes possible." Her emphasis, however, was show business: "The public will apply the same entertainment yardstick to this medium that it applies to radio, the theater and motion pictures. Poor shows will mean receivers not in use or people tuned-in to other stations. Good programming will have ready acceptance." Dupuy argued that television would have to learn all that radio and the movies had learned and more: "That is why this handbook has been written—for only television experience can answer television's show problems completely."[90] She contended that direct audience feedback was the measure of good television. Thus, she explained the need for producer authority: "The producer, responsible for the dramatic quality, rhythm and presentation of a show, works with cameras, lights and sets and equipment as well as with story material and performers. How well he combines these ingredients can be measured by how well the program is received in the home and how much the audience likes the show" (10). Much of the discussion that followed reflected specifically on the reception of experimental programming in the home and drew on WRGB's audience-measurement project.

Most experimental broadcasters engaged in some audience measurement, but WRGB was particularly frank in its publicity materials' discussion of its practices and results. Keeping "a constant finger on the televiewer's pulse," the station used three techniques: each week it sent schedules with "space for reaction ratings" to the owners of television receivers; the station conducted specific studies of audience reactions to certain programs and commercials; and it sent a "comprehensive questionnaire" to all television owners "in the Albany-Troy-Schenectady area during the winter of 1943–44" (204). In contrast to Sarnoff, Dupuy readily conceded that audience measurement could "indicate only what people think of what has been offered to them," but she argued that "their opinions . . . are sign posts for future program planning and the imaginative, visual-minded producer will study viewers' suggestions, adapting those that add to the pictorial presentation of commercials and shows" (204).

Perhaps the most remarkable thing about the audience-measurement practices at WRGB was the specific solicitation of evaluations. Commercial audience measurement was for most of television's and radio's existence relatively unconcerned with audience reactions beyond tuning in. This disparity also suggests that experimental audiences, who were admittedly only able to respond to what was put before them, had a dramatic impact on the ratification of the emerging logics of television programming. Roughly 10 percent of the estimated three hundred set owners returned weekly evaluation cards, giving a much greater sample size relative to presumed audience than any conventional commercial ratings (204).[91] In terms of audience composition, Dupuy's findings from the winter 1943–1944 questionnaires indicate that at least a third of those solicited and more than half of the respondents were General Electric employees (207). This data helps account for survey responses that took up already developed public relations tropes, as in this testimony: "I believe that popular large scale acceptance of television must stand or fall on its entertainment value and its ability to transmit spot pick-ups of items which do not now reach the public except by stills or newsreels, but its major field is entertainment. There the pressing need is for the well staged shows of high entertainment value which the movie industry has carried to a high degree of perfection in two-dimensional presentation" (210). Similarly, another anonymous respondent honed in on the intersection of content and technological limitations: "We often have company to see the television programs and we frequently have to apologize for the program material shown. So far, the boxing and wrestling and certain movies have been the best. Musical programs cannot be fully appreciated because of unsuitability or inability of present receivers to reproduce FM" (210). In sum, the subjects of these experiments were among those most likely to have been already engaged in the discourse of what television should be.

Perhaps the relatively rich audience feedback—particularly from coworkers—amplified the discourse of television's intimacy. Regardless of the reasons, Dupuy drew conclusions similar to those of many other theorists about television's role in the home. It had to be a well-behaved guest: "It can be gay or bold but never raucous, informative or entertaining but never bawdy" (5). It had special powers to breach the home and touch the audience's emotions: "Television gives space and movement to a story. It can project mental conflict and show its devastating effect. It can bring charming people into a living room without overstaying its welcome and it can realistically present spine-chillers" (36). It demanded close-ups, yet when broadcasting a simple dance show, those close-ups threatened cultural disruption: "But the television camera with its intimate picture quality emphasized the girls' bare thighs in panning shots and gave the routine a burlesque flavor" (54). And it brought the racist imagery of minstrelsy off the stage and into the home:

The one minstrel show, produced with local talent, *WRGB Minstrels* (July 3, 1942), achieved the gaudy and flamboyant atmosphere of minstrelsy by use of very elaborate costumes. This was especially effective for close-up shots which were staged with an interesting set but was enjoyed more by the studio audience than by the home viewers who rated it simply as "good." To put over a minstrel show requires professional talent, an excellent interlocutor and superb camera takes which catch and reflect the gag-tossing repartee of the endmen. Comedy, particularly the gag routine, does not lend itself readily to the intimacy of television without perfect timing and well executed camera sequences. (15)

Dupuy's claims about the difficulty of comedy tap into a wellspring of performer folk wisdom, but it is also possible that home viewing partially disrupted the racist solidarity stoked by the minstrel show.[92] Certainly, comedy would find a relatively secure home on television, with elements of minstrelsy intermittently repurposed from *The Amos 'n' Andy Show* to the present. However, Dupuy's articulation of timing, intimacy, and the orchestration and execution of camera work and switching speak to the emerging consensus on the nature of the medium and how programming could best fulfill its promise.

Drawing on audience feedback, Dupuy outlined several hypotheses about the shape of future television programming. Complicating the question of filmed versus live programming, GE's research indicated that a quarter of the audience identified films as their favorite program form, while it was also identified as the most disagreeable. In terms of genre, Dupuy noted, "Surveys indicate that variety shows are the first choice of WRGB's television audience, but simply bringing together a group of acts or putting a master of ceremonies before the camera with a collection of vaudeville artists does not make a television variety show. A producer must learn this quickly. Unity of theme and unity of staging are the secrets of a successful television variety show. As a matter of fact unity is one of the basic factors required for any visual production" (13). Dupuy grounded this claim in an internally contradicted set of claims about viewers' capacity to follow variety programs by sound and vision, but her central point emphasized unity imposed by the producer.

This position meshed well with the arguments for integrity put forth by Eddy and others, but it was also supported by detailed reporting on audience and staff reactions to experimental variety programs. Among the most successful was *Barstow's Sketches*, which used drawings by an artist superimposed upon vaudevillians in a matching tableau to give the effect of still pictures coming to life. This was "the magic of television," where "the acts in themselves were not Radio City Music Hall quality—a ventriloquist, a girl trio, a boy playing a miniature organ, and a singer and a dancer—but the effect of the drawings coming to life gave the show spontaneity and zip which held home and studio audience attention" (13).[93] Other successes were *Hoe-Down Night* (July 16, 1943), a western theme in which "the spirit of gaiety and informality was projected through the ad lib spontaneity of the actors and encouraged by the square dance caller who led the party"; *Russian Hour* (June 24, 1943), "an excellent example of a theme setting the mood of a program" that earned "the consensus of opinion of both the studio and the home audience . . . that the 'whole program was excellent'"; and *A Day at the Circus* (July 23, 1943), which "topped all variety shows for enthusiastic home audience enjoyment as was indicated by the weekly rating forms filled in by set owners. Here, too, it was felt that the quality of individual acts would not have justified the high rating of 'excellent' without the novelty of presentation. The studio was turned into a big top with large cutout animal silhouettes festooning the walls where they gave atmosphere without being in the way of cameras and lights" (13–14). In addition to endorsing thematic unity, careful planning, and rehearsals, Dupuy took pains to emphasize that "performances must end" and opined that "too much television today fades out for no good reason—leaving the audience wondering if it's all over—until an announcer or a slide signs-off the show" (17). Even in experimental variety programming, coherence was a paramount value, and audience confusion was to be avoided at all costs. This desire for clarity and stability speaks not only to actual audience reaction and adaptation to television's modes of presentation but also to the expectations of broadcasters, as well as those of sponsors and advertising agencies. At the end of the war the sort of stability sought by television's business interests was still far off, but as the manuals by Hubbell, Eddy, and Dupuy indicate, the push for the medium's rationalization and discipline was well under way.

The Corner at Last: On the Folly of Quality

The theories and practices of television that had been worked out during World War II and before were subject to both revision and reinforcement as television was adapted to dominant constructions of the nation's postwar cultural and economic needs. The corner may have been in sight in 1946, but it took another half decade for television to become truly established and more than a full decade to round into the relatively stable network system that typified US television in the second half of the century. In standard conceptions of television history, these moments are linked to the lifting of the FCC license freeze in 1952 and the shift away from sponsor control of advertising with the quiz show scandals of 1957. While US television—with its mosaic of local, regional, and national programming practices, coupled with contending corporate agendas— was much more diverse than can be described by the arc between these two points in history, the cultural, regulatory, professional, and institutional values analyzed in this and the previous chapters buttressed consolidated control of the medium and found their realization in the emerging network system.

As the war ended and economic and cultural focus shifted, television was not yet the key institution in forging the postwar order that historians such as George Lipsitz have argued it would become by the early 1950s.[94] The period between the end of the war and lifting of the freeze remains underexplored, but recent scholarship points to the continued salience of quality. Media scholar Chad Dell has examined NBC's ambivalence about programming marked as culturally high and low, formulated specifically as a contrast between quality and popularity, during this era. In particular, he found that NBC managed its programming so as to enhance its long-term market identity to the detriment of its television operations' near-term profitability, that is, ultimately choosing quality over the popularity of such programming as wrestling and roller derby.[95] Likewise, Mike Mashon has recounted the struggles in the later 1940s and 1950s among NBC programming personnel and the advertisers at the J. Walter Thompson agency, in which the network, under the aegis of expanded issues of quality control supposedly demanded by the new medium, sought to assure its singular position in programming by making the sponsors and agency work through NBC employees.[96] The divergence between network and advertiser/sponsor interests would ultimately facilitate the shift to spot advertising and network control of programming in the late 1950s, but throughout the 1940s, questions of evaluation and authority were not simply answered by the rough calculus between near- and long-term interests.

Instead, as *New York Times* television critic Jack Gould asserted in 1952, "Television [could finally] be judged fairly by its performance rather than its promise. If the phenomenal expansion of television has proved one unarguable point, it is the futility of broad generalities on its overall quality."[97] Questions of evaluation and authority were rendered complex even as the medium was showing some stability. The overarching cultural hierarchies of gender, nation, and critical authority described by historians such as Lynn Spigel and William Boddy would certainly come to structure the system that was coalescing during the 1950s, yet the logics of quality were contingently adapted to industrial and cultural circumstance. Examples range from NBC's opportunistic arguments with admen described by Mashon to television's embrace of "documentary melodrama" in the late 1940s as recounted by Michael Kackman in his analysis of the spy genre to the networks' expansion of actual documentary in the face of cold war imperatives and the emergent cultural and industrial critique epitomized by Minow's "Vast Wasteland" speech as detailed by Michael Curtin.[98] Even during the long period of relative stability that some scholars call "The Classic Network System," loosely bounded by the quiz show scandals of 1957 and the rise of FOX in the mid-1980s, discourses of quality were called upon to shore up the system and rearticulate the nature of television.[99] The sheer number of uses of quality across historical periods or simply across the daily television schedule speaks to the folly of seizing on a singular vision of the televisual good or excellent.

Nevertheless, Gould's warning against blanket assertions about television's quality has been little heeded for most of the medium's history, and this has been, at least in part, because television's promise and its performance have been and are bound up in one another. Television programs in 1952 were not simply being evaluated for what they were, in some intrinsic sense, nor were they being viewed simply in comparison to what had come over the airwaves in the preceding six years. Instead, television was enmeshed in a set of expectations and competing cultural values that had been articulated and disputed in preceding decades. The conceptions of the nature of television programs and audiences developed in the 1930s and 1940s were reiterated during the early commercial era and became the common sense about the medium. Former WRGB program manager Hoyland Bettinger's 1947 manual *Television Techniques* took up the position laid out by Sarnoff before the war, claiming, "Television is classified as either a medium of communication or an entertainment medium. But these are narrow terms. It is in a real sense a powerful sociological force. Like radio, it reaches into the home and thus into the heart of the nation. It forms attitudes. It conditions thinking. It establishes and nurtures cultural standards." Bettinger affirmed the "rigid control" of the FCC to safeguard "the best interests of the public in this field of influence . . . against abuse." He further argued that television was such "a potent factor in home life, in the formation of attitudes, in setting standards of taste and judgement, and in molding public opinion" that "all who work in it" must be aware of their power and "use it wisely." Bettinger emphasized television's potency in the conjuncture of its presumed placement in the home and its demand on not one but two senses, which "accounts for its double effectiveness as an entertainment and advertising medium."[100] Similarly, Seldes's 1952 guide on television writing imagined television swarming the senses: "As he watches his television screen the spectator is affected in many different ways: he is surprised by a joke, worried by a news broadcast, emotionally stirred by a pretty face or a patriotic sentiment, astonished by an acrobat, caressed by musical sounds, irritated by a personality to which he is allergic, persuaded to buy one kind of gasoline, dissuaded from trying a brand of cigarettes different from his present one, uplifted, diverted, excited, soothed. Whatever the arts of entertainment and persuasion can do is done to him."[101] Television's supposed ability to transfix and transform its audience placed it in a matrix of expectations where its presumed highest quality was integrity—both being true and being complete.

Nevertheless, for most of its history, television had a troubled relationship with claims to truth and completeness. In the interest of economy and control, liveness and actuality were plowed under as dominant prime-time values by the end of the 1950s, while series television, built on the ruins of classical Hollywood's B-movie production, rose to prominence.[102] Yet most series on US television have lacked conclusive conclusions.[103] Moreover, prior to the widespread penetration of recording technologies in the 1980s, approximating a complete experience of television programs required a strict scheduling regimen and either a hermetic viewing space or the significant indulgence of housemates. Likewise, television's budget-conscious adaptation of continuity style from cinema worked to undermine its claims on immediacy and realism. A paradox of the continuity system is that it must break up space and time so as to give the semblance of temporal and spatial coherence. It must disarticulate the continuum in which perception and reality meet in order to render its representations symbolically legible. The seamlessness of a text relies on skill in building the seams. This moves beyond being merely a philosophical point as the television text has been subjected to the dual challenges (relative to Hollywood cinema) of hurried, underfunded production and harried, undisciplined reception. Thus, fictional dramatic television fell into the trap of being regularly defined as debased cinema (and less often as sterile or puerile theater).

With the culture of cable, recording, and niche programming, the presumption of debasement may be somewhat diminished or even inverted, but fictional dramatic television has also become more thoroughly anchored to cinematic textual expectations and Aristotelian values of coherence and endurance partly through contrast with adjacent television genres such as reality TV that are marked as low others. Yet actuality formats from reality to news to sports are what sustain the traditional broadcast networks both economically and as a shared, roughly simultaneous audience experience. In these circumstances it is tempting to conclude that Seldes was, to some extent, right about the nature of television programs—that the medium just took a while to catch up. But the lesson should be that television and its audiences never had a nature but rather a multitude of actual and potential uses. The aesthetic hierarchies and generic definitions used to make common sense of the relations among programs and viewers are power-laden "cultural categories" that work to rationalize and coordinate systems of exchange and identification.[104] And although as labels they do not have essence, as discourse they most certainly have substance.

Conclusions

Why Not Quantity Television?

The realization of television—its authorities and audiences, its textual forms and technical articulation—was presented not on a "blank canvas" but amid an existing panorama of contending institutions and expectations.[1] Made manifest in a vacuum tube but not in a vacuum, the medium's relationship with the Arnoldian vision of culture as "a study of perfection" has been conflicted, with discourses of perfection, excellence, and quality both indulged and confounded by the compulsion to standardize, rationalize, and secure.[2] Evaluative discourse has also often included gestures of contingency, a claim of perfection not made, that has inscribed television in more local narratives of progress and brokered deals between aspiration and economy. Commercial systems, aesthetic systems, and technical systems are all ultimately cultural, not in the Arnoldian sense but in that they are all concerned with the circulation of values and meanings.[3] In the specific case of television the language of evaluation served not only as an articulated set of meanings and values but also as a set of rules and expectations that worked to structure the larger systems of exchange.

This book has examined the ways in which cultural authority and evaluative discourse helped shape the technical form, institutional structures, and programming practices of US television in the period before its successful commercial introduction. These workings of culture and language were not independent of institutional imperatives or the choices of historical actors, but neither were they entirely determined by them. Rather, there was a series of reciprocal inflections. For example, CBS's strategy for competing with NBC and RCA in the 1940s shaped Gilbert Seldes's developing philosophy on the nature of television programs, but the imagination of programming he articulated both continued earlier conceptions of television's essence and resounded into future televisual practice in ways that were largely independent of the interests of the man or company. Such "mutual shaping" occurs across all facets of a system and practice such as television, and as historians of science and technology have argued, these interdependent interactions can explain much about the development of our modern material world.[4] But nuancing determination is not the only notable feature of this model of culture, particularly as applied to aspirational language and planning. Although the specific imaginations of television and its uses were dependent on institutional, economic, and social context, there has also been a significant persistence of evaluative tropes and habits of authority even to the present moment of media convergence. Some of their configurations have changed. Rhetoric and seats of critical power that used to work in concert now may act in tension. Still, many remain potent.

Certainly the experimental period set the stage for the immediate practices and decisions of the late 1940s, such as the programming choices made by NBC analyzed by Chad Dell, as well as the later cultural and industrial logics examined by scholars such as William Boddy and Lynn Spigel.[5] However, the early acts of affirmatively imagining the medium at the intersection of cultural authority, commercial calculation, and the much theorized but never wholly disciplined everyday practices of production and consumption—have as much bearing on the present as the intermediate past. Over the past quarter of a century many of the paradigms that gave the semblance of stability and coherence to television as a cultural construct (and television history as a set of articulated disciplines and knowledges) have given way to uncertainty. Yet quality, for example, remains salient, and this is not accidental. Quality has long been a favored treatment to palliate if not remedy the scourge of uncertainty that plagues the interests that would have broadcasting be a rationalized system for the production of subjects and the rendering of those subjects into profitable objects of exchange and control. Nevertheless, the stable conception of quality that arose in the later portion of what some historians term the Classic Network System was rearticulated into an instrument of that system's dismemberment, as forces within and outside of television's main institutions transformed it from a defense of the oldest broadcast network into a vanguard of narrowcasting. We are again at a juncture where the medium's identities are being defined, and each of the preceding chapters has revealed questions of evaluation and authority from television's early period that can tell us something significant about the debates of the present and the crafting of the future.

The first chapter showed that definitional practice was bound up in evaluative discourse that expressed cultural values and commercial expectations as scientific fact. The discursive positioning of mechanical and electronic television depended on an emerging regime of knowledge and power that rephrased perfection in terms of pragmatic and contingent value—good (enough)—that worked to valorize standardization, predictability, and thereby control. The particular technologies endorsed by the emergent evaluative language have had, at best, historically contingent advantages over alternatives, and the return of once-abandoned and derided televisions, as with the moving mirrors in the DLP chips of modern digital cinema projectors and the arrays of wired picture elements as in LCD and LED HD TVs, testifies powerfully to the social construction of technology. The door has not yet closed on the current era of standardization. Indeed, the convergence of television with networked computer technologies along with audience reluctance disrupted the timetables for the switch to high definition and has facilitated a significant reconsideration of the virtues of smaller and lower-definition pictures. Presently, definitional practice is again working to articulate true television to forms of imaging and types of content that winnow opportunities to broadcast, to make distinctions at the level of technology and technique among uses even as such practices as video blogging are broadcast in intent. While in the widening gyre of video platforms television may fail to hold the cultural centrality that justified unitary and exclusionary systems of standards, acts of technical definition are still very much imbricated with matters of managing cultural hierarchy, pursuing institutional interests, and valuing of particular users and uses.

As I argued in chapters 2 and 3, systems of professionalization and institutional control were erected, in part, in response to the perceived threat that radio and then television would become media of mere anarchy rather than bastions of enterprise and ennoblement. Television was rendered culturally coherent at a moment when hierarchical distinctions among engineers, aficionados, and audiences were drawn in ever sharper relief. To tinker with television would not offer the same promise of discovery as early radio. Amateurs were cropped out of the picture by regulatory fiat by the early 1930s. Despite the thrilling opportunities to build your own set offered again in the late 1940s and the later promises of guerilla video, cable access, and interactivity, when television has given way to individual visions, they have generally been marginalized as idiosyncratic and often narcissistic. Though various forms of expertise and exceptionalism were cultivated over the second half of the twentieth century, these worked more to define the acceptable boundaries of audience activity, direct the investment of viewers' passions, and distinguish particular audience segments as salable commodities than to establish the television public, or even a fraction of connoisseurs, as stake-holding participants. The early, gendered ordering of technical authority presaged the largely unidirectional model of communication that followed.

As television's second coming is bound up with Web 2.0 (or 3.0 or 1.2 depending on whom you consult), we should not be surprised to see a rhetoric of juvenile and feminized self-absorption reappear, as with Caitlin Flanagan's attribution of MySpace's success to the "fathomless narcissism of the young" that she sees exemplified by "today's girls [who] spend hours looking at their MySpace profiles, fiddling and tinkering with them—much as I once sat in front of my vanity mirror, holding my hair up and letting it fall, smiling one way and then the other."[6] Flanagan's ultimate point about social networking sites' potential for facilitating stalking and worse—a point she proves by purportedly using MySpace to stalk a neighborhood teenager—completes the pattern of articulation echoing back to early broadcasting, in which cultural dynamics of gender and age mobilized as vanity and vulnerability are ascribed to media users. Historically, these discourses have been voiced as part of assertions and justifications of technical, legal, and cultural authority.

The digital commons are unlikely to remain a space either amiable or properly shared without governance. The historical examples of early radio and television broadcasting in the United States, however, speak to a pattern of trusting in private oligopoly coupled with ultimately friendly regulation to rationalize and manage communications in the name of protecting the masses from demagogues, charlatans, and—most of all—themselves. In keeping with the logics of US capitalism, centralized commercial control and competition were posed as the mechanisms for ensuring quality and the guarantors of the paradoxical sovereignty of the audience. Today, media concentration is marked by horizontal integration and "global flows" of money, people, technology, ideas, and media themselves in a manner where the complexity of organization and interaction sometimes obscures the continuing appeal of oligopoly to national regulators and constituencies seeking cultural control.[7] Quality continues to be marshaled in the interests of a select few. This was exemplified by the arguments of former FCC chair Michael Powell, for whom the commercial and critical successes of HBO testified to the decline of broadcast television and served as evidence for expanding the reach of HBO's corporate sibling the WB (now the CW) by raising station ownership caps.[8] Thus, the solution to concentrated media's branding and distribution practices is asserted to be greater concentration. The cultural work that enabled these discursive contortions was begun long ago.

As we saw in chapter 4, television's evaluative criteria are shaped by complex contextual factors and reconfigured in times of institutional disruption, yielding protean evaluation of television's textual features. Variance from the classical Hollywood style has been both a badge of honor and a mark of shame. Filmed programs were low then high and then challenged in the cultural hierarchy by a series of emergent video aesthetics. Seriality has been damned as characteristic of daytime soap operas and praised as a hallmark of the "prime-time novel."[9] Conclusions are good, unless they are pat "sitcom endings."[10] The notion of television being an engrossing source of sensory fulfillment has been imagined as both its highest potential and a source of cultural abasement.[11] There is no singular, coherent continuity between the present and the aesthetic precepts that emerged from television's experimental period. There are instead many persistent truisms and tropes, but they have been intermittently dis- and re-articulated. What has remained fairly constant, however, is the tendency to articulate television's value in terms of the nature of the medium and its audiences, who are for the most part expected to be acted upon by television, whether fiction or actuality, recorded or live—but always standing in for life. Among the significant consequences of this tendency have been conceptions of quality content that aspire to universality and endurance and draw on deterministic models of the relationships among institutions, audiences, and texts.

The preceding chapters encourage ongoing reflection and investigation, particularly as they bear on media policy and television criticism. In terms of policy, the examples of the past suggest that a general lowering of the stakes—including a move away from expecting each instance of television to stand in for all television, from a centralized, standardized quality to diverse qualities—would, on its own, be in the interest of a more democratic television. That said, the televisions of the future are just as much enmeshed in institutional interests and broad cultural hierarchies as the televisions of the past, and the contemporary articulations of paedocracy and intellectual property generally work to label and limit our choices. Oft-repeated threats of predators and pirates are culturally productive just as much as the affirmative imagination of television has been restrictive. Moreover, expanded surveillance is not likely to yield a bounty of innovative or diverse programming, nor will it deliver greater access to the means of representation.[12] The openings created by the convergence of television and networked computing will be constrained or maintained in part by how they are framed through evaluative discourse and by established and emergent cultural authority, and it is worth renegotiating the bargains struck between access and excellence, between flexibility and endurance, and between the promises of communicational equality and quality control.

These issues of policy also point to the need for a reappraisal of television criticism's continued reliance on the text as primary object of analysis and proving ground for critical authority. To treat television programming as merely a text and evaluate it on those terms ignores what it has historically been very good at—quantity. The sheer scope of US television is nearly imponderable. Only by imposing the categorical blinders of national networks or prime time can we make a history of its programs from a textualist perspective, and coherence collapses under the weight of local broadcasts and commercials and syndication.[13] As it was for those who spoke and wrote of television in the 1930s and 1940s, so essentialisms may be a necessity for modern historians and critics to make sense of this vast terrain. Yet television's rhythms, its pattern of what Jane Feuer, reconciling concepts from Raymond Williams and John Ellis, called "segmentation and flow," point not just to consistencies of political economy but also to a poetics of experience, a delicate dance between television's ephemerality and the other exigencies of our lives.[14] Television and its programs may have been designed to command our attention and continuously structure and account for time—airtime and our time economically linked and reciprocally laden with cultural expectations—but the vision of the person as always already waiting to be disciplined is a peculiar conceit in these models of human nature. It may be pleasant for critics and media professionals to think of the viewers as conditioned, responding to stimuli in a predictable manner, but this is both somewhat counterfactual and a narrowing of human experience in the interest of order.

Yet the era of convergence has also been one of intensified legitimation of television, fixing its texts and its forms through processes and rhetoric that echo those explored in this study.[15] As media scholars Michael Z. Newman and Elana Levine argue, some television scholarship has been complicit in the "perpetuation of hierarchies of taste and cultural value and inequalities of class and gender" in efforts to reframe the medium as worthy of esteem.[16] I share Levine and Newman's ambivalence about the general thrust of this legitimation and distress at its reinscription of disparities of cultural power, and I find in the current era the exercise of cultural authority and deployment of evaluative language in patterns quite similar to the beginnings of Television 1.0. But because evaluation and decision-making power are necessary for the planning and coordination of complex human interactions, I also see such problematic hierarchies as stemming from attempts to corral uncertainties about iterative technologies, fluid social and business relations, and the somewhat invisible audience. Critics, regulators, businesspeople, and inventors have sought to dispel doubts by erecting aspirational norms on the scaffolding of existing axes of cultural power such that television seems to be an unassailable fact, an essence realized.[17] But claims to the essence of the medium and its audience have historically worked to create unity and stability at the expense of quantity and variety. Thus, the search for and assertion of television's nature as a set of stable and clearly definable characteristics from which its textual features should flow denies its very real potential for flexibility and diversity that defy exclusionary concentrations of cultural power. There is much to be gained from an appreciation of television, its audiences, and modern life as immeasurable and fleeting. Thus, as we continue to rethink television and its place in our culture and lives, we might want to ask why television's vastness and wastefulness have been regarded as things to be tamed rather than as two of the medium's more estimable qualities.

NOTES

INTRODUCTION

1. Hugo Gernsback, "Television to the Front," *Radio News*, June 1927, 1419.
2. James W. Carey, *Communication as Culture: Essays on Media and Society* (New York: Routledge, 1989), 86–87.
3. See Joseph H. Udelson's *The Great Television Race: A History of the American Television Industry, 1925–1941* (Tuscaloosa: University of Alabama Press, 1982), which provides an illuminating account of the technical and economic struggles that roiled this era. In addition, there are a number of quite thorough technical histories from the past few decades. See, e.g., Albert Abramson's *The History of Television, 1880–1941* (Jefferson, NC: McFarland, 1987); and David E. Fisher and Marshall Jon Fisher's *Tube: The Invention of Television* (Washington, DC: Counterpoint, 1996). William Hawes's *American Television Drama: The Experimental Years* (Tuscaloosa: University of Alabama Press, 1986) exhaustively chronicles the dramatic programming of NBC and CBS prior to 1946, as well as other key early moments in television drama.
4. Jonathan Sterne, *The Audible Past: Cultural Origins of Sound Reproduction* (Durham, NC: Duke University Press, 2003), 7.
5. Ibid., 210.
6. In particular, this transposition borrows from his analysis of the telephone and the AT&T system (ibid., 209–214).
7. Thomas Streeter, *Selling the Air: A Critique of the Policy of Commercial Broadcasting in the United States* (Chicago: University of Chicago Press, 1996), 25.
8. Ibid., 10.
9. Ibid., 107 (emphasis in original).
10. Hugh Aitken, *The Continuous Wave: Technology and American Radio, 1900–1932* (Princeton, NJ: Princeton University Press, 1985), 16–17.
11. See Michel Foucault, *The Archaeology of Knowledge*, trans. A. M. Sheridan Smith (New York: Pantheon, 1972). For Foucault the phrase "discursive formation" describes the system of dispersion or organization among a group of discourses (38). These discourses are not merely groups of signs but instead are utterances or practices within systems of power that can form and change the objects they purport to describe (49).
12. Within a formation, discourses are subject to certain "rules of formation" that describe and govern their existence and exchange and efface their service of power. To defy the attempts of these utterances in power to naturalize themselves, Foucault advocated the principles of *reversal, discontinuity, specificity,* and *exteriority* (emphasis in the original) to accentuate the constructedness and contingency of discourse. In this scheme,

"reversal" consists of examining the ways in which activities and functions generally thought to be creative can act to restrict, narrow, and police the bounds of discourse and thereby the possible. The principle of "discontinuity" requires the researcher to recognize that discourse is a heterogeneous, interrupted mosaic of signs and practices, that the unities offered by a historical narrative of stability work both to stamp out other traces of the past and foreclose alternative interpretations of the present. Attention to the principle of "specificity" allows one to escape prior significations, and it demands that discourse be recognized as a practice or process as opposed to a description. Finally, the principle of "exteriority" would preclude the analyst from looking for a core meaning in a discourse and instead oblige her or him to attend to its conditions of existence. In sum, this method is an argument for attention to context and specificity and a refusal to accept totalizing narratives that render history in the interests of power. See Foucault, *The Archaeology of Knowledge*, Appendix: "The Discourse on Language," 229.

13. Carolyn Marvin, *When Old Technologies Were New: Thinking About Electric Communication in the Late Nineteenth Century* (Oxford: Oxford University Press, 1988), 9–62.

14. Hugh Aitken, *Syntony and Spark—The Origins of Radio* (New York: John Wiley and Sons, 1976), 327.

15. Ibid., 20.

16. Marvin, *When Old Technologies Were New*, 44–45.

17. Roland Marchand, *Advertising the American Dream: Making Way for Modernity, 1920–1940* (Berkeley: University of California Press, 1985), 359.

18. Here I am drawing on Nancy Fraser's discussion of "subaltern counterpublics" (60) in "Rethinking the Public Sphere: A Contribution to the Critique of Actually Existing Democracy," *Social Text* 25/26 (1990): 56–80.

19. Although I am not specifically drawing on the model for cultural studies described by the Open University's series on cultural studies and modeled in Paul du Gay, Stuart Hall, Linda Janes, Hugh Mackay, and Keith Negus's *Doing Cultural Studies: The Story of the Sony Walkman* (London: Sage, 1997), their conception of a circuit model and call for attention to the processes of regulation, representation, production, consumption, and identification certainly informs my project and is broadly congruent with its aims and claims.

20. I draw here on the work of Pierre Bourdieu, who observed that the dominance of the dominant was naturalized by the leveraging of cultural capital. See Pierre Bourdieu, *Distinction: A Social Critique of the Judgement of Taste*, trans. Richard Nice (Cambridge, MA: Harvard University Press, 1984).

21. See James W. Carey with John J. Quirk, "The Mythos of the Electronic Revolution," in Carey, *Communication as Culture*, 120–123.

CHAPTER 1   QUESTIONS OF DEFINITION

1. Thus, in discussing television's meaning, my point is not to echo Marshall McLuhan's universalizing "the medium is the message" but rather to offer a variation on Raymond Williams's theories that reinscribe intention and limited, local determination on theories of television. See Marshall McLuhan, *Understanding Media: The Extensions of Man* (New York: Signet, 1966); and Raymond Williams, *Television: Technology and Cultural Form* (London: Fontana, 1974).

2. Richard W. Hubbell, *4000 Years of Television: The Story of Seeing at a Distance* (New York: G. P. Putnam's Sons, 1942). See also E.F.W. Alexanderson, "Radio-Photography and

Television," *Radio News*, Feb. 1927, 944–945; Berthold Laufer, "The Prehistory of Television," *Scientific Monthly*, Nov. 1928, 455–459; and Orrin E. Dunlap Jr., *The Outlook for Television* (New York: Harper and Brothers, 1932), 3–17.

3. Carolyn Marvin, *When Old Technologies Were New: Thinking About Electric Communication in the Late Nineteenth Century* (Oxford: Oxford University Press, 1988), 222–231; and Brian Winston, "How Are Media Born and Developed?" in *Questioning the Media*, ed. John Downing and Annabelle Sreberny-Mohammadi, 2nd ed. (London: Sage, 1995), 54–74. Marvin argues that the application and development of nineteenth-century media technologies such as the telephone depended greatly on both the immediate social and industrial contexts in which their uses were invented and the competition of adjacent media technologies and institutions. Winston opposes "technological determinism" with his preferred "cultural determinism." The latter theorizes a consistent historical pattern, in which a media technology undergoes a moment of "ideation" or imagining, is called into technical being by the force of "supervening social necessity," and is subjected to a "suppression of radical potential," in which economic and cultural forces discipline the technology and its users. For his specific application of this theory to television's history see Brian Winston, *Media Technology and Society, a History: From the Telegraph to the Internet* (New York: Routledge, 1998), 88–143.

4. See Hugh Slotten, *Radio and Television Regulation: Broadcast Technology in the United States, 1920–1960* (Baltimore: Johns Hopkins University Press, 2000).

5. David E. Fisher and Marshall Jon Fisher, *Tube: The Invention of Television* (New York: Harvest, 1996), 357.

6. Hubbell, *4000 Years of Television*, 70–71. Hubbell also notes Hugo Gernsback's 1928 claim to coining the term in December 1909 in an article in *Modern Electrics*. Elsewhere, Gernsback, a publisher and author for electronics-enthusiast and science fiction magazines, claimed to have been using the term since 1912 or 1913. See Hugo Gernsback, "Television to the Front," *Radio News*, June 1927, 1419.

7. William Uricchio, "Television, Film and the Struggle for Media Identity," *Film History* 10, no. 2 (1998): 118–127, 120. Notably, this imagination was crucially linked to the experience of simultaneity provided by the telephone (119), a characteristic that would become a point of dispute around television technologies that relied on intermediate film processes and broadcast practices that replayed filmed content.

8. This proliferation of discourse on television can be tracked through the indexes of periodicals during the era. For example, statistical analysis of the database generated from the *Readers' Guide to Periodical Literature* yields a distinctive pattern of peaks and troughs showing three booms in articles about television, with the first two peaking in 1928 and 1940 and the third starting at the end of World War II and lasting through television's wide-scale commercial release. Wilson Web: Readers' Guide Retrospective (1890–). The *Readers' Guide* and the *New York Times* have their own processes of inclusion and exclusion about which sources and topics count. In particular, inconsistencies in journals indexed and a relatively late adoption of the new generation of news magazines such as *Time*, which was not indexed until 1935, twelve years after its launch, makes the data from the *Readers' Guide* at best a rough tool. However, the general pattern is borne out by other sources and an analysis of those journals consistently indexed throughout the period. Likewise, ProQuest's database of the *New York Times* shows a similar pattern for articles referring to television. ProQuest Historical Newspapers: The *New York Times* (1851–2001). Notably, data from the *New York Times* includes classified ads, which complicate the statistical comparison.

9. Joseph H. Udelson, *The Great Television Race: A History of the American Television Industry, 1925–1941* (Tuscaloosa: University of Alabama Press, 1982), 50.

10. "New Scheme for Distance Vision," *Literary Digest*, Jan. 6, 1912, 17; and "Doubts About Television," *Literary Digest*, Nov. 6, 1926, 72–74.

11. "Notes," *Time*, March 30, 1925, 17.

12. Another form of acknowledging television's contingency was to refer to the "problem of television." For early instances see "A Partial Solution of the Problem of Television," *Scientific American*, August 7, 1909, 94; Fernand Honore, "Rignoux-Fournier System of Television," *Scientific American*, Jan. 1, 1910, 13; and "Important Step in the Problem of Television," *Scientific American*, Dec. 23, 1911, 574. The construction was still in use in the late 1920s. A typical instance is "Dr. Alexanderson is seeking to solve the problem of television," in Edgar H. Felix's article, "Television: Europe or America First?" *Radio Broadcast*, March 1927, 460.

13. J. H. Morecroft, "Wireless Vision Achieved," *Radio Broadcast*, June 1925, 205–206. Additionally, indexes of the era sometimes cross-referenced the as yet unrealized television with facsimile or tele-photography, as in the *Readers' Guide* listing "Visible Radio for the Amateur," *Literary Digest*, June 6, 1925, 28–29, an article concerned exclusively with wireless facsimile, under its television heading.

14. See "Partial Solution of the Problem of Television," 94; Honore, "Rignoux-Fournier System of Television," 13; and "Important Step in the Problem of Television," 574.

15. In contrast to cinematographic methods for producing the illusion of movement, in which a whole image is produced through sequential exposures of individual frames of raw film stock to an image projected onto the stock by the lens and then reproduced when the developed stock is projected as a succession of whole, still pictures, the picture elements that make up the television frame are not strictly contemporaries but rather are produced in sequence.

16. Sean Cubitt, *Timeshift: On Video Culture* (London: Routledge, 1991), 30–31, cited in and expanded upon by Philip Auslander, "Against Ontology: Making Distinctions Between the Live and the Mediatized," *Performance Research* 2, no. 3 (1997): 52.

17. Alfred Dinsdale, "And Now, We See by Radio!" *Radio Broadcast*, Dec. 1926, 139. Dinsdale, a member of the Royal Radio Society of Great Britain, was particularly invested in the system developed by John Logie Baird, one of the two most commonly recognized claimants to having developed working, lower-resolution television.

18. Morecroft, "Wireless Vision Achieved," 206. See also James Nevin Miller, "Latest in Television," *Popular Mechanics*, Sept. 1929, 474, which reported on the Federal Radio Commission's figures for visual broadcasting: "While they do not divide television into its still and movie chapters, they show that twenty-two visual broadcast stations, probably, by the time this is read, will be transmitting pictures and television on channels assigned by the radio commission."

19. E.F.W. Alexanderson, "Radio Photography and Television," *Radio News*, Feb. 1927, 944–945, 1030–1034.

20. Fisher and Fisher, *Tube*, 42–43.

21. See Hubbell, *4000 Years of Television*, 86; Udelson, *The Great Television Race*, 27; Orrin Dunlap, "Seeing Around the World by Radio," *Scientific American*, March 1926, 162–163; and Miller, "The Latest in Television," 472–476.

22. W. B. Arvin, "See with Your Radio," *Radio News*, Sept. 1928, 278 (emphasis mine). In this article the author espouses an engineering aesthetic founded on twin principles of simplicity and excellence, which presage the trope of elegance in what I will call "the electronic aesthetic."

23. "What Television Offers You," *Popular Mechanics*, Nov. 1928, 822. See also Dinsdale's "And Now, We See by Radio!" in which he states "shadowgraphs are not television" (140).

24. "Televisionary," *Radio News*, June 1927, 1484; and Dorinda Hartmann, University of Wisconsin–Madison, Media and Cultural Studies Colloquium Presentation, Nov. 9, 2000. Baird's usage of "televisor" to denote the projecting and receiving apparatuses was also a source of considerable agitation.

25. "New Visions: Television, Noctovision, and the Phonovisor," *Living Age*, Nov. 15, 1927, 933–934. Noctovision was a Baird flying-spot method using infrared rays that allowed for television in the dark, thereby relieving the strain placed on human models by extremely bright visible flying-spot scanning. The phonovisor recorded the analog television signal onto a wax phonograph record in the same manner as a sound signal would be recorded. *Living Age* made a practice of placing *televise* in quotation marks while awaiting its replacement. See "Sciences and Society," *Living Age*, April 1935, 179; and Alan Patrick Herbert, "Some Thoughts on Television," *Living Age*, Nov. 1936, 208–210.

26. Betty McGee, "WGBS-W2XCR Television Invades Broadway," *Radio Digest*, Sept., 1931, 15; and "And Now Television Gives Form to the Radio Voice," *Literary Digest*, May 16, 1931, 40–43. McGee found "visience" problematic as it only accounted for sight. *Literary Digest* favored "looker in" but also noted the *New York Times*' report on alternatives.

27. See also John Wallace, "The Announcer as English Teacher," *Radio Broadcast*, May 1926, 37; Beatrice Leigh, "Good Diction: Radio Demands Perfect Articulation, Says Dagmar Perkins, Expert Advisor on Committee for Diction Medal Award," *Radio Digest*, Nov. 1930, 66; and Charles M. Adams, "Radio and Our Spoken Language," *Radio News*, Sept., 1927, 208.

28. Marvin, *When Old Technologies Were New*, 50–51.

29. W. G. Walton, "A New Method of Television," *Radio News*, April 1925, 1872.

30. Orrin Dunlap, "Seeing Around the World by Radio," *Scientific American*, March 1926, 162–163.

31. Gernsback, "Television to the Front," 1419.

32. This is not to say that these distinctions were the product of unambiguous maneuvering by electronics giants, or at least not wholly so. Inventors like Jenkins and populist publishers like Gernsback had substantial incentives to participate. For Jenkins, "radio movies" could function as a sales name. Moreover, the ability to make technical distinctions as expressed through words was crucial to claiming competence within his field of invention and in prosecuting patent applications. Gernsback's publishing enterprise was built on the production of science fiction and fact, and these acts of distinction produced new knowledges to attract readers who would buy the magazine and in turn themselves be sold to advertisers. While their particular televisions suffered, Jenkins and Gernsback were active participants in and beneficiaries of a broad cultural valorization of notions of technical progress.

33. In writing about events that occur in sequence, the reporter or historian faces a challenge in that the modal biases of storytelling all but impose a narrative of progress or decline. With technology or art, the tendency toward tales of progress is exacerbated by the limited verbs—*develop, evolve, invent, elaborate*, to pick a few from the preceding paragraphs—available to express the goal-oriented change of a technological artifact.

34. "Literalism and Illiteracy," "'Monkey War' Collapses," and "Televisionary," in *Science News-Letter*, April 16, 1927, 241. See also "Radiovision on Air Across Country" and "Seven-Inch Tail on Baby," *Science News-Letter*, Nov. 17, 1928, 307–308.

35. For a popular account of Einstein's work from this period in television's development see "Einstein's New Ideas of Space," *Literary Digest*, July 5, 1930, 29, which ran adjacent to "Television on the Theater Screen," 28. Einstein's already iconic status within the world of physics made him a frequent subject of reportage and commentary in both the scientific and radio-enthusiast publications. Of particular interest is George Bernard Shaw's "The Universe of Einstein," in *Radio Digest*, Jan. 1931, 54 and 103, in which Shaw assigns Einstein the hero's role in the story of scientific progress and triumph over the irrationality of religion.

36. John Arnold, "Photoelectricity, the Means of Television," *Radio News*, Dec. 1927, 640.

37. "A Tree of Electricity," *Scientific American*, March 1926, 171.

38. Carroll Pursell, *The Machine in America: A Social History of Technology* (Baltimore: Johns Hopkins University Press, 1995), 203.

39. Carl Dreher, "How Radio Has Progressed," *Radio Broadcast*, April 1926, 672.

40. Jay Hollander, "Hammatorial: Put It on Paper First," *Radio News*, April 1925, 1892.

41. J. H. Morecroft, "The March of Radio: Why the Radio Industry Will Not Be Revolutionized," *Radio Broadcast*, August 1925, 483–485.

42. Jonathan Sterne, *The Audible Past: Cultural Origins of Sound Reproduction* (Durham, NC: Duke University Press, 2003), 181–182.

43. "Latest Television Developments," *Radio Broadcast*, June 1927, 81.

44. See Udelson, *The Great Television Race*, 2.

45. Harold Brown, "Science Brings Radio Close to Movietone," *Radio Digest*, Oct. 1928, 24.

46. See "Radio Vision Forges Ahead but Slowly," *New York Times*, Feb. 3, 1929, 147, which reported on a David Sarnoff speech with the lead "Television for Home Not Around the Corner, Says Sarnoff—He Predicts Colored Scenes." This was typical of Sarnoff's strategy for holding television at bay in that it both downplayed television's present and hyped its future.

47. Theodore H. Nakken, "Complex Nature of Sight Retards Seeing by Radio," *New York Times*, May 27, 1928, 132.

48. Anna Nyus, "Just Around the Corner, Reincarnation: Transmuter Rejuvenates," *Radio Digest*, Feb. 1932, 46–47, 49.

49. The apparent time travel recounted in this article could be accounted for either by using filmed content for the before or after segments or by exploiting quirks in the color spectrum used by a specific flying-spot system to create the appearance of costume or makeup change while maintaining a continuous performance before the cameras. Specifically, this account describes a costume change from "formal dress" to a "checkered coat, plaid vest, a prodigious tie and tight collar," and these pattern changes can be accounted for strictly by a change in the color of the scanning spot.

50. "Why Should Radio Appeal Only to the Auditory Sense?" *Radio Broadcast*, May 1925, 81.

51. Edgar H. Felix, "Television: Europe or America First?" *Radio Broadcast*, March 1927, 461. Gernsback and a few others imagined sensors that would simultaneously detect all of the waves of light that made up an image and render it into a complex signal that could be transmitted along a relatively narrow bandwidth, but this certainly has not happened in the manner he described. See Gernsback, "Television to the Front," 1419. Of course, today we do have video compression—anticipated by Farnsworth and achieved through digital processing—but this still does not match the elegance of sound transmission, in part because sound is perceived through the process of measuring changes in intensity and frequency. That is, sound perception is in some sense a compression scheme.

52. Nakken, "Complex Nature of Sight Retards Seeing by Radio," 132.

53. Sterne, *The Audible Past*, 15, 3, 15.

54. Ibid., 5.

55. Ibid., 31–84.

56. Louis S. Treadwell, "Practical Television Demonstrated," *Scientific American*, June 1927, 385.

57. Alden Armagnac, "Human-Eye Camera Opens New Way to Television," *Popular Science*, Sept. 1933, 11–13. In the 1920s, Zworykin's photocell was also referred to as the "radio 'eye.'" See also Orrin E. Dunlap Jr., "Seeing Around the World by Radio," *Scientific American*, March 1926, 162–163, which reported on the work of Jenkins and Zworykin with the lead, "The Development of a New Combination Photo-electric Cell and Vacuum Tube Has Created an 'Eye' for Wireless."

58. "Eye Sees like Television Camera," *Literary Digest*, Oct. 3, 1931, 17.

59. James Stokely, "Television, Though Crude, Has Arrived," *Science News-Letter*, Feb. 2, 1929, 60.

60. For a few examples see Dinsdale, "And Now, We See by Radio!" 142–143; H. Winfield Secor, "Radio Vision Demonstrated in America," *Radio News*, June 1927, 1424; and Joseph Alexander Gray, "Television," *Queen's Quarterly*, April 1929, 285–293.

61. Uricchio, "Television, Film and the Struggle for Media Identity," 121. Uricchio draws a distinction between the discursive uses of liveness and simultaneity, finding that while cinema and film historians made claims to liveness, "a look at broader cultural practices, at the telephone, at the ideas sparked by electricity, at the fantasies of new media, all suggest that simultaneity stood as a powerful anticipation which film could simulate but never deliver" (119).

62. William Uricchio, "Television's First Seventy-Five Years: The Interpretive Flexibility of a Medium in Transition," *The Oxford Handbook of Film and Media Studies*, ed. Robert Kolker (Oxford: Oxford University Press, 2008), 286. See also the section "Rethinking Media Sequence: Television Before Film?" 294–297.

63. Carl Dreher, "The Place of Television in the Progress of Science," *Radio Broadcast*, July 1927, 167.

64. Ibid., 168 (quotations in the following two paragraphs are *ibidem*). Here Dreher anticipates Harold Innis's theorization of the time and space biases of various communications forms. Also, Steve J. Wurtzler intriguingly notes in *Electric Sounds: Technological Change and the Rise of Corporate Mass Media* (New York: Columbia University Press, 2007) that Dreher was concurrently involved in an ongoing dispute about the "appropriate content for radio" in which one side argued for the transmission or transcription of events of general social import and interest, while the other argued for the crafting of programs specifically for radio presentation (230–231). In this debate, where the salient distinction was not live vs. recorded but rather the constructedness of representation vs. independent existence of the represented event, Dreher endorsed construction.

65. See Walter Benjamin, "The Work of Art in the Age of Mechanical Reproduction," in *The Routledge Critical and Cultural Theory Reader*, ed. Neil Badmington and Julia Thomas (New York: Routledge, 2008), 34–56.

66. Notably, Dreher omits other purposes, such as surveillance, and pleasures, such as voyeurism, in which the absence of the original is a central part of the power play that makes looking or listening worthwhile.

67. This image also serves as a latter-day corollary of both the cruel and sometimes deadly pranks played on native peoples by nineteenth-century electricians, as documented by Carolyn Marvin in *When Old Technologies Were New* (36–37), and the use of recording

technologies to memorialize native languages that were dying as a result of colonialism or genocide, as examined by Jonathan Sterne in *The Audible Past* (311–325).

68. Timothy Taylor, "Music and the Rise of Radio in Twenties America: Technological Imperialism, Socialization, and the Transformation of Intimacy," in *Engineering and Technologies in Sonic Cultures*, ed. Paul D. Greene and Thomas Porcello (Middletown, CT: Wesleyan University Press, 2005), 247.

69. Ibid., 249–250.

70. "Hope of Seeing by Radio Brought Nearer Fact," *Popular Mechanics*, March 1927, 359.

71. Quoted in William J. Brittain, "Television in Europe," *Radio Broadcast*, Dec. 1927, 102–104.

72. Quoted in Lawrence W. Corbett, "What Prospects of Television Abroad?" *Radio Broadcast*, Nov. 1928, 13.

73. "Television at Stage of 1921 Radio," *Science News-Letter*, Jan. 12, 1929, 19. Goldsmith's report to the Science News Service as quoted in *Science News-Letter* is largely identical in content and phrasing to his brief to the FRC, filed May 14, 1928, and published as Appendix M to the *Second Annual Report of the Federal Radio Commission to the Congress of the United States for the Year Ended June 30, 1928*, 252–253.

74. "Television Prefers Red-Heads," *Science News-Letter*, Feb. 23, 1929, 115.

75. "Television at Stage of 1921 Radio," 19.

76. Stokely, "Television, Though Crude, Has Arrived," 59.

77. During the last years of the 1920s this express articulation was conspicuously common, occurring in at least one-eighth of the articles on television indexed by the *Readers' Guide* for 1928–1929. Wilson Web: Readers' Guide Retrospective (1890–) and document coding done in preparation for this work.

78. Military and industrial surveillance and "theater television" were the next most common.

79. Trevor J. Pinch and Wiebe E. Bijker, "The Social Construction of Facts and Artefacts: Or How the Sociology of Science and the Sociology of Technology Might Benefit Each Other," *Social Studies of Science* 14, no. 3 (August 1984): 399–441. See the section "Interpretive Flexibility—the Technology Case" (421–424).

80. See Marvin, *When Old Technologies Were New*, 222–231.

81. James Hamilton, "Unearthing Broadcasting in the Anglophone World," in *Residual Media*, ed. Charles R. Acland (Minneapolis: University of Minnesota Press, 2007), 291.

82. Ibid., 296.

83. H. Winfield Secor, "Radio Vision Demonstrated in America," *Radio News*, June 1927, 1424.

84. It is instructive to reflect on the odd set of circumstances that shaped the adjacent developments in television and cinema. When Baird and Jenkins demonstrated their schemes for transient image transmission in 1925, synchronized sound in a motion picture was not a cultural commonplace, but within a few months of the AT&T demonstrations talking pictures such as *Don Juan* and *The Jazz Singer* catalyzed the conversion to sound. As theaters were wired, the commercial potential for very low-definition synchronous broadcasts was diminished—as a higher resolution and fidelity analogue could be obtained elsewhere; moreover, visual simulcasts of sponsored radio programs were soon forbidden by the FRC. See Betty McGee, "Chicago Asks License," *Radio Digest*, Sept. 1931, 14; and Keith Henney, "When Will Television Come?" *Review of Reviews*, Jan. 1932, 44. As chapters 3 and 4 will discuss in greater detail, this left television pursuing an entertainment and informational model established by the cinema and set forth a mission for television in which it would complement radio and cinema

and serve to reconcile the contradictions among modernity, capitalist industry, and the idealized patriarchal home. Television has been repeatedly damned to this day for its failure to meet these goals.

85. Dinsdale, "And Now, We See by Radio!" 143. During this early period there were alternative analogues, as when Baird's experiments with color and stereoscopic television were posed as attempts to solve "the problem of perfect television" conceived in terms of a complete mimicry of human vision, yet at a distance. "Pictures in Color Are Sent by Television," *Popular Mechanics*, Nov. 1928, 750.

86. Dinsdale, "Television Needs New Ideas—and Less Ballyhoo," *Scientific American*, Nov. 1930, 367.

87. Gernsback, "Television to the Front," 1419.

88. A. P. Peck, "Television Enters the Home," *Scientific American*, March 1928, 247.

89. "Jenkins Discusses Television," *Radio Digest*, March 1929, 50.

90. James N. Miller, "The Latest in Television," *Popular Mechanics*, Sept. 1929, 473.

91. William Hoyt Peck, "What Constitutes Perfect Detail in Television?" *Scientific American*, Dec. 1933, 273.

92. Udelson, *The Great Television Race*, 51–72.

93. Ibid., 52–53.

94. Quoted in McGee, "Chicago Asks License," 14.

95. Henney, "When Will Television Come?" 44.

96. McGee, "Chicago Asks License," 14.

97. FRC, *Sixth Annual Report of the Federal Radio Commission to the Congress of the United States for the Fiscal Year 1932* (Washington, DC: United States Government Printing Office, 1932), 42–43 (repr., New York: Arno, 1971).

98. Paul Traugott, "Some Aspects of High-Quality Reproduction, Part I," *Radio News*, July 1927, 26–27, 68; and Paul Traugott, "Some Aspects of High-Quality Reproduction, Part II," *Radio News*, August 1927, 126–127, 179.

99. "Radiovision in Homes This Fall," *Science News-Letter*, August 25, 1928, 113.

100. Howard E. Rhodes, "Television—Its Progress To-day," *Radio Broadcast*, Oct. 1928, 331–333.

101. Charles C. Henry, "A New Method of Transmitting Pictures by Wire of Radio," *Radio Broadcast*, May 1925, 27.

102. R. Clarkeson, "What Hope for Real Television?" *Radio Broadcast*, July 1928, 125–126.

103. R. Clarkeson, "What Can Be Seen by Radio?" *Radio Broadcast*, August 1928, 185–187.

104. C. W. Horn to M. H. Aylesworth, memorandum, April 1, 1930, box 102, folder 1, Mass Communications History Collections, National Broadcasting Company records, 1921–2000, Wisconsin Historical Society, Madison, Wisconsin (hereafter cited as NBC). See also the letter from C. W. Horn to Roy D. Chapin, Dec. 22, 1933, box 102, folder 2, NBC, in which Horn argued, "To be worthwhile and to be of general service to the public [television] must have sufficient detail and clarity to compare favorably with moving pictures." Horn also brings in teleological notions about the development of television, saying it must "grow along natural lines."

105. Vladimir K. Zworykin, "Television with Cathode Ray Tubes," June 9, 1933, box 102, folder 3, NBC. For a non-NBC source see "Report: New RCA Victor Television Quality like Television Parlor Films," *Variety Television Reviews*, Sept. 18, 1934, in which the transition from 180 to 340 lines of scansion is discussed.

106. Even the opposition between a scanned moving image and one relying on multichannel relay of picture elements has some roots in US broadcasting practices, where broadcasters have relatively narrow spectrum allocations. However, other causes

include early attempts to send pictures by wire (e.g., single-channel relay, which required scanning).

107. Zworykin, "Television with Cathode Ray Tubes," 1–2,

108. Zworykin's method for scanning images involved an array of picture elements that were synchronically depolarized (i.e., hit with a stream of electrons) in a manner that provided a scanning effect. Zworykin and others used a system that exploited the ability to electronically scan an image in much more detail—i.e., a greater number of picture elements and "frames."

109. Zworykin, "Television with Cathode Ray Tubes," 12.

110. Sterne, *The Audible Past*, 218.

111. See Michele Hilmes, *Radio Voices: American Broadcasting, 1922–1952* (Minneapolis: University of Minnesota Press, 1997), 6–33. See also William Boddy, *Fifties Television: The Industry and Its Critics* (Urbana: University of Illinois Press, 1990), 80–92.

112. Pursell, *The Machine in America*, 203.

113. James W. Carey with John J. Quirk, "The Mythos of the Electronic Revolution," in *Communication as Culture: Essays on Media and Society* (New York: Routledge, 1989), 120–123.

114. Boddy, *Fifties Television*, 28–62.

115. Michael Ritchie, *Please Stand By: A Prehistory of Television* (New York: Overlook, 1995), 31. Most contemporary histories of television are more reserved in their claims about mechanical television, and Udelson argued to the contrary (77–78). Additionally, Sterne in *The Audible Past* instructs that the standards of fidelity or "good enough" are culturally determined and owe much to the underlying anticipated social relations (218–219).

116. Here, again, Sterne's *Audible Past* is instructive in its rethinking of sound fidelity as a "shifting standard" relying on faith and understanding of specific networks by listeners (282). Certainly, the resolution that mechanical television could produce in the 1920s and 1930s does not keep the faith with our current common beliefs about television's uses and the social relations in which it is inscribed, but in the definitional struggles recounted in this chapter, the criterion of being "good enough" was contingent on the particular television and concomitant network of relations being imagined.

117. In Erik Barnouw's *Tube of Plenty: The Evolution of American Television*, 2nd rev. ed. (New York: Oxford University Press, 1990), a commonly used text for television history courses, mechanically scanned television and its inventors warranted mention on eight pages, supplemented by a few photographs, for less than 2 percent of the total page count. J. Fred MacDonald's *One Nation Under Television: The Rise and Decline of Network TV* (New York: Pantheon, 1990) gives mechanical television six pages in setting the stage for his discussion of television as a national institution. Michele Hilmes's *Only Connect: A Cultural History of Broadcasting in the United States*, 3rd ed. (Boston: Wadsworth, 2011) describes the consequences of early television's silencing: "television slid smoothly out of the retooled factories of the major electronics firms and into American living rooms, complete with established corporate owners, regulatory structures, and even programming" (179). However, she subordinates the early struggles in television to the more broadly contested cultural and regulatory disputes in sound broadcasting.

118. Orrin E. Dunlap, "Removing Radio's Blinders," *New York Times*, Nov. 25, 1934, X13.

119. Mark Hertsgaard provides an exemplary instance of this critique of the press's "abdication of responsibility" in favor of a story that is easier to tell and fit within the institutional logics of both the press and the institutions being covered. See Mark Hertsgaard, "Washington's Court Press," *Nation*, June 10, 1996, 10.

120. Dunlap, "Removing Radio's Blinders," X13.

121. Frank C. Waldrop and Joseph Borkin, *Television: A Struggle for Power* (New York: William Morrow, 1938).

122. Hubbell, *4000 Years of Television*, 17–19, 84–86, 96–97.

123. Lisa Gitelman, *Scripts, Grooves, and Writing Machines: Representing Technology in the Edison Era* (Stanford, CA: Stanford University Press, 1999), 5–6.

124. In the case of early television, mechanical broadcasters and audiences persisted well into the 1930s, after the FRC and FCC had decided against a mechanical standard, and more recently some users and collectors of Sony Betamax—and a bit later VHS—VCRs and tapes were remarkably reluctant to assent to televisual change. See Kim Bjarkman's "To Have and to Hold: The Television Collector's Relationship with an Ethereal Medium," *Television & New Media* 5, no. 3 (2004): 217–246, for a discussion of some of the appeals of video collecting and the barriers to conversion in the face of technological change.

CHAPTER 2   ENGENDERING EXPERTISE AND ENTHUSIASM

1. There is no enumerated power to protect general safety, and the definition of broadcasting as commerce rather than communication or assembly seems a careful circumvention of the First Amendment. While amateurs and others contested the FRC's basic authority, the courts largely stood behind Congress's new regulatory edifice. Again, this stems as much from arguments about the cultural role and technical limitations of radio as from clear constitutional power.

2. See Michele Hilmes, "Who We Are, Who We Are Not: Battle of the Global Paradigms," in *Planet TV: A Global Television Reader*, ed. Lisa Parks and Shanti Kumar (New York: New York University Press, 2003), 53–73; and Michele Hilmes, "British Quality, American Chaos: Historical Dualisms and What They Leave Out," *Radio Journal: International Studies in Broadcast & Audio Media* 1, no. 1 (2003): 2–17. Though more concerned with UK uses of "American Chaos" in framing the supposed superiority of British broadcasting, Hilmes lays out the ways in which discourses of chaos were used to advocate stricter regulatory regimes. For stateside uses of *chaos* see "Is There a Monopoly in Radio?" *Radio Broadcast*, Oct. 1926, 472; and "The March: Reviewing the Commission's Reign, Too Much Politics in Radio Licensing—The Jellyfish Commission," *Radio Broadcast*, March 1930, 258. In the latter, this American radio-enthusiast publication heartily endorsed forceful regulation to counteract "chaotic . . . conditions" but compared the FRC only somewhat favorably to what could be expected of "a committee of high school seniors."

3. See Thomas Streeter, *Selling the Air: A Critique of the Policy of Commercial Broadcasting in the United States* (Chicago: University of Chicago Press, 1996), 54–55.

4. Ibid., 29, 45.

5. Ibid., 47.

6. Mark Goodman and Mark Gring, "The Radio Act of 1927: Progressive Ideology, Epistemology, and Praxis," *Rhetoric & Public Affairs* 3, no. 3 (2000): 397–418.

7. See Streeter, *Selling the Air*, 107; and Hugh R. Slotten, *Radio and Television Regulation: Broadcast Technology in the United States, 1920–1960* (Baltimore: Johns Hopkins University Press, 2000).

8. Carolyn Marvin, *When Old Technologies Were New: Thinking About Electric Communication in the Late Nineteenth Century* (Oxford: Oxford University Press, 1988), 61.

9. It is a generic feature of patent applications in established fields such as radio engineering to detail the "prior art" and distinguish one's invention from those that came

before. In addition, applications are evaluated in terms of priority (if someone else claims invention, you have to prove you did it first) and the appearance of practicability (it has to seem like it will work, according to generally understood scientific principles). Thus, for Baird or Jenkins or Alexanderson to claim to have invented something, they had to prove that they had done something new and different and that it worked. For a contemporaneous commentary see Leo T. Parker, "How Inventors May Guard Their Rights," *Radio News*, Dec. 1928, 543, 578–580.

10. For such journalists as Alfred Dinsdale and Orrin Dunlap, access to particular inventors gave them special status to make assertions about television and its prospects. While it makes superficial sense that those who interviewed the inventors were able to comment from a privileged position, who gets in the door is certainly a matter of power.

11. Alfred Dinsdale, "And Now, We See by Radio!" *Radio Broadcast*, Dec. 1926, 143.

12. Susan Douglas, *Inventing American Broadcasting, 1899–1922* (Baltimore: Johns Hopkins University Press, 1987). In particular, see "Marconi and the America's Cup: The Making of the Inventor Hero" (2–28) and "Popular Culture and Populist Technology: The Amateur Operators, 1906–1912" (187–215) for a discussion of the adaptation of Alger's masculine ideal to the radio amateur.

13. Alexanderson, "Radio Photography and Television," *Radio News*, Feb. 1927, 944–945.

14. Ibid. (emphasis in original). See also Orrin Dunlap, "Radio's Silver Screen: Cluster of Seven Lights Carries Inventor Toward the Goal of Wireless Vision," *Scientific American*, Feb. 1927, 106–107; and John Arnold, "Photoelectricity, the Means of Television," *Radio News*, Dec. 1927, 640. Interestingly, in reporting on Alexanderson's address to the convention of the American Institute of Electrical Engineers, Dunlap uses the Shaw play as an introduction to an account praising Alexanderson as an inventor hero. In contrast, Arnold expressly downplays genius, situating invention within the wide and learned body of science. The play was also invoked in Berthold Laufer's "The Prehistory of Television," *Scientific Monthly*, Nov. 1928, 455–459; and Joseph Alexander Gray's "Television," *Queen's Quarterly*, April 1929, 285–293.

15. Alexanderson's argument is one with which I—following Raymond Williams, *Television: Technology and Cultural Form* (London: Fontana, 1974); Carolyn Marvin, *When Old Technologies Were New*; and Brian Winston, *Media Technology and Society, a History: From the Telegraph to the Internet* (New York: Routledge, 1998), among others—am largely in agreement. However, although such a theory of technological development may comport with our understanding of innovation as it occurs within complex social relations, we should also be mindful that similar historiographic theories can be put to dramatically different uses in varying contexts—a tool of institutional power in one moment can be a critique of institutional power in another.

16. "Free Geniuses, Says Hoover," *Science News-Letter*, Jan. 8, 1927, 17.

17. H. Olken, "Invention—A Coming Profession," *Scientific American*, Jan. 1933, 28.

18. Jay Hollander, "Hamitorial: Put It on Paper First," *Radio News*, April 1925, 1892–1893.

19. Jay Hollander, "Wanted—A New Thrill," *Radio News*, July 1925, 65.

20. Hollander, "Hamitorial," 1893.

21. See Douglas, *Inventing American Broadcasting*, 174–176; and Michele Hilmes, *Radio Voices: American Broadcasting, 1922–1952* (Minneapolis: University of Minnesota Press, 1997), 38–41.

22. Hollander, "Wanted—A New Thrill," 65.

23. Carroll Pursell, *The Machine in America: A Social History of Technology* (Baltimore: Johns Hopkins University Press, 1995), 226. Pursell notes, "Between 1893 and 1933 the number of engineering schools increased from 100 to 160, and the estimated number of

students grew from about twelve or thirteen thousand to perhaps sixty-five thousand, including by this time a sprinkling of women. During these same years the number of graduate students in engineering, a better indicator of possible research activity, rose from practically none to about four thousand."

24. See Slotten, *Radio and Television Regulation.*

25. Pursell, *The Machine in America*, 203.

26. Advertisements in *Radio News*, May 1928, 1275; Oct. 1928, 386; and Nov. 1928, 475.

27. Ien Ang, with Joke Hermes, "Gender and/in Media Consumption," in *Mass Media and Society*, ed. James Curran and Michael Gurevitch (London: Arnold, 1991), 307–328.

28. Carl Dreher, "University Offerings in Radio Education," *Radio Broadcast*, March 1928, 339.

29. Quoted in ibid.

30. Ibid., 342.

31. Carl Dreher, "Opportunities in the Audio and Radio Arts," *Radio News*, July 1929, 52. Dreher's article appears relatively early in the period following Gernsback's ousting as publisher and editor of *Radio News*, a period in which the magazine took a decidedly less populist approach to television and sound broadcasting.

32. Ibid.

33. FRC, *Annual Report of the Federal Radio Commission to the Congress of the United States for the Fiscal Year Ended June 30, 1927* (Washington, DC: United States Government Printing Office, 1927 [repr., New York: Arno, 1971]), 3–8. The prominent persons were given an opportunity to testify in hearings. The public and listeners were spoken for and about in a speech to the League of Women Voters by Commissioner Bellows that was included in this first annual report. The fans' suggestions for regulating radio were processed and recapitulated by an employee of the Department of Commerce.

34. See "Prominent Persons Offer Suggestions," in ibid., 3.

35. FRC, *Third Annual Report of the Federal Radio Commission to the Congress of the United States: Covering the Period from October 1, 1928 to November 1, 1929* (Washington, DC: United States Government Printing Office, 1929 [repr., New York: Arno, 1971]), 55–56.

36. National Archives, Record Group 173, FCC Office of the Executive Director, "Microfilm Copies of Minutes, 3/15/27–12/29/71," Box 1, Reel 1, 127. Meeting of Oct. 31, 1928, 2:30 p.m.

37. FRC, *Third Annual Report*, 58.

38. FRC, *Fourth Annual Report of the Federal Radio Commission to the Congress of the United States for the Fiscal Year 1930* (Washington, DC: United States Government Printing Office, 1930 [repr., New York: Arno, 1971]), 68.

39. Louis S. Treadwell, "Practical Television Demonstrated," *Scientific American*, June 1927, 385.

40. FRC, *Second Annual Report of the Federal Radio Commission to the Congress of the United States for the Year Ended June 30, 1928, Together with a Supplemental Report for the Period from July 1, 1928 to Sept. 30, 1928* (Washington, DC: United States Government Printing Office, 1930 [repr., New York: Arno, 1971]), 232. Dellinger's testimony comes from Appendix L (2), "Discussion of High-Frequency Spectrum by Dr. J. H. Dellinger, January 17, 1928."

41. Ibid., 254. Goldsmith's testimony comes from Appendix M (2), "Brief of Dr. Alfred N. Goldsmith, filed May 14, 1928, on Subject of Television."

42. John Hartley, "Invisible Fictions: Television Audiences, Paedocracy, Pleasure," in *Television Studies: Textual Analysis*, ed. Gary Burns and Robert J. Thompson (New York: Praeger, 1989), esp. 227–231.

43. Ibid., 230.

44. "Trade Notes and Comment," *New York Times*, Dec. 3, 1928, 102.

45. "Trade Notes and Comment," *New York Times*, Dec. 16, 1928, XX18.

46. Ibid.

47. H. P. Davis, "Television Hopes Are Over-Played," *New York Times*, Sept. 16, 1928, 162.

48. National Archives, Record Group 173, FCC Office of the Executive Director, "Microfilm Copies of Minutes, 3/15/27–12/29/71," Box 1, Reel 1, 127. Meeting of Oct. 31, 1928, 2:30 p.m.

49. Lawrence W. Corbett, "What Prospects of Television Abroad?" *Radio Broadcast*, Nov. 1928, 12.

50. Richard Butsch, *The Making of American Audiences: From Stage to Television, 1750–1990* (New York: Cambridge University Press, 2000), 181.

51. Ibid., 183–186.

52. Orrin E. Dunlap Jr., "New Sets Called Musical Marvels," *New York Times*, Sept. 22, 1929, R1.

53. *Radio News* in particular made frequent fun of domestic struggles over the set, with jokes like "Neighbor: 'How many controls are there on your radio?' Owner: 'Three, my mother-in-law, my wife, and my daughter'" ("Broadcastatics," *Radio News*, Dec. 1927, 614).

54. Some television theorists would argue that these acts of imagination and fragmentation are paralleled in the processes of identification of actual viewers. See Ang and Hermes, "Gender and/in Media Consumption."

55. Ronald Kline and Trevor Pinch, "Users as Agents of Technological Change: The Social Construction of the Automobile in the Rural United States," *Technology and Culture* 37, no. 4 (Oct. 1996): 763–795.

56. It is worth noting that Gernsback's populism evidenced a lack of commitment to true equality along the lines of race in a manner similar to the co-optation of turn-of-the-twentieth-century populist movements. For example, his wife Dorothy Gernsback's story "The Dark Side of Radio" (*Radio News*, Jan. 1929, 641, 684–687) was riddled with vicious stereotypes, abusive use of dialect, and a construction of black technical ignorance tailored in the tradition of minstrelsy to foster a sense of inclusion among white readers.

57. Hugo Gernsback, "Needs of the Radio Industry," *Radio News*, Dec. 1927, 593.

58. Charles Francis Jenkins to Hon. Herbert Hoover, Department of Commerce, March 14, 1925, Herbert Hoover Presidential Library (West Branch, IA), Commerce Papers—Radio: Pictures by Radio, Box 502. See also Douglas, *Inventing American Broadcasting*; as well as Kline and Pinch, "Users as Agents of Technological Change."

59. Charles Francis Jenkins, "Jenkins Discusses Television: Famous Scientist Says Visual Broadcasts Will Supplement, Not Supplant, Tomorrow's Programs," *Radio Digest*, March 1929, 51.

60. Both men foundered on the unforgiving shoals of capitalism in the Great Depression. Gernsback went bankrupt, and Jenkins died broke.

61. Dinsdale, "And Now, We See by Radio!" 140, 143.

62. Jenkins, "Jenkins Discusses Television," 50.

63. See Mikhail Bakhtin, *Rabelais and His World*, trans. Hélène Iswolsky (Cambridge, MA: MIT Press, 1968).

64. Hugo Gernsback, "Needs of the Radio Industry," *Radio News*, Dec. 1927, 593. This position also fit with *Radio News*' periodic crusades against manufacturers and repairmen for ripping off home users.

65. Jenkins, "Jenkins Discusses Television," 50.

66. See Michel Foucault, *Discipline and Punish: The Birth of the Prison*, trans. Alan Sheridan (New York: Vintage, 1995), 58–65, where Foucault explains the potential for revolt or disorder brought forth by the display of power in the public execution.

67. "Why Should Radio Appeal Only to the Auditory Sense?" *Radio Broadcast*, May 1925, 81.

68. "Radiotics: Television Outdone," *Radio News*, July 1927, 55.

69. "Broadcastatics: Paregorically Speaking," *Radio News*, Dec. 1927, 614.

70. "Broadcastatics: Shadowed to His Doom," *Radio News*, Nov. 1928, 445.

71. "The Humorists Begin Worrying for Us," *Radio News*, Oct. 1928, 373. See Dorinda Hartmann's forthcoming dissertation (University of Wisconsin–Madison) for a further discussion of the anxiety of television's invasion of the domestic sphere.

72. "Broadcastatics: A Tragedy of 1929," *Radio News*, Oct. 1928, 309.

73. "A Proposed Television Set—'The Motorist's Friend,'" *Radio News*, April 1928, 1154.

74. George Wall, "Radio News of the Month Illustrated," *Radio News*, Oct. 1927, 330.

75. George Wall, "Radio News of the Month," *Radio News*, Nov. 1925, 586–587; and Coleman Galloway, "Radio and Movies Are Now Linked," ibid., 740–743. The latter article reports on new developments in sound pictures and reprints Gernsback's "Grand Opera by Wireless" from Sept. 1919.

76. C. Sterling Gleason, "Rays of Justice," *Radio News*, Nov. 1928, 432–433, 479–481. A later "serious consideration" by Gleason, "High Frequencies for Color Television," *Radio News*, Jan. 1929, 632–633, 678–680, indicates that he was well enough known for his technique as a "contriver of humorous stories, each of which, however, is based on a phenomenon of radiation," that a brief note to readers highlighting a shift in tone was considered necessary (632).

77. "$300 Prize Contest: What's Wrong with Our Cover Picture?" *Radio News*, May 1927, cover, 1328, 1382.

78. "Can You Find the 34 Mistakes on Our Cover," *Radio News*, Nov. 1925, cover, 593.

79. "$300 Prize Contest," 1328.

80. Ibid., 1382.

81. Likewise, since this was the future being envisioned, it was not considered a mistake that the picture far exceeded the resolution and depth-of-field of any system just around the corner.

82. See John Berger's *Ways of Seeing* (London: British Broadcasting Corporation, 1972), esp. 51.

83. William Boddy, *New Media and Popular Imagination: Launching Radio, Television, and Digital Media in the United States* (New York: Oxford University Press, 2004), 42.

84. Charles A. Siepmann, *Radio's Second Chance* (Boston: Little, Brown, 1946), 254 (quoted in Boddy, *New Media and the Popular Imagination*, 51). Concerns over and attempts to account for women's attention to both radio and television persisted throughout the midcentury. See also Alexander Russo, *Points on the Dial: Golden Age Radio Beyond the Networks* (Durham, NC: Duke University Press, 2010), 156–166; Jennifer Hyland Wang, "'The Case of the Radio-Active Housewife': Relocating Radio in the Age of Television," in *The Radio Reader: Essays in the Cultural History of Radio*, ed. Michele Hilmes and Jason Loviglio (New York: Routledge, 2002), 343–366; James Schwoch, "Selling the Sight/Site of Sound: Broadcast Advertising and the Transition to Television," *Cinema Journal* 30, no. 1 (Fall 1990): 55–66, 61.

85. Butsch, in *The Making of American Audiences*, notes that "tuning was typically depicted as a masculine skill" (179).

86. Lynn Spigel, *Make Room for TV: Television and the Family Ideal in Postwar America* (Chicago: University of Chicago Press, 1992).

87. Russo, *Points on the Dial*, 153; and Roland Marchand, *Advertising the American Dream: Making Way for Modernity, 1920–1940* (Berkeley: University of California Press, 1985).

88. "Awards of the $300 'What's Wrong?' Contest, Based on Our Television Cover Picture of May, 1927," *Radio News*, Sept. 1927, 206, 278–279. For example, a typical error in the radio contest is that the horn is connected to the terminals for the phones and vice versa. An outlying error was that the man's cigar is not lit, yet he blows smoke rings. In contrast, for the 1927 contest seven of the errors were principally concerned with furniture.

89. For instance, the television camera appearing in the picture was identified as impossible "as it cannot transmit its own picture," but this presumes single-camera shooting. Catching another camera in the shot might violate the codes of professionalism for studio production, but it certainly was not impossible for the near future. As early as September 1928 multiple-camera productions were being broadcast. The first live American drama, *The Queen's Messenger*, used several image-pickup devices, which were fed into a switcher in a manner roughly analogous to studio cameras in a modern live production. See Albert Abramson, *The History of Television, 1880–1941* (Jefferson, NC: McFarland, 1987), 125–127; David E. Fisher and Marshall Jon Fisher, *Tube: The Invention of Television* (Washington, DC: Counterpoint, 1996), 96; and William Hawes, *American Television Drama: The Experimental Years* (Tuscaloosa: University of Alabama Press, 1986), 21–25. Abramson is reluctant to call these devices "cameras" as they did not involve the projection of an image through an aperture onto a plane within a box (*camera* being the Italian/Latin for "room," and the modern usage deriving from the Renaissance drawing technique of the *camera obscura*, in which light from a scene to be painted was let into an enclosure where the artist or assistant would trace the image on a canvas) but instead sequentially projected light onto parts of the subject and picked up reflections from the subjects with freestanding photocells. This terminological issue does not change the underlying nature of emergent studio practice.

90. The three top contestants chose to remark on Fips as did many others among the published responses. For example, the third-place winner, N. Chamberlain, wrote, "Tell Fips I went one better and found 17 (*Wrong! or you would have had first prize*—Editor). Let's have his picture so we can see how many mistakes we can find on him" ("Awards of the $300 'What's Wrong?' Contest," 278).

91. Many of the other published reader comments chose to express solidarity with Fips over his lost raise, hoping that their gains should not continue to be his loss. But here again, Fips serves as a defining other for the expert enthusiast cultivated by *Radio News*.

92. "Awards of the $300 'What's Wrong?' Contest," 206.

93. Ibid., 206, 278–279. Based on *Radio News'* reporting, it is likely that "Ovila Duquet," who placed fourth, was Andrea's father or brother, while another unidentified family member earned honorable mention. Page numbers hereinafter cited in text.

94. Gaylyn Studlar, *This Mad Masquerade: Stardom and Masculinity in the Jazz Age* (New York: Columbia University Press, 1996), 151.

95. Dinsdale, "And Now, We See by Radio!" 142.

96. "New Visions," *Living Age*, Nov. 15, 1927, 934.

97. W. T. Meenam, "Strange 'Tongue' Greets Listeners," *New York Times*, Jan. 20, 1929, XX18.

98. See Doty Hobart's "It Won't Be Long Now Until We'll Be Seeing Things," *Radio Digest*, July 1930, 20; and Boyd Phelps's "Unscrambling Television," *Radio Broadcast*, Jan. 1929, 157–158. The aspiration toward this skill intriguingly prefigures contemporary

portrayals of computer aptitude as in *The Matrix* in which certain adept users no longer require the interface and interact with programs directly from the code.

99. "Second Issue Just Out: Television," *Radio News*, Oct. 1928, 384.

100. Jenkins, "Jenkins Discusses Television," 50.

101. Howard E. Rhodes, "Television—Its Progress To-day: Table II," *Radio Broadcast*, Oct. 1928, 333.

102. "Television Receiver Run by Fan Motor," *Popular Mechanics*, Feb. 1929, 305; and Frank L. Brittin, "Here Is Your Television Receiver!" *Popular Mechanics*, Dec. 1928, 1004–1007. The *Popular Science* series by George Waltz Jr. began with "Get in on Television," July 1931, 16–17, 136, and continued monthly until "Enlarging the Picture," April 1932, 85–86.

103. "Announcing a New, Practical, Inexpensive Televisor," *Radio News*, July 1930, 49–50.

104. "Television: 'Seeing' Music with a Television Receiver," *Radio News*, Oct. 1928, 314.

105. Zeh Bouck, "Building Receivers for Television," *Radio Broadcast*, Nov. 1928, 35.

106. Phelps, "Unscrambling Television," 157–158.

107. Boyd Phelps, "Some Useful Standards: Transmitting Amateur Television," *Radio Broadcast*, Feb. 1929, 247–248.

108. "Commission Permits Limited Picture Broadcasting," *Radio Broadcast*, May 1929, 9.

109. "Television Broadcasters Licensed," *Science News-Letter*, March 9, 1929, 142.

110. Joseph H. Udelson, *The Great Television Race: A History of the American Television Industry, 1925–1941* (Tuscaloosa: University of Alabama Press, 1982), 52–53.

111. FRC, *Fourth Annual Report of the Federal Radio Commission to the Congress of the United States for the Fiscal Year 1930* (Washington, DC: United States Government Printing Office, 1930 [repr., New York: Arno, 1971]), 68.

112. Kline and Pinch, "Users as Agents of Technological Change."

113. Carl Dreher, "As the Broadcaster Sees It: Who Shall Judge the Quality of Our Broadcasting Stations?" *Radio Broadcast*, Jan. 1926, 326–327.

114. See Elena Razlogova, *The Listener's Voice: Early Radio and the American Public* (Philadelphia: University of Pennsylvania Press, 2011); Jason Loviglio, *Radio's Intimate Public: Network Broadcasting and Mass-Mediated Democracy* (Minneapolis: University of Minnesota Press, 2005); and Bruce Lenthall, *Radio's America: The Great Depression and the Rise of Modern Mass Culture* (Chicago: University of Chicago Press, 2007).

CHAPTER 3   PROGRAMMING THE SYSTEM FOR QUALITY

1. Thomas Streeter, *Selling the Air: A Critique of the Policy of Commercial Broadcasting in the United States* (Chicago: University of Chicago Press, 1996), 7.

2. See Jennifer Daryl Slack, "The Theory and Method of Articulation in Cultural Studies," in *Stuart Hall: Critical Dialogues in Cultural Studies*, ed. David Morley and Kuan-Hsing Chen (New York: Routledge, 1996), 113–129; and Lawrence Grossberg, "On Postmodernism and Articulation," in ibid., 131–150; Raymond Williams, "Base and Superstructure in Marxist Cultural Theory," *New Left Review* (Nov.-Dec. 1973): 3–16; and Raymond Williams, *Marxism and Literature* (Oxford: Oxford University Press, 1979).

3. Susan Smulyan, *Selling Radio: The Commercialization of American Broadcasting, 1920–1934* (Washington, DC: Smithsonian Institution Press, 1994); and Michele Hilmes, *Network Nations: A Transnational History of British and American Broadcasting* (New York: Routledge, 2011).

4. Stuart Hall, "Gramsci's Relevance for Race and Ethnicity," in *Stuart Hall: Critical Dialogues in Cultural Studies*, ed. David Morley and Kuan-Hsing Chen (New York: Routledge, 1996), 411–440, 423.

5. This is a partial account, and as cultural critics John Frow and Meaghan Morris would advise, partial in both the sense of being limited and in the sense of taking a side. See John Frow and Meaghan Morris, "Introduction," *Australian Cultural Studies*, ed. John Frow and Meaghan Morris (Urbana: University of Illinois Press, 1993), vii–xxxi. The documents surveyed for this chapter draw heavily from a few newspapers, particularly the *New York Times* but also the *Chicago Tribune* and *Los Angeles Times*. One of the primary reasons for this emphasis is the availability of full text, Boolean searches for these dailies (via ProQuest's historical newspapers database between Nov. 2003 and February 2004), which allowed me to limit my initial survey of past utterances on broadcasting and its hierarchies to those that actually used the word *quality* in specific configurations. These sources were supplemented with articles from enthusiast and popular magazines that (a) directly invoked quality, (b) engaged with the central defining terms for quality that emerged from my survey of the daily newspapers, or (c) contained commentary directly bearing on cultural hierarchy from key figures in the production, criticism, and regulation of broadcast content. Thus, a letter to the editor complaining of a program's quality because of an irritating announcer was certainly considered, but an article on the artistic challenges of synthesizing radio and cinema by noted cultural critic and later head of CBS's television programming department Gilbert Seldes would also make the cut. In the main, however, I have chosen to hew closely to statements that invoke quality because my investigation is concerned with not only the uses of the specific term *quality* to obscure the workings of cultural and economic power but also the particular problems and opportunities questions of quality provoke for the institutions and groups that take up the language of quality.

   The costs of this choice are a certain degree of synthesis and, more significantly, a bias toward the urban and cosmopolitan that doubles down on the FRC and FCC's favoritism toward certain manufacturers and other notables in broadcasting in allocating licenses, while the rewards are a greater appreciation of the contradictions and discontinuity in early uses of quality, which gives a better sense of not only the shape of the discursive struggle but also how specific articulations and repeated terms work to shape culture and institutional structures. My reliance on the *New York Times* had several additional, though not wholly unanticipated, consequences. First, the paper's midcentury practice of what I have followed others in describing as stenographic journalism had the result of providing relatively large and uninterrupted statements by regulators, entertainers, industrialists, and activists, where judgments of whose opinions did and did not count certainly foreclosed the debate but can reasonably be considered to capture the dominant discourse on broadcasting at the time. Second, the regional character of US broadcasting and resistance to centralization during the 1920s and 1930s is not adequately captured; indeed, there was often better and more comprehensive reporting on the rest of the Americas than the rest of the United States, particularly the much-derided South. This lack is somewhat ameliorated by the contrasts with the Chicago and Los Angeles papers, but the primary contrasts among the three are their positions within entertainment communities. Finally, and related to the first two, the discourse examined does not give a broad perspective on the contingent quality of the subaltern. Although the letters to the editor provide liminal articulations, they are still those that made it through the paper's screening process.

6. See Erik Barnouw, *The Golden Web: A History of Broadcasting in the United States, 1933–1953* (New York: Oxford University Press, 1968); and William Boddy, *Fifties Television: The Industry and Its Critics* (Urbana: University of Illinois Press, 1993). In particular,

see Boddy's chapters "Regulating the Early Television Industry" (28–41) and "UHF, the Television Freeze, and Network Monopoly" (42–62).

7. "Continuance of Broadcasting Depends upon Paying Talent: David Sarnoff Says Consumers Will Not Have to Pay If Only Three Super-Stations Entertain the Entire Country—Radio Industry Can Support Broadcasting," *New York Times*, Feb. 3, 1924, X9.

8. Ibid.

9. Ibid.

10. Ibid.

11. "Fund to Improve Quality of Radio Programs," *New York Times*, Feb. 24, 1924, XX15.

12. Ibid. This is the first use of *narrowcasting* among the *New York Times*, *Los Angeles Times*, and *Chicago Tribune*. The term turns up in searches only seven times (there are eight hits, but one is a result of a bad scan of a report on Chicago livestock) prior to debates over pay television and cable starting in the 1960s—with all but one of the early uses from 1932 or before. Sarnoff's use of the term was broad and pejorative, applying generally to a reconfiguration of the relationship between radio and audience members, but others used the term to specifically discuss John Hays Hammond's system for scrambling radio signals for military and commercial purposes. Interestingly, the *Chicago Tribune*, the self-proclaimed "World's Greatest Newspaper" and owner of WGN broadcasting, eschewed the term entirely until the dawn of the cable era in 1972. Its coverage and corporate interests are suggested by the first two articles mentioning narrowcasting: Nicholas von Hoffman, "Public Access to Cable TV," *Chicago Tribune*, Dec. 18, 1972, 26; and Richard D. Heffner, "Smut in the Home; TV's Newest Moral Crisis," *Chicago Tribune*, August 30, 1980, S8.

13. See Erik Barnouw, *A Tower in Babel: A History of Broadcasting in the United States to 1933* (New York: Oxford University Press, 1966), 105–114.

14. Orrin E. Dunlap Jr., "Further Radio Developments Expected to Come with 1926; Six Outstanding Improvements in 1925—New Tube May Make Television a Reality—Low Waves Lead Progress of Old Year," *New York Times*, Dec. 27, 1925, XX12.

15. Ibid.

16. "Radio Impresarios Outline Their Winter Plans; International Exchange of Programs This Winter—Phonograph Stars to Be Heard on the Air," *New York Times*, Sept. 13, 1925, R4.

17. The Voice, "Quality of Radio Programs Displeasing to Performer: He Doubts If Microphone Is an Aid to Singers Who Aim at Finer Things—Another Opinion on the General Subject of Broadcasting," *New York Times*, Nov. 7, 1926, X16.

18. George M. Purver, "Musicians and Idealism," *New York Times*, Nov. 7, 1926, X16.

19. Michele Hilmes, "British Quality, American Chaos: Historical Dualisms and What They Leave Out," *Radio Journal: International Studies in Broadcast & Audio Media* 1, no. 1 (Spring 2003): 2–17.

20. Hugh Slotten, *Radio and Television Regulation: Broadcast Technology in the United States, 1920–1960* (Baltimore: Johns Hopkins University Press, 2000).

21. Michele Hilmes, *Only Connect: A Cultural History of Broadcasting in the United States* (Belmont, CA: Wadsworth, 2002), 43–44.

22. "Continuance of Broadcasting Depends upon Paying Talent."

23. Steve J. Wurtzler, *Electric Sounds: Technological Change and the Rise of Corporate Mass Media* (New York: Columbia University Press, 2007), 175.

24. "Hoover Offers Plan to Regulate Radio," Special to the *New York Times*, Nov. 10, 1925, 27. At the Fourth National Radio Conference in 1925, Hoover delivered both an admonition and call for distinction on the question of advertising: "If we can distinguish on the one hand between unobtrusive publicity that is accompanied by a direct service

and engaging entertainment to the listener and obtrusive advertising on the other, we may find a solution." Such a solution proved illusory, but the quest has persisted to this day and has held considerable consequence for broadcasting's structure, economics, and programming.

25. "Hoover Opposes More Radio Control," Special to the *New York Times*, Dec. 6, 1924, 4.
26. "Rural Listeners Hail Radio Ruling; Send Thanks to Commission for Regulation of Stations to Give Diverse Programs," Special to the *New York Times*, Nov. 22, 1927, 27. See also "Long-Term Licenses Planned to Stabilize Broadcasting," *New York Times*, Dec. 11, 1927, XX20, in which FRC commissioner, and later CBS executive, Sam Pickard lauded regulatory scarcity, claiming that "never before has the radio set afforded its owner as much as it does now in quality of reception and quality of program."
27. Clifford John Doerksen, *American Babel: Rogue Radio Broadcasters of the Jazz Age* (Philadelphia: University of Pennsylvania Press, 2005), 124.
28. "Radio Board Resumes Work with New Law as Tool; Radio Power Reductions Here Will Intensify 'Dead Spots,'" *New York Times*, April 8, 1928, XX13.
29. Saxe H. Hanford, "What the Listener Thinks," *New York Times*, April 29, 1928, XX17.
30. "The March of Radio," *Radio Broadcast*, April 1929, 372.
31. "R.C.A. Companies File License Suits: Four Seek Injunction Against the Radio Board to Test Law Denying Renewals," Special to the *New York Times*, June 6, 1931, 12.
32. For the case of Australia see "Australia Moves to Improve Radio; Government Says Program Quality Not Commensurate with Receiving Tax—National Control of Broadcasting Proposed," *New York Times*, Sept. 9, 1928, 127; and "Australia Plans to Control Radio; Government Ownership of Broadcasting Is Announced for 1929," *New York Times*, Oct. 7, 1928, X20. For the Case of Canada see V. M. Kipp, "Radio Advertising Hit by New Canadian Body; League Moves for Nationalization of Broadcasting in the Dominion," *New York Times*, Dec. 21, 1930, 52; and V. M. Kipp, "Nationalized Radio Urged in Dominion," *New York Times*, Jan. 18, 1931, 60. Notably, in both the press and in private these questions of definition centered on mostly Anglophonic nations and to a lesser extent Western Europe. The significance and dynamics were quite different when it came to other parts of the world. For example, in *The American Radio Industry and Its Latin American Activities, 1900–1939* (Urbana: University of Illinois Press, 1990), historian James Schwoch found in NBC's interactions with Latin America, the goals were not the installation of an "American model' that included private ownership, advertising, and entertainment" but rather "how to deal with the strengths and weaknesses of Latin American market economies and to integrate them rationally into a larger, global system of capitalism" (142).
33. Hilmes, *Network Nations*, 63–79.
34. This agreement also relies on significant though rarely supported assumptions that broadcast programs should have an effect on audiences—be that entertainment, uplift, or something else—thus broadcast programs along with the individuals and institutions that produce and distribute them are conceived of as the subjects in a transitive process, acting on the object, the audience.
35. Robert McChesney, "Conflict, Not Consensus," in *Ruthless Criticism: New Perspectives in U.S. Communication History*, ed. William Solomon and Robert McChesney (Minneapolis: University of Minnesota Press, 1993), 222–258.
36. See Hilmes, "British Quality, American Chaos."
37. "A Londoner Visits the Studios: Over-Commercialism Is Called Stumbling-Block to Progress in American Broadcasting—Few Morning Programs in England," *New York Times*, March 15, 1931, 136.

38. "Letters to the Editor: Our Radio Programs Suffer by Comparison with British; They Are, It Is Held, Made Up by Inexperienced Persons and Shriek Commercialism," *New York Times*, Nov. 8, 1931, E2. A similar proposition was explicitly framed in terms of "quality or lack of quality in radio programs" by Sydney Greenbie in a letter to the *New York Times* arguing that radio had not yet learned the lessons of magazine publishing's past in that its dependence on advertising vitiated the cohesive point of view and quality control that make up editorial policy in publishing and, further, that radio's continued dependence on unpaid talent ran counter to the necessary professionalization of a maturing medium. See Sydney Greenbie, "Letters to the Editor: Quality in Radio Program. Broadcasters Should Pay for All Participants to Improve Talent," *New York Times*, June 2, 1931, 28.

39. "Letters to the Editor: Our Radio Programs Suffer by Comparison with British," E2.

40. Edward F. Thomas, "Letters from Readers of the Times on Topics in the News: Defending Our Broadcasting," *New York Times*, Nov. 15, 1931, E2.

41. Stanley Rayfield, "Letters to the Editor from Readers of The Times on Topics in the News: Tiresome Radio Programs Advertisers Not Concerned with Art, Critic Holds, Praising British System," *New York Times*, Nov. 29, 1931, E58.

42. "Sidelights on England's Radio," *New York Times*, Nov. 9, 1930, XXII. As an example of the BBC's overinvestment, the article noted a performance of Mahler's Eighth Symphony at a cost of $10,000 with four backup soloists. It is unclear whether the primary complaint was the extravagance or the Mahler.

43. "Listening-in: De Forest and the Future," *New York Times*, Nov. 9, 1930, XXII.

44. Dunlap, "What Is the Ideal System? Students Throughout the Country Debate Whether English Radio Is Superior to the American Plan," *New York Times*, Dec. 17, 1933, X15. See B. Charles-Dean's "Letters to the Times: Broadcasting in Britain," *New York Times*, August 9, 1937, 18, for a self-interested example of the persistence of these strands of discourse beyond the political debates on the communications act. Charles-Dean, president of British American Productions, argued that the BBC could not "hold a candle to American broadcasting, either in quantity or quality of programs," and attributed Britain's "amateurish" "technique and showmanship" to "British broadcasting [being] an autocracy unto itself."

45. "Radio Impresarios Outline Their Winter Plans"; and "Fund to Improve Quality of Radio Programs."

46. Doerksen, *American Babel*; David Goodman, *Radio's Civic Ambition* (New York: Oxford University Press, 2011), 77–93.

47. See Randall Patnode's "'What These People Need Is Radio': New Technology, the Press, and Otherness in 1920s America," *Technology and Culture* 44, no. 2 (April 2003): 285–305, for a discussion of the "othering" of rural audiences and particularly his observation that "in focusing on radio's promise to redeem the farm, the popular press acknowledged the degree of American ambivalence about the trajectory of modern advances and the loss of comforting traditions" (289). Doerksen's *American Babel* (21–48) details the ways in which racial mixing through jazz along with blurring and crossing of gender and sexual norms through the broadcast of cabaret culture were met with calls for regulation and reform.

48. Freeman Hopwood, "Uplift Is Sought in Radio Programs," *New York Times*, Oct. 31, 1926, X16. This letter was a reply to several letters defending commercial radio against earlier condemnations by Hopwood, who advocated that broadcasting focus on various great works of literature, philosophy, and sciences such as psychoanalysis. An emblematic response to this earlier letter was William A. Johnson's comment:

"Frankly I do not find anything objectionable in the commercialism. I do not know anything about Schopenhauer—unless it's a new brand of cheese. . . . The only thing familiar about Voltaire is 'Volt'—did Voltaire discover the volt or did he invent it? . . . As for psychoanalysis, who in the name of tarnation cares about knowing that I don't like cocoanut because my grandfather's pet rabbit was a white one, and cocoanut is white? . . . I appreciate the fact that broadcasting costs money, and that someone must pay the bill, and that I am one of the 15,000,000 who must do their share. I will do it gladly and readily by purchasing the products of those persons and firms that bring me music each night" ("Backdraft from a Radio Fan," *New York Times*, Oct. 24, 1926, X16). See also Freeman Hopwood, "Flutterings of a Radio Fan May Stir Up Quite a Breeze; He Pines for Programs Untainted by Commercialism—Present Trend of Broadcasting Gives His Set a Five-Months' Rest," *New York Times*, Oct. 10, 1926, X16; and Magda Leigh, "The Air Needs Clearing," *New York Times*, Oct. 17, 1926, X16.

49. Hopwood, "Flutterings of a Radio Fan May Stir Up Quite a Breeze."

50. "Dangers Threatening Radio Are Seen by Commissioner; Stations Must Keep Pace with Public Demand for Quality Programs, Says Bellows—Manufacturers Told That They Should Aid," *New York Times*, June 12, 1927, XX18.

51. Ibid.

52. Eileen Meehan, "Why We Don't Count," in *Logics of Television: Essays on Cultural Criticism*, ed. Patricia Mellencamp (Bloomington: Indiana University Press, 1990), 117–137.

53. Elena Razlogova, *The Listener's Voice: Early Radio and the American Public* (Philadelphia: University of Pennsylvania Press, 2011), 56–57, 69–74.

54. Ibid., 75.

55. Ibid., 85–97.

56. Jason Loviglio, *Radio's Intimate Public: Network Broadcasting and Mass-Mediated Democracy* (Minneapolis: University of Minnesota Press, 2005), 38.

57. "Education by Radio," *New York Times*, August 24, 1932, 16. See also "Women's Group Resumes Radio Reviews," *New York Times*, Oct. 18, 1936, X12.

58. Olin Downes, "Substantial Music on the Radio: Finest Artists Asked by Sponsors to Play Best Works—Schnabel's Beethoven Raises Questions of Interpretations," *New York Times*, Dec. 10, 1933, X8.

59. Bruce Lenthall, *Radio's America: The Great Depression and the Rise of Modern Mass Culture* (Chicago: University of Chicago Press, 2007), 51–52.

60. Marian S. Carter, "Professionally Speaking: Women Listen Because," *Radio Digest*, Summer 1932, 43.

61. Ibid.

62. Ibid., 44.

63. Doerksen, *American Babel*; and Alexander Russo, *Points on the Dial: Golden Age Radio Beyond the Networks* (Durham, NC: Duke University Press, 2010).

64. H. P. Davis, "Television Hopes Are Over-Played; H. P. Davis Warns Against Purchase of Premature Vision Apparatus," *New York Times*, Sept. 16, 1928, 162.

65. Orrin E. Dunlap Jr., "Who Will See the Images?" *New York Times*, August 10, 1930, XX9.

66. Ibid.

67. William S. Paley, "Radio and the Humanities," *Annals of the American Academy* (1935): 94–104, 94.

68. Ibid., 95.

69. Ibid., 102.

70. "Television Gives a Real Show," *Business Week*, Nov. 14, 1936, 46.

71. Seldes, "The 'Errors' of Television," 536.

72. Ibid., 541.

73. Goodman's *Radio's Civic Ambition* finds a complex and contradictory set of dispositions toward US broadcasting's potential for and attempts at uplift, a paradigm more associated with Walter Lippmann and the "propaganda" school that held an "interest in [both] how to influence and the civic goal of how to create critical, propaganda-proof individuals" (93).

74. See Mark Jancovich and James Lyons, eds., *Quality Popular Television: Cult TV, the Industry and Fans* (London: BFI, 2003) for discussions of contemporary television programs' negotiation and synthesis of aspirations to quality and the imperative and appeal of both popularity and intense viewer attachment to specific programs.

75. For an extended example of this argument see Gilbert Seldes, *The Great Audience* (New York: Viking, 1950). In particular, his chapter "Myth: Movies" (9–104), with its discussion of the Production Code and his proposed "Criteria of Maturity," and his chapter "A Nation of Teen-Agers" (233–249) capture his critical stance on paedocratization. Butsch, in *The Making of American Audiences*, notes the persistence throughout the 1930s of advocacy groups and institutions from the National Advisory Council on Radio in Education to the Women's National Radio Committee to the Payne Fund seeking to determine and root out radio's threat to children (232–233).

76. Roy L. Albertson, "Too Many 'Crocodile' Tears," *New York Times*, May 12, 1935, XII.

77. "Behind the Scenes: No Place for Brazen Broadcasts in American Air, Good Taste Is Keynote of Radio Etiquette," *New York Times*, April 11, 1937, 12.

78. Ibid.

79. See Lynn Spigel, *Make Room for TV: Television and the Family Ideal in Postwar America* (Chicago: University of Chicago Press, 1992).

80. This is not to say that the nationality of distant stations did not matter to dx-ers. It did and gave a regularly remarked upon sense of the exotic to sitting in the radio shack, especially with the transition to wireless telephony from telegraphy.

81. Susan Douglas, *Inventing American Broadcasting, 1899–1922* (Baltimore: Johns Hopkins University Press, 1987), 206.

82. See Barnouw's *A Tower in Babel*; Douglas's *Inventing American Broadcasting*; and Michele Hilmes's *Radio Voices: American Broadcasting, 1922–1952* (Minneapolis: University of Minnesota Press, 1997) for thorough descriptions of the nationalization of US broadcasting.

83. Barnouw, *A Tower in Babel*, 59. RCA's articles of incorporation contained provisions expressly designed to mark it as an institution of the nation, including prohibition of foreign citizens on the board of directors, a 20 percent limitation on foreign ownership of stock, and a seat on the board for a representative of the US government.

84. James Hamilton, "Unearthing Broadcasting in the Anglophone World," in *Residual Media*, ed. Charles R. Acland (Minneapolis: University of Minnesota Press, 2007), 283–300.

85. Hilmes, *Radio Voices*.

86. Ibid.; see chapter 3, "Who We Are, Who We Are Not: The Emergence of National Narratives" (75–96). See also Wurtzler, *Electric Sounds*, 180.

87. Smulyan, *Selling Radio*, 58–61.

88. Display ad, *New York Times*, Sept. 14, 1926, 27. Reprinted in full in Erik Barnouw's *Tube of Plenty: The Evolution of American Television*, 2nd rev. ed. (New York: Oxford University Press, 1990), 55; excerpted in Hilmes, *Radio Voices*, 10.

89. See Smulyan, *Selling Radio*, 58–59; and Hilmes, *Radio Voices*, 10. Smulyan observes that crucial for RCA "was the question of national radio and how it could be achieved with

a maximum of profit and a minimum of public fuss over monopoly." Hilmes argues that RCA positioned its new network as an institution that would "fulfill the technical and cultural promise of radio and set restraints on its potential dangers if left in the hands of scattered, unsupervised small stations" while staving off the threat of government seizure of broadcasting.

90. Russo, *Points on the Dial*, 20.

91. David Sarnoff, "Report to Stockholders," May 7, 1935, box 102, folder 4, Mass Communications History Collections, National Broadcasting Company records, 1921–2000, Wisconsin Historical Society, Madison, Wisconsin (hereafter cited as NBC), 5. See also Sarnoff's comments in White's "What's Delaying Broadcasting?" *Collier's*, Nov. 30, 1935, 40, where he argues that audiences will demand national coverage, and RCA will provide it, no matter the expense.

92. Julius Weinberger, "Treatise on Television," Feb. 5, 1934, box 102, folder 5, NBC, 2, 6, 11. See also O. B. Hanson to Baker, May 31, 1935, box 102, folder 6, NBC.

93. Russo, *Points on the Dial*, 106–114.

94. Weinberger, "Treatise on Television," 2.

95. Sarnoff, "Report to Stockholders," 6. Of course, later in the decade the FCC would make a similar complaint about NBC and RCA's plans for commercial television, but, by that time, concerns about freezing the art seem to have been abandoned. See, e.g., Associated Press report of March 23, 1939, in box 102, folder 26, NBC.

96. Hilmes, *Radio Voices*, 45–48. Unsurprisingly, the prohibition of broadcasting phonograph records benefited established music interests and hindered African American broadcasting efforts.

97. Michele Hilmes, *Hollywood and Broadcasting: From Radio to Cable* (Urbana: University of Illinois Press, 1990), 143.

98. Ibid.

99. Russo, *Points on the Dial*, 87.

100. Keith Henney, "When Will Television Come?" *Review of Reviews*, Jan. 1932, 44–46.

101. Bill Schudt, "Columbia Turns the Corner," *Radio Digest*, Sept. 1931, 13–14; Betty McGee, "Chicago Asks License," *Radio Digest*, Sept. 1931, 14–15, 86; and Bill Schudt, "Scanning," *Radio Digest*, Oct. 1931, 18, 60.

102. Eliza Schallert, "Television Is an Actuality," *Los Angeles Times*, Jan. 12, 1936, H29.

103. Ibid, H30.

104. Benn Hall, "What's Happened to Television?" *Review of Reviews*, June 1935, 52–53.

105. Ibid, 53–54. This fact was also seized on in "Television Tasks," *Business Week*, June 8, 1935, 20, which remarked, "Experience of Germany and England in this field illustrate one advantage the closely-populated nation has over our own great open space. Britain has appropriated $900,000 for a program including an experimental transmitting station in London. Nine more are planned and are expected to bring television to 50% of the English population."

106. Hall, "What's Happened to Television?" 54.

107. Ibid.

108. This was much to the enrichment of Desi and Lucy, who had retained syndication rights. See Thomas Schatz's "Desilu, *I Love Lucy*, and the Rise of Network TV," in *Making Television: Authorship and the Production Process*, ed. Robert J. Thompson and Gary Burns (New York: Praeger, 1990), esp. 120–122.

109. Orrin E. Dunlap Jr., "Rivalry Speeds the Television Race over New York: A Spring Tonic, New Competition Spurs Television in Leap from Manhattan's Lofty Spires," *New York Times*, April 11, 1937, 12.

110. A partial exception was L. Marsland Gander's "Is America Right in Television? After 17 Months Wonders If Uncle Sam Has the Solution," *New York Times*, May 8, 1938, 166, which reported on "dissatisfaction in the Midlands and the North Country."

111. William Uricchio, "Television's First Seventy-Five Years: The Interpretive Flexibility of a Medium in Transition," in *The Oxford Handbook of Film and Media Studies*, ed. Robert Kolker (Oxford: Oxford University Press, 2008), 297.

112. Ibid, 298.

113. There were, of course, plans for theater television, videophones, and televisual surveillance being discussed and developed throughout the 1930s in the United States, but by the mid-1930s the primacy of broadcasting to the home was relatively secure.

114. Privately, NBC kept tabs on developments in Britain, France, Germany, and Holland, sending employees on regular tours of Europe in order to define and defend itself against the threat of alternative broadcasting systems, open markets and form strategic alliances, combat the installation of low-resolution television systems as national or international standards to protect RCA patents, and appraise the need for cross-licensing agreements. In their confidential internal communications, employees of RCA and NBC expressed more pragmatic and opportunistic views on European television. For example, in response to Dutch broadcaster Algemeer-Vereen Radio Omroep's (AVRO) subscription system, one employee noted, "The association method of financing broadcasting may have some possibilities for television, and should be kept in mind" ("Report on Television Observations in Europe," by C. W. Farrier, July 15, 1937, pp. 2–3, box 102, folder 15, NBC). Likewise, observations of EMI's work were met first with satisfaction since it was "practically the RCA system" ("Observations on Broadcasting and Television in Europe," by O. B. Hanson, Sept. 10, 1936, cover letter, box 102, folder 8, NBC). Later, Hanson would send a shopping list of parts to request from EMI for "improving the performance of our apparatus" (O. B. Hanson to Lenox R. Lohr, July 20, 1937, box 102, folder 13, NBC).

115. "Television Prices Drop: Important Market Factors," *New York Times*, April 4, 1937, 182.

116. Ibid.

117. See Meehan, "Why We Don't Count."

118. For an examination of the emergence of this concept see David A. Cook's "The Birth of the Network: How Westinghouse, GE, AT&T, and RCA Invented the Concept of Advertiser-Supported Broadcasting," *Quarterly Review of Film Studies* 8, no. 3 (Summer 1983): 3–8. Cook concludes that the corporations with governmental support determined that "American broadcasting would be publicly financed in the private interest" (8).

119. Gander, "Is America Right in Television?"

120. L. Marsland Gander, "Lessons in Television: Two Years of Telecasting in London Give Americans Practical Pointers," *New York Times*, Nov. 27, 1938, 180.

121. Ibid.

122. Ibid.

123. Ron Becker, "'Hear-See Radio' in the World of Tomorrow: RCA and the Presentations of Television at the World's Fair, 1939–40," *Historical Journal of Film, Radio, and Television* 21, no. 4 (2001): 369–370.

124. "FCC Cautions on Speedy Prospect of Commercializing Television: Report Stresses Sale of Only 1,000 Sets Since May," *New York Times*, Nov. 15, 1939, 25.

125. Russell Maloney, "The Age of Television," *New Yorker*, July 27, 1940, 22–23.

126. Ibid, 22.

127. Ibid.

128. Ibid, 23.

129. Ibid. Hewing to a traditional means of establishing sophistication when writing about television, Maloney also took the opportunity to tweak rural audiences with his description of "the Charlie McCarthy Riots of 1949, when the backward people of the Kentucky mountains became emotionally upset by the discovery that one of their television idols was a wooden dummy."

130. See Goodman, *Radio's Civic Ambition*, 245–285.

CHAPTER 4   SEEING AROUND CORNERS

1. Compared to theater or cinema audiences, broadcast audiences are relatively complex in terms of negotiations between public and private. With the majority of the listening or viewing public receiving the programs in the private sphere of the home or, in the cases of the automobile and the Walkman, in a state of mobile privatization, the audience straddles presumably divided and opposed facets of life, engaging in acts of imagination to both join a community and believe they are isolated.

2. See, e.g., William Boddy's *Fifties Television: The Industry and Its Critics* (Urbana: University of Illinois Press, 1990). In particular, the chapter "Live Television: Program Formats and Critical Hierarchies" (81–92) documents the uses of critical hierarchies in the 1950s through the articulation of liveness as the culturally high, best fulfillment of television's essential nature and proclamations about the nature of the home viewing experience to elevate the character-driven, live drama and position the writer as the hero of a noble struggle with the Goliaths of networks.

3. Michael Kammen, *The Lively Arts: Gilbert Seldes and the Transformation of Cultural Criticism in the United States* (New York: Oxford University Press, 1996), notes that Seldes stood out from other cultural critics of the time in his enthusiasm for popular media as—at least potentially—democratic arts and his lively ambivalence and impulsive but moderate iconoclasm (8–9). Bruce Lenthall, *Radio's America: The Great Depression and the Rise of Modern Mass Culture* (Chicago: University of Chicago Press, 2007), 159–165, details the work of academic researchers, "commercial pragmatists," who saw broadcasting as an effective aid to modern democracy.

4. Rod Serling, "The Happy Medium," in *How to Write for Television*, ed. William I. Kaufman (New York: Hastings House, 1955), 67–73.

5. Kammen, *The Lively Arts*.

6. Gilbert Seldes, "A Note on Television," *New Republic*, Dec. 2, 1931, 71–72.

7. Gilbert Seldes, "Errors of Television," *Atlantic*, May 1937, 531.

8. William Boddy, *New Media and Popular Imagination: Launching Radio, Television, and Digital Media in the United States* (New York: Oxford University Press, 2004), 42.

9. C. W. Horn to M. H. Aylesworth, memorandum, April 1, 1930, box 102, folder 1, Mass Communications History Collections, National Broadcasting Company records, 1921–2000, Wisconsin Historical Society, Madison, Wisconsin (hereafter cited as NBC). See also Zworykin's "Television with Cathode Ray Tubes," June 9, 1933, box 102, folder 3, NBC, which anticipates a dedicated viewer sitting rapt in the darkness.

10. Alexander Russo, *Points on the Dial: Golden Age Radio Beyond the Networks* (Durham, NC: Duke University Press, 2010), 151–183.

11. Owen Payne White, "What's Delaying Television?" *Collier's*, Nov. 30, 1935, 40.

12. Seldes, "Errors of Television," 535.

13. Ibid. On the same page Seldes argues that while a car radio may be enhancing or annoying based on the individual, attending to television in the automobile "will be in practice impossible."

14. Rick Altman, "Television Sound," in *Television: The Critical View*, ed. Horace Newcomb, 4th ed. (Oxford: Oxford University Press, 1987), 566–584.

15. Television scholar Elana Levine, drawing on Richard Johnson, has argued that the audience is present at the "moment" of production in the "circuit of culture," both in the producer's conceptions and uses of the audience but also in their own role as a first set of meaning makers. See Elana *General HospitalCritical Studies in Media Communication* 18, no. 1 (March 2001): 66–82. By 1937 the role of producers as audience was amplified with NBC's use of seventy-five to one hundred employee families as test audiences, as reported in "NBC-RCA Tele Demonstration Again Points Up It's Still in the Future," *Variety*, Feb. 17, 1937, *Variety Television Reviews*, vol. 3.

16. See Michele Hilmes, *Radio Voices: American Broadcasting, 1922–1952* (Minneapolis: University of Minnesota Press, 1997), 78–82, for a discussion of the anxiety produced by the indeterminacy of race in the voices of radio.

17. George Engles to Bertha Brainard, memorandum, Dec. 15, 1930; Brainard's response is attached, as is Engles's reply, box 102, folder 1, NBC.

18. Engles's reply to Brainard, box 102, folder 1, NBC.

19. "Philco's Latest Demonstration Sets Television Back Further in the Future," *Variety*, Feb. 17, 1937, *Variety Television Reviews*, vol. 3 (New York: Garland, 1989); "Video Bars Hefty Singers," *New York Times*, August 19, 1945, SM15.

20. "'Dumb' Acts Solve Television Talent Problem—and Cheaper: 2½ Hours Daily on W9AXO," *Variety*, Feb. 25, 1931, *Variety Television Reviews*, vol. 3.

21. See "Television Startling," *Variety*, May 28, 1930, *Variety Television Reviews*, vol. 3; and "Don Lee Video Hailed as Nearing Perfection," *Variety*, June 24, 1946, *Variety Television Reviews*, vol. 3. The latter article's "Uncle Tom" comment referred to live transmission of a swimming event and suggested the difficulties television would have maintaining racial hierarchies with sports in particular.

22. See Richard Dyer's *White* (London: Routledge, 1997) for a thorough discussion of the construction of whiteness.

23. "'Dumb' Acts Solve Television Talent Problem—and Cheaper." *Dumb* refers not to the intellectual content, but the vaudeville practice of beginning and ending bills with silent acts, in part to accommodate the noise made by late or hasty audience members, but "freak" and "peekshow" are certainly used pejoratively. In addition to this overt impugning of WTC's programming, *Variety* also described the company as "laboratory nursemaid to an electrical offspring of his own invention."

24. Shawn VanCour, "Popularizing the Classics: Radio's Role in the American Music Appreciation Movement, 1922–34," *Media, Culture & Society* 31, no. 2 (2009): 289–307, details the attempts at uplifting tastes and lives through classical music programming on popular radio, as well as the frustrations of classical music advocates with those presentations.

25. Robert Hertzberg, "Television Makes the Radio Drama Possible," *Radio News*, Dec. 1928, 524–526. This article reported on General Electric's broadcast of *The Queen's Messenger*, considered to be the first drama televised in the United States. See William Hawes, *American Television Drama: The Experimental Years* (Tuscaloosa: University of Alabama Press, 1986), for more on the full range of experimental drama.

26. Shawn VanCour, "The Sounds of 'Radio': Aesthetic Formations of 1920s American Broadcasting" (PhD diss., University of Wisconsin–Madison, 2008), 337–339.

27. "Television's Dilemma," *Literary Digest*, July 4, 1931, 20. The dilemma being "Now that we have television, what shall we do with it?"

28. Ibid.

29. Bill Schudt, "Columbia Turns the Corner," *Radio Digest*, Sept. 1931, 13–14; Betty McGee, "Chicago Asks License," *Radio Digest*, Sept. 1931, 14–15, 86; and Bill Schudt, "Scanning," *Radio Digest*, Oct. 1931, 18, 60.

30. Schudt, "Columbia Turns the Corner," 14.

31. Julius Weinberger, "Treatise on Television Planning," box 102, folder 5, NBC, 2.

32. Ibid., 3, 6–7, 11.

33. William F. Fairbanks to Bertha Brainard, memorandum, July 17, 1935, box 102, folder 5, NBC, 2. Although film had some obvious advantages, and notions of film quality still were an important consideration in defining television, additional investigation into using filmed programming had introduced new concerns about the choice of 16 mm or 35 mm film. Among the advantages of 35 mm film were superior image quality and sound. However, 35 mm prints were more costly, would require union projectionists, and, significantly, were more flammable, which resulted in critical restrictions on their transport—in essence some of the same issues that made the dream of theater television attractive to the Hollywood studios. See Hilmes, *Hollywood and Broadcasting*, 120–123, for a discussion of theater television.

34. "Report of the First Meeting of the Television Program Committee," June 4, 1935, box 102, folder 5, NBC.

35. William F. Fairbanks to Bertha Brainard, memorandum, July 17, 1935, box 102, folder 5, NBC.

36. "Report on Television Observations in Europe," by C. W. Farrier, July 15, 1937, 7–8, box 102, folder 15, NBC.

37. C. W. Fitch to all department heads, memorandum, Nov. 16, 1937, box 102, folder 12, NBC.

38. T. H. Hutchinson to J. F. Royal, memorandum, Feb. 26, 1938, box 102, folder 18, NBC.

39. Ron Becker, "'Hear-See Radio' in the World of Tomorrow: RCA and the Presentations of Television at the World's Fair, 1939–40," *Historical Journal of Film, Radio, and Television* 21, no. 4 (2001): 361–378.

40. Ibid., 372–373. Becker notes weak sales and independent polling that suggest the public was not persuaded by RCA's pitch.

41. See Boddy, *Fifties Television.*

42. Gilbert Seldes, "The Nature of Television Programs," and David Sarnoff, "The Possible Social Effects of Television," both in *Annals of the American Academy of Political and Social Science* 213 (Jan. 1941): 138–144 and 145–152, respectively.

43. Sarnoff, "The Possible Social Effects of Television," 147. With the phrase "power invention" Sarnoff is drawing on the work of William F. Ogburn, specifically his article "National Policy and Technology," in *Technological Trends and National Policy* (Washington, DC: National Resources Committee, 1937).

44. Sarnoff, "The Possible Social Effects of Television," 145–146; see also Marshall McLuhan, *Understanding Media: The Extensions of Man* (New York: Signet, 1966).

45. Sarnoff, "The Possible Social Effects of Television," 150–151; and Raymond Williams, *Television: Technology and Cultural Form* (London: Fontana, 1974), 26. Moreover, Sarnoff described this phenomenon in terms strikingly similar to those Williams would use years later to explain why McLuhan's model of determinism lacked sufficient attention to intention.

46. Sarnoff, "The Possible Social Effects of Television," 151. In the same vein he asserted, "We may also anticipate a rising level of culture, with universal education of both adults and children," without much in the way of evidence.

47. Ibid., 147–148. Sarnoff's intimation that the audience played a major role in programming decisions does not jibe with other accounts of NBC's television production during this period. William Hawes's *American Television Drama* reports a four-month hiatus on drama leading up to the date of publication of the Sarnoff article (90) and gives no indication of the dramatic programming being driven by audience feedback. Instead, Sarnoff's assertion that NBC's programming was "guided by audience response, as expressed by returns of special post cards," is best viewed through the lens of public relations, a careful circumlocution working to maintain the necessary fictions of programming driven by popularity and the implication of legitimacy conferred on the commercial system by this suggestion of media democracy.

48. Sarnoff, "The Possible Social Effects of Television," 149. See also Michele Hilmes, *Only Connect: A Cultural History of Broadcasting in the United States* (Belmont, CA: Wadsworth, 2002), 63–65, for an analysis of the FRC's distinction between "propaganda" stations like the Chicago Federation of Labor's WCFL and private commercial broadcasters who were considered to better serve the public interest.

49. Sarnoff, "The Possible Social Effects of Television," 152.

50. Seldes, "The Nature of Television Programs," 138.

51. Gilbert Seldes, *The Seven Lively Arts* (New York: A. S. Barnes, 1962), 287.

52. Seldes, "The Nature of Television Programs," 139.

53. Ibid., 138–139.

54. Kammen, *The Lively Arts*, 274. Seldes attributed his firings by both CBS and Paramount to his failure to convince his employers of the potential of his ventures, a failure of leadership (his) rather than ideas.

55. Seldes, "The Nature of Television Programs," 139. Except where otherwise noted, directly quoted material appearing in the next four paragraphs is taken from this article (140–144, 274).

56. John Caldwell, "Prime-Time Fiction Theorizes the Docu-Real," in *Reality Squared: Televisual Discourse on the Real*, ed. James Friedman (New Brunswick, NJ: Rutgers University Press, 2002), 259–292; and Seldes, "The Nature of Television Programs."

57. Christian Metz ties epistemophilia to "voyeuristic sadism" in a psychoanalytic scheme that similarly relies on essentialist theorizations of human drives and pleasures but neatly writes the theorist into its account. See Christian Metz, *The Imaginary Signifier*, trans. Celia Britton, Annwyl Williams, Ben Brewster, and Alfred Guzzetti (Bloomington: Indiana University Press, 1982). See "The Imaginary and the 'Good Object' in the Cinema and in the Theory of the Cinema," 3–16, for the specific discussion of pleasure and desire in the practice of film theory.

58. A thoroughgoing Marxist critique might even argue that in provoking an unquenchable thirst for expanded perception, a set of unfulfilled desires was created that could conveniently be palliated by the products soon to be sold through television, but that fits together a bit too nicely.

59. Erik Barnouw, *The Golden Web: A History of Broadcasting in the United States, 1933–1953* (New York: Oxford University Press, 1968), 127–128.

60. See Barnouw, *The Golden Web*; and Erik Barnouw, *Tube of Plenty: The Evolution of American Television*, 2nd rev. ed. (New York: Oxford University Press, 1990); J. Fred McDonald, *One Nation Under Television: The Rise and Decline of Network TV* (Chicago: Nelson-Hall, 1994); Hilmes, *Only Connect*; Christopher H. Sterling and John M. Kitross, *Stay Tuned: A History of American Broadcasting*, 3rd ed. (Mahwah, NJ: Lawrence Erlbaum, 2002). Barnouw's *Golden Web* set the precedent: "Most television stations left the air. Six

hung on with skeleton programming to serve the 10,000 sets—they would soon be museum pieces—that had already been sold" (127–128). Boddy gives this period somewhat greater attention in *Fifties Television*; William Hawes's *American Television Drama* and Michael Ritchie's *Please Stand By: A Prehistory of Television* (New York: Overlook, 1995) give the period considerable attention.

61. Hawes, *American Television Drama*, 186.

62. Ibid., 219.

63. Ritchie, *Please Stand By*, 143–153; and Hawes, *American Television Drama*, 114, report on the station's closing, with Hawes reporting an autumn relaunch. David Weinstein, *The Forgotten Network: Dumont and the Birth of American Television* (Philadelphia: Temple University Press, 2004), 15, reports Dumont's free time for sponsors as a summer practice.

64. Gilbert Seldes, "Regarding Video Experiments," *New York Times*, Dec. 24, 1944, 35.

65. Ibid. See also Hawes, *American Television Drama*, 51–53. The title of the adapted radio program suggests elements of minstrelsy, but neither of these sources gives further indication of the content beyond the generic description.

66. Seldes, "Regarding Video Experiments," 35.

67. Hawes, in *American Television Drama*, paraphrases CBS producer Worthington Miner's articulation of television camera work and its divergence from cinema: "The basic difference between television and motion pictures was that, in pictures, actors for the most part moved in and out of a fixed frame; in television, they often remained still, while the frame around them moved" (53). Here, Miner sees the pragmatic adaptations of cinematic style as creating an essential distinction.

68. Seldes, "Regarding Video Experiments," 35.

69. See John Thornton Caldwell, *Televisuality: Style, Crisis, and Authority in American Television* (New Brunswick, NJ: Rutgers University Press, 1995).

70. Seldes, "Regarding Video Experiments," 35.

71. Richard W. Hubbell, "Programming," *Television: The Magazine of Video Fact*, Fall 1944, 26.

72. Ibid., 26–27.

73. Ibid. Hawes also uses this quote in his discussion of CBS's mid-1940s dramas in *American Television Drama* (53).

74. Hubbell, "Programming," 28.

75. Richard Hubbell, *Television Programming and Production* (New York: Little and Ives, 1945), 14 (emphasis in original). This comes from the chapter titled "The Nature of Television."

76. Ibid., 14–15. Interestingly, Hubbell saves his discussion of Sergei Eisenstein for a much later discussion of camera technique (88).

77. Schwoch, "The Selling Sight/Site of Sound," *Cinema Journal* 30, no. 1 (Fall 1990): 60–61; and Boddy, *New Media and Popular Imagination*, 49–53.

78. Hubbell, *Television*, 136. This position was rearticulated as applied to television three years later by N. Ray Kelly, who "took violent issue" with the suggestion that television was a "new 'art medium'" and argued that "with television we have opened up only a new medium of communication." N. Ray Kelly, "Television Production Facilities," in *Television Production Problems*, ed. John F. Royal (New York: McGraw-Hill, 1948), 53–54.

79. Hubbell, *Television*, 138–139.

80. Ibid., 141–146. The chapter "Toward a Video Technique" lays out seven steps to developing a distinctive and appropriate visual style for television.

81. Ibid., 144, vi–vii. Of Seldes's cadre, Hubbell reports that the so-called "nine old men of television" were actually "ten young men and a woman: Ruth Norman, Worthington

Miner, Rudolf Bretz . . . Phillip Booth, Edward Anhalt, Paul Mowrey, Stephen Marvin, Marshall Diskin, James Leaman, Richard Rawls and I."

82. Judy Dupuy, *Television Show Business* (Schenectady, NY: General Electric, 1945); and William C. Eddy, *Television: The Eyes of Tomorrow* (New York: Prentice Hall, 1945).

83. Boddy, *New Media and Popular Imagination*, 49–53; and Jennifer Hyland Wang, "'The Case of the Radio-Active Housewife': Relocating Radio in the Age of Television," in *The Radio Reader*, ed. Michele Hilmes and Jason Loviglio (New York: Routledge, 2002), 343–366.

84. Schwoch, "Selling the Sight/Site of Sound," 60–61. Most interesting was a set of television trials for soap operas produced by Irna Phillips at NBC with the goal of determining and demonstrating television's potential for engaging the woman working in the home.

85. Eddy, *Television*, 14–29.

86. Ibid., 188. Lacking reliable electronic character generators, and decades removed from the complex video manipulation capability of modern switchers, experimental producers and programmers were bound to cuts, dissolves, and that which could be placed in front of a camera; this included the film chain that enabled the integration of filmed segments and the broadcast of motion pictures.

87. Ibid., 317 (emphasis in original).

88. See Dupuy's foreword to *Television Show Business*; see also Bernice Brown McCullar, "Book Reviews," *Southern Speech Journal* 12, no. 3 (1947): 77.

89. Dupuy, *Television Show Business*, 3.

90. Ibid., 3–4. In quick succession, Dupuy reeled off a litany of televisual truths. "Visual broadcasting is developing a creative form all its own." "Television is an intimate medium which goes into the home and must be welcomed as a fireside guest." "The use of multiple cameras [is] a fundamental of good television."

91. The mid-2000s enlargement of Nielsen's main national sample provides some perspective on typical sample size. In 2004 Nielsen Media Research announced the planned expansion of its National People Meter Sample to "nearly 10,000" in a nation of more than one hundred million television households. See Lisa de Moraes, "Coming Clean About Sweeps: A Messy Little Detail About Ratings Periods," *Washington Post*, Feb. 29, 2004, N12.

92. See Steven Classen's "Southern Discomforts: The Racial Struggle over Popular TV," in *The Revolution Wasn't Televised: Sixties Television and Social Conflict*, ed. Lynn Spigel and Michael Curtin (New York: Routledge, 1997), 305–326, for a discussion of the fraying of the segregationist boycott of *Bonanza* in part because of the potential for private backsliding.

93. Seldes reported the success of a similar program at CBS in 1944: "The other day we got it in another experiment—we took a series of drawings of a Wac giving jiu-jitsu to an apache dancer. We got two dancers to re-enact the strip, and as they reached certain high-spots, we dissolved from them to the appropriate sections of the original strip of drawings. It wasn't an esthetic discovery; it was only something that could not be done anywhere except in television; it had a unique quality. And our audience responded to it immediately" (Seldes, "Regarding Video Experiments," 35).

94. George Lipsitz, "The Meaning of Memory: Family, Class, and Ethnicity in Early Network Television," in *Private Screenings: Television and the Female Consumer*, ed. Lynn Spigel and Denise Mann (Minneapolis: University of Minnesota Press, 1992), 71–108.

95. Chad Dell, "Wrestling with Corporate Identity: Defining Television Programming Strategy at NBC, 1945–1950," in *Transmitting the Past: Historical and Cultural Perspectives on Broadcasting*, ed. J. Emmett Winn and Susan L. Brinson (Tuscaloosa: University of Alabama Press, 2005), 68–91.

96. Mike Mashon, "NBC, J. Walter Thompson, and the Struggle for Control of Television Programming, 1946–1958," in *NBC: America's Network*, ed. Michele Hilmes (Berkeley: University of California Press, 2007), 135–152.

97. Jack Gould, "TV at the Crossroads: A Critic's Survey," *New York Times*, March 9, 1952, SM12.

98. See Mashon, "NBC, J. Walter Thompson, and the Struggle for Control of Television Programming, 1946–1958"; Michael Kackman, *Citizen Spy: Television, Espionage, and Cold War Culture* (Minneapolis: University of Minnesota Press, 2005), particularly the first two chapters, 1–48; and Michael Curtin, *Redeeming the Wasteland: Television Documentary and Cold War Politics* (New Brunswick, NJ: Rutgers University Press, 1995).

99. See Michele Hilmes, *Only Connect: A Cultural History of Broadcasting in the United States* (Belmont, CA: Wadsworth, 2002), 194–195, 228–229; and Jason Mittell, "The 'Classic Network System' in the US," in *The Television History Book*, ed. Michele Hilmes (London: BFI, 2003), 44–49.

100. Hoyland Bettinger, *Television Techniques* (New York: Harper and Brothers, 1947), 11, 14.

101. Gilbert Seldes, *Writing for Television* (New York: Doubleday, 1952), 21.

102. See Boddy's *Fifties Television*; and Christopher Anderson's *Hollywood TV: The Studio System in the Fifties* (Austin: University of Texas Press, 1994).

103. Here I am primarily referring to cancellation, but it is worth noting that, Dupuy's warning notwithstanding, *The Sopranos* recently and somewhat notoriously ended its critically acclaimed run with an abrupt cut to black that left some viewers thinking their cable had gone out. See Martin Miller and Carmen Gentile, "'The Sopranos'; 'We Wuz Robbed,' Fans Complain," *Los Angeles Times*, June 11, 2007, E1; Mike McDaniel, "Sopranos a Hit or Miss?" *Houston Chronicle*, June 11, 2007, A1; and Tim Goodman, "An Ending That Befits Genius of 'Sopranos,'" *San Francisco Chronicle*, June 11, 2007, A1, which began, "No, your cable—or satellite—didn't go out."

104. Jason Mittell, *Genre and Television: From Cop Shows to Cartoons in American Culture* (New York: Routledge, 2004).

CONCLUSIONS

1. See James W. Carey, *Communication as Culture: Essays on Media and Society* (New York: Routledge, 1989), 86–87.

2. Matthew Arnold, *Culture and Anarchy*, edited with an introduction by J. Dover Wilson (Cambridge: Cambridge University Press, 1950), 44–45.

3. Stuart Hall, *Representation: Cultural Representations and Signifying Practices* (London: Sage, 1997), 1–11.

4. Nelly Oudshoorn and Trevor Pinch, "How Users and Non-users Matter," in *How Users Matter: The Co-construction of Users and Technology*, ed. Nelly Oudshoorn and Trevor Pinch (Cambridge, MA: MIT Press, 2005), 3. Oudshoorn and Pinch specifically use "mutual shaping" and "co-construction" to conceive of the interactions of technologies and social groups, but the concept can be profitably extended across other relationships to imagine multivalent and interdependent impacts.

5. Chad Dell, "Wrestling with Corporate Identity: Defining Television Programming Strategy at NBC, 1945–1950," in *Transmitting the Past: Historical and Cultural Perspectives on Broadcasting*, ed. J. Emmett Winn and Susan L. Brinson (Tuscaloosa: University of Alabama Press, 2005), 68–91; William Boddy, *Fifties Television: The Industry and Its Critics* (Urbana: University of Illinois Press, 1990); and Lynn Spigel, *Make Room for TV: Television and the Family Ideal in Postwar America* (Chicago: University of Chicago Press, 1992).

6. Caitlin Flanagan, "Babes in the Woods," *Atlantic*, July/August 2007, 124.

7. See Arjun Appadurai's "Disjuncture and Difference in the Global Cultural Economy," in *Modernity at Large: Cultural Dimensions of Globalization* (Minneapolis: University of Minnesota Press, 1998), 27–47, for his schematic analysis of global flows and complication of theories of cultural imperialism.

8. Michael K. Powell, "New Rules, Old Rhetoric," *New York Times*, July 28, 2003, A17.

9. Charles McGrath, "The Triumph of the Prime-Time Novel," *New York Times*, Oct. 22, 1995, SM52–57.

10. The derision of "sitcom endings" can often be found in theatrical criticism, such as Neil Genzlinger's "A Louse's Animal Magnetism (The Sex Appeal of the Jerk)," *New York Times* July 28, 2006, E3.

11. For examples of the latter see Jason Mittell's analysis of the discourse of the "plug-in drug," in "The Cultural Power of an Anti-television Metaphor: Questioning the 'Plug-In Drug' and a TV-Free America," *Television & New Media* 1, no. 2 (2000): 215–238; and Dorinda Hartmann's analysis of dystopian nightmares in films such as *Videodrome* (David Cronenberg, 1983), in "Reach In and Touch Someone: Communication Technology and Cultural Fears of Sexual Predation" (PhD diss., University of Wisconsin–Madison, 2013).

12. See John Thornton Caldwell, *Televisuality: Style, Crisis, and Authority in American Television* (New Brunswick, NJ: Rutgers University Press, 1995), 267–268. Caldwell regards user-generated content in shows like *America's Funniest Home Videos* as a recuperation—access transmogrified into panopticism—of portable video's threat to network television.

13. It is partly for this reason that John Caldwell turns to political-economic and corporate-cultural explanations when he considers prime-time events, such as the live *ER* episode, in conjunction with the other network and local broadcast materials that directly invoke them, such as the newscast that came on directly after that *ER*. See John T. Caldwell, "Critical Industrial Practice: Branding, Repurposing, and the Migratory Patterns of Industrial Texts," *Television & New Media* 7, no. 2 (2006): 99–134.

14. Jane Feuer, "The Concept of Live Television: Ontology as Ideology," in *Regarding Television: Critical Approaches*, ed. E. Ann Kaplan (Frederick, MD: University Publications of America, 1983), 15–16.

15. Michael Z. Newman and Elana Levine, *Legitimating Television: Media Convergence and Cultural Status* (New York: Routledge, 2011). See also Max Dawson, "TV Repair: New Media 'Solutions' to Old Media Problems" (PhD diss., Northwestern University, 2008), for an analysis of the various ways in which television has of late been fixed and has been considered in need of it.

16. Newman and Levine, *Legitimating Television*, 171.

17. Stanley Cavell, "The Fact of Television," in *Daedalus* 111, no. 4 (Fall 1982): 75–77. See also Thomas Streeter's *Selling the Air: A Critique of the Policy of Commercial Broadcasting in the United States* (Chicago: University of Chicago Press, 1996), which begins his critical analysis of broadcast policy with a consideration of Cavell's observation that television seems obvious but remains mysterious (and in Cavell's estimation conspicuously underinvestigated), a phenomenon Streeter explains, contra Cavell, as a function of the political and cultural work done by corporate liberals to construct a regulatory regime and set of social and economic relations in support of a particular, centralized vision of broadcasting.

SELECTED BIBLIOGRAPHY

Abramson, Albert. *The History of Television, 1880–1941*. Jefferson, NC: McFarland, 1987.

Adorno, Theodor, and Max Horkheimer. "The Culture Industry: Enlightenment as Mass Deception." In *Cultural Studies*, edited by Lawrence Grossberg, Cary Nelson, and Paula Treichler, 29–43. New York: Routledge, 1992.

Aitken, Hugh. *The Continuous Wave: Technology and American Radio, 1900–1932*. Princeton, NJ: Princeton University Press, 1985.

———. *Syntony and Spark—The Origins of Radio*. New York: John Wiley and Sons, 1976.

Allen, Robert C. *Horrible Prettiness: Burlesque and American Culture*. Chapel Hill: University of North Carolina Press, 1991.

Altman, Rick. "Television Sound." In *Television: The Critical View*, edited by Horace Newcomb, 4th ed., 566–584. Oxford: Oxford University Press, 1987.

Anderson, Benedict. *Imagined Communities: Reflections on the Origin and Spread of Nationalism*. New York: Verso, 1991.

Anderson, Christopher. *Hollywood TV: The Studio System in the Fifties*. Austin: University of Texas Press, 1994.

Ang, Ien. "In the Realm of Uncertainty: The Global Village and Capitalist Postmodernity." In Mackay and O'Sullivan, *The Media Reader*, 366–384.

———, with Joke Hermes. "Gender and/in Media Consumption." In *Mass Media and Society*, edited by James Curran and Michael Gurevitch, 307–328. London: Arnold, 1991.

Appadurai, Arjun. *Modernity at Large: Cultural Dimensions of Globalization*. Minneapolis: University of Minnesota Press, 1998.

Arnold, Matthew. *Culture and Anarchy*. Edited with an introduction by J. Dover Wilson. Cambridge: Cambridge University Press, 1950.

Auslander, Philip. "Against Ontology: Making Distinctions Between the Live and the Mediatized." *Performance Research* 2, no. 3 (1997): 50–55.

Bakhtin, Mikhail. *Rabelais and His World*. Translated by Hélène Iswolsky. Cambridge, MA: MIT Press, 1968.

Barker, David. "Television Production Techniques as Communication." In *Television: The Critical View*, edited by Horace Newcomb, 4th ed., 179–196. Oxford: Oxford University Press, 1987.

Barnouw, Erik. *The Golden Web: A History of Broadcasting in the United States, 1933–1953*. New York: Oxford University Press, 1968.

———. *The Image Empire: A History of Broadcasting in the United States from 1953*. New York: Oxford University Press, 1970.

———. *A Tower in Babel: A History of Broadcasting in the United States to 1933*. New York: Oxford University Press, 1966.

———. *Tube of Plenty: The Evolution of American Television*. 2nd rev. ed. New York: Oxford University Press, 1990.

Baughman, James L. *The Republic of Mass Culture*. 2nd ed. Baltimore: Johns Hopkins University Press, 1997.

Becker, Ron. "'Hear-See Radio' in the World of Tomorrow: RCA and the Presentations of Television at the World's Fair, 1939–40." *Historical Journal of Film, Radio, and Television* 21, no. 4 (2001): 361–378.

Benjamin, Walter. "The Work of Art in the Age of Mechanical Reproduction." In *The Routledge Critical and Cultural Theory Reader*, edited by Neil Badmington and Julia Thomas, 34–56. New York: Routledge, 2008.

Berger, John. *Ways of Seeing*. London: British Broadcasting Corporation, 1972.

Bettinger, Hoyland. *Television Techniques*. New York: Harper and Brothers, 1947.

Bjarkman, Kim. "To Have and to Hold: The Television Collector's Relationship with an Ethereal Medium." *Television & New Media* 5, no. 3 (2004): 217–246.

Boddy, William. *Fifties Television: The Industry and Its Critics*. Urbana: University of Illinois Press, 1990.

———. *New Media and Popular Imagination: Launching Radio, Television, and Digital Media in the United States*. New York: Oxford University Press, 2004.

Bourdieu, Pierre. *Distinction: A Social Critique of the Judgement of Taste*. Translated by Richard Nice. Cambridge, MA: Harvard University Press, 1984.

Brunsdon, Charlotte. "Problems with Quality." *Screen* 31, no. 1 (Spring 1990): 67–90.

———. "What Is the Television in Television Studies?" In *The Television Studies Book*, edited by Christine Geraghty and David Lusted, 95–113. New York: Arnold, 1998.

Butsch, Richard. *The Making of American Audiences: From Stage to Television, 1750–1990*. New York: Cambridge University Press, 2000.

Caldwell, John. "Critical Industrial Practice: Branding, Repurposing, and the Migratory Patterns of Industrial Texts." *Television & New Media* 7, no. 2 (2006): 99–134.

———. "Prime-Time Fiction Theorizes the Docu-Real." In *Reality Squared: Televisual Discourse on the Real*, edited by James Friedman, 259–292. New Brunswick, NJ: Rutgers University Press, 2002.

———. *Televisuality: Style, Crisis, and Authority in American Television*. New Brunswick, NJ: Rutgers University Press, 1995.

Calhoun, Craig. "Introduction: Habermas and the Public Sphere." In *Habermas and the Public Sphere*, edited by Craig Calhoun, 1–48. Cambridge, MA: MIT Press, 1992.

Carey, James W. "Abolishing the Old Spirit World." In *Critical Studies in Mass Communication—Colloquy* (March 1995): 82–95.

———. *Communication as Culture: Essays on Media and Society*. New York: Routledge, 1989.

Carey, James W., with John J. Quirk. "The Mythos of the Electronic Revolution." In Carey, *Communication as Culture*, 113–141.

Cavell, Stanley. "The Fact of Television." *Daedalus* 111, no. 4 (Fall 1982): 75–96.

Classen, Steven. "Southern Discomforts: The Racial Struggle over Popular TV." In *The Revolution Wasn't Televised: Sixties Television and Social Conflict*, edited by Lynn Spigel and Michael Curtin, 305–324. New York: Routledge, 1997.

Cook, David A. "The Birth of the Network: How Westinghouse, GE, AT&T, and RCA Invented the Concept of Advertiser-Supported Broadcasting." *Quarterly Review of Film Studies* 8, no. 3 (Summer 1983): 3–8.

Cubitt, Sean. *Timeshift: On Video Culture*. London: Routledge, 1991.

Curtin, Michael. *Redeeming the Wasteland: Television Documentary and Cold War Politics*. New Brunswick, NJ: Rutgers University Press, 1995.

Dawson, Max. "TV Repair: New Media 'Solutions' to Old Media Problems." PhD diss., Northwestern University, 2008.

De Certeau, Michel. *The Writing of History*. Translated by Tom Conley. New York: Columbia University Press, 1988.

Dell, Chad. "Wrestling with Corporate Identity: Defining Television Programming Strategy at NBC, 1945–1950." In *Transmitting the Past: Historical and Cultural Perspectives on Broadcasting*, edited by J. Emmett Winn and Susan L. Brinson, 68–91. Tuscaloosa: University of Alabama Press, 2005.

Doerksen, Clifford John. *American Babel: Rogue Radio Broadcasters of the Jazz Age*. Philadelphia: University of Pennsylvania Press, 2005.

Douglas, Susan. *Inventing American Broadcasting, 1899–1922*. Baltimore: Johns Hopkins University Press, 1987.

du Gay, Paul, Stuart Hall, Linda Janes, Hugh Mackay, and Keith Negus. *Doing Cultural Studies: The Story of the Sony Walkman*. London: Sage, 1997.

Dunlap, Orrin E., Jr. *The Outlook for Television*. New York: Harper and Brothers, 1932

Dupuy, Judy. *Television Show Business*. Schenectady, NY: General Electric, 1945.

Dyer, Richard. *White*. London: Routledge, 1997.

Eddy, William C. *Television: The Eyes of Tomorrow*. New York: Prentice Hall, 1945.

Fisher, David E., and Marshall Jon Fisher. *Tube: The Invention of Television*. Washington, DC: Harvest, 1996.

Fiske, John. "Popularity and the Politics of Information." In *Journalism and Popular Culture*, edited by Peter Dahlgren and Colin Sparks, 45–63. London: Sage, 1992.

———, and John Hartley. *Reading Television*. London: Methuen, 1978.

Flichy, Patrice. "The Wireless Age: Radio Broadcasting." In Mackay and O'Sullivan, *The Media Reader*, 73–90.

Foucault, Michel. *The Archaeology of Knowledge*. Translated by A. M. Sheridan Smith. New York: Pantheon, 1972.

———. *Discipline and Punish: The Birth of the Prison*. Translated by Alan Sheridan. New York: Vintage, 1995. Originally published as *Surveiller et punir: Naissance de la prison* (Paris: Gallimard, 1975); first English translation Harmondsworth, UK: Penguin, 1977.

———. "Nietzsche, Genealogy, History." In *The Foucault Reader: An Introduction to Foucault's Thought*, edited by Paul Rabinow, 76–100. London: Penguin, 1984.

Fraser, Nancy. "Rethinking the Public Sphere: A Contribution to the Critique of Actually Existing Democracy." *Social Text* 25/26 (1990): 56–80.

Frow, John, and Meaghan Morris. "Introduction." In *Australian Cultural Studies*, edited by John Frow and Meaghan Morris, vii–xxxi. Urbana: University of Illinois Press, 1993.

Gitelman, Lisa. *Scripts, Grooves, and Writing Machines: Representing Technology in the Edison Era*. Stanford, CA: Stanford University Press, 1999.

Goodman, David. *Radio's Civic Ambition*. New York: Oxford University Press, 2011.

Goodman, Mark, and Mark Gring, "The Radio Act of 1927: Progressive Ideology, Epistemology, and Praxis." *Rhetoric & Public Affairs* 3, no. 3 (2000): 397–418.

Grossberg, Lawrence. "History, Politics and Postmodernism." In Morley and Chen, *Stuart Hall*, 151–173.

———, ed. "On Postmodernism and Articulation: An Interview with Stuart Hall." In Morley and Chen, *Stuart Hall*, 131–150.

Habermas, Jürgen. *The Structural Transformation of the Public Sphere: An Inquiry into a Category of Bourgeois Society*. Translated by Thomas Burger with the assistance of Frederick Lawrence. Cambridge, MA: MIT Press, 1989.

Hall, Stuart. "Gramsci's Relevance for Race and Ethnicity." In Morley and Chen, *Stuart Hall*, 411–440.

———. *Representation: Cultural Representations and Signifying Practices*. London: Sage, 1997.

Hamilton, James. "Unearthing Broadcasting in the Anglophone World." In *Residual Media*, edited by Charles R. Acland, 283–300. Minneapolis: University of Minnesota Press, 2007.

Hartley, John. "Invisible Fictions: Television Audiences, Paedocracy, Pleasure." In *Television Studies: Textual Analysis*, edited by Gary Burns and Robert J. Thompson, 223–244. New York: Praeger, 1989.

Hawes, William. *American Television Drama: The Experimental Years*. Tuscaloosa: University of Alabama Press, 1986.

Hilmes, Michele. "British Quality, American Chaos: Historical Dualisms and What They Leave Out." *Radio Journal: International Studies in Broadcast & Audio Media* 1, no. 1 (2003): 2–17.

———. *Hollywood and Broadcasting: From Radio to Cable*. Urbana: University of Illinois Press, 1990.

———. *Network Nations: A Transnational History of British and American Broadcasting*. New York: Routledge, 2011.

———. *Only Connect: A Cultural History of Broadcasting in the United States*. Belmont, CA: Wadsworth, 2002.

———. *Radio Voices: American Broadcasting, 1922–1952*. Minneapolis: University of Minnesota Press, 1997.

———. "Who We Are, Who We Are Not: Battle of the Global Paradigms." In *Planet TV: A Global Television Reader*, edited by Lisa Parks and Shanti Kumar, 53–73. New York: New York University Press, 2003.

Hubbell, Richard W. *4000 Years of Television: The Story of Seeing at a Distance*. New York: G. P. Putnam's Sons, 1942.

———. *Television Programming and Production*. New York: Little and Ives, 1945.

Jancovich, Mark, and James Lyons, eds. *Quality Popular Television: Cult TV, the Industry and Fans*. London: BFI, 2003.

Jaramillo, Deborah L. "The Family Racket: AOL Time Warner, HBO, *The Sopranos*, and the Construction of a Quality Brand." In *Television: The Critical View*, edited by Horace Newcomb, 7th ed., 579–594. Oxford: Oxford University Press, 2007.

Jenkins, Henry. *Textual Poachers: Television Fans and Participatory Culture*. New York: Routledge, 1992.

Jenkins, Keith. *Re-thinking History*. New York: Routledge, 1991.

Kackman, Michael. *Citizen Spy: Television, Espionage, and Cold War Culture*. Minneapolis: University of Minnesota Press, 2005.

Kammen, Michael. *The Lively Arts: Gilbert Seldes and the Transformation of Cultural Criticism in the United States*. New York: Oxford University Press, 1996.

Kline, Ronald, and Trevor Pinch. "Users as Agents of Technological Change: The Social Construction of the Automobile in the Rural United States." *Technology and Culture* 37, no. 4 (Oct. 1996): 763–795.

Lacey, Kate. *Feminine Frequencies: Gender, German Radio, and the Public Sphere, 1923–1945*. Ann Arbor: University of Michigan Press, 1996.

Lenthall, Bruce. *Radio's America: The Great Depression and the Rise of Modern Mass Culture*. Chicago: University of Chicago Press, 2007.

Lentz, Kirsten Marthe. "*Quality* versus *Relevance*: Feminism, Race, and the Politics of the Sign in 1970s Television." *Camera Obscura* 15, no. 1_43 (2000): 45–93.

Levine, Elana. "Toward a Paradigm for Media Production Research: Behind the Scenes at *General Hospital*." *Critical Studies in Media Communication* 18, no. 1 (March 2001): 66–83.

Levine, Lawrence. *Highbrow/Lowbrow*. Cambridge, MA: Harvard University Press, 1988.

Lipsitz, George. "The Meaning of Memory: Family, Class, and Ethnicity in Early Network Television." In *Private Screenings: Television and the Female Consumer*, edited by Lynn Spigel and Denise Mann, 71–108. Minneapolis, University of Minnesota Press, 1992.

Loviglio, Jason. *Radio's Intimate Public: Network Broadcasting and Mass-Mediated Democracy*. Minneapolis: University of Minnesota Press, 2005.

MacDonald, J. Fred. *One Nation Under Television: The Rise and Decline of Network TV*. Chicago: Nelson-Hall, 1994.

Mackay, Hugh, and Tim O'Sullivan, eds. *The Media Reader: Continuity and Transformation*. London: Sage, 1999.

MacLaurin, W. Rupert. *Invention and Innovation in the Radio Industry*. New York: Arno, 1971.

Marchand, Roland. *Advertising the American Dream: Making Way for Modernity, 1920–1940*. Berkeley: University of California Press, 1985.

Marvin, Carolyn. *When Old Technologies Were New: Thinking About Electric Communication in the Late Nineteenth Century*. Oxford: Oxford University Press, 1988.

Mashon, Mike. "NBC, J. Walter Thompson, and the Struggle for Control of Television Programming, 1946–1958." In *NBC: America's Network*, edited by Michele Hilmes, 135–152. Berkeley: University of California Press, 2007.

McChesney, Robert. "Conflict, Not Consensus: The Debate over Broadcast Communications Policy, 1930–1935." In *Ruthless Criticism: New Perspectives in U.S. Communication History*, edited by William Solomon and Robert W. McChesney, 222–258. Minneapolis: University of Minnesota Press, 1993.

McGuigan, Jim. *Culture and the Public Sphere*. London: Routledge, 1996.

McLuhan, Marshall. *Understanding Media: The Extensions of Man*. New York: Signet, 1966.

Meehan, Eileen. "Why We Don't Count." In *Logics of Television: Essays on Cultural Criticism*, edited by Patricia Mellencamp, 117–137. Bloomington: Indiana University Press, 1990.

Metz, Christian. *The Imaginary Signifier*. Translated by Celia Britton, Annwyl Williams, Ben Brewster, and Alfred Guzzetti. Bloomington: Indiana University Press, 1982.

Meyrowitz, Joshua. "No Sense of Place: The Impact of Electronic Media on Social Behavior." In Mackay and O'Sullivan, *The Media Reader*, 99–120.

Mittell, Jason. "The 'Classic Network System' in the US." In *The Television History Book*, edited by Michele Hilmes, 44–49. London: BFI, 2003.

———. "The Cultural Power of an Anti-television Metaphor: Questioning the 'Plug-In Drug' and a TV-Free America." *Television & New Media* 1, no. 2 (2000): 215–238.

———. *Genre and Television: From Cop Shows to Cartoons in American Culture*. New York: Routledge, 2004.

Morley, David, and Kuan-Hsing Chen, eds. *Stuart Hall: Critical Dialogues in Cultural Studies*. New York: Routledge, 1996.

Mulgan, Geoff, ed. *The Question of Quality*. London: BFI, 1990.

Nelson, Cary, Paula Treichler, and Lawrence Grossberg. "Cultural Studies: An Introduction." In *Cultural Studies*, edited by Lawrence Grossberg, Cary Nelson, and Paula Treichler, 1–16. New York: Routledge, 1992.

Newcomb, Horace, and Paul M. Hirsch. "Television as Cultural Forum." In *Television: The Critical View*, edited by Horace Newcomb, 4th ed., 455–470. Oxford: Oxford University Press, 1987.

Newman, Michael Z., and Elana Levine. *Legitimating Television: Media Convergence and Cultural Status*. New York: Routledge, 2011.

Ong, Walter. "Print, Space, and Closure." In *Communication in History: Technology, Culture, Society*, edited by David Crowley and Paul Heyer, White Plains, NY: Longman, 1995.

Oudshoorn, Nelly, and Trevor Pinch. "How Users and Non-users Matter." In *How Users Matter: The Co-construction of Users and Technology*, edited by Nelly Oudshoorn and Trevor Pinch, 1–25. Cambridge, MA: MIT Press, 2005.

Paley, William S. "Radio and the Humanities." *Annals of the American Academy* (1935): 94–104.

Patnode, Randall. "'What These People Need Is Radio': New Technology, the Press, and Otherness in 1920s America." *Technology and Culture* 44, no. 2 (April 2003): 285–305.

Pinch, Trevor J., and Wiebe E. Bijker. "The Social Construction of Facts and Artefacts: Or How the Sociology of Science and the Sociology of Technology Might Benefit Each Other." *Social Studies of Science* 14, no. 3 (August 1984): 399–441.

Pursell, Carroll. *The Machine in America: A Social History of Technology*. Baltimore: Johns Hopkins University Press, 1995.

Razlogova, Elena. *The Listener's Voice: Early Radio and the American Public*. Philadelphia: University of Pennsylvania Press, 2011.

Ritchie, Michael. *Please Stand By: A Prehistory of Television*. New York: Overlook, 1995.

Russo, Alexander. *Points on the Dial: Golden Age Radio Beyond the Networks*. Durham, NC: Duke University Press, 2010.

Schatz, Thomas. "Desilu, *I Love Lucy*, and the Rise of Network TV." In *Making Television: Authorship and the Production Process*, edited by Robert J. Thompson and Gary Burns, 117–135. New York: Praeger, 1990.

Schwoch, James. *The American Radio Industry and Its Latin American Activities, 1900–1939*. Urbana: University of Illinois Press, 1990.

———. "Selling the Sight/Site of Sound: Broadcast Advertising and the Transition to Television." *Cinema Journal* 30, no. 1 (Fall 1990): 55–66.

Seldes, Gilbert. *The Great Audience*. New York: Viking, 1950.

———. *The Seven Lively Arts*. New York: A. S. Barnes, 1962.

———. *Writing for Television*. New York: Doubleday, 1952.

Slack, Jennifer Daryl. "Contextualizing Technology." In *Rethinking Communications*. Vol. 2, *Paradigm Exemplars*, edited by Brenda Dervin, Lawrence Grossberg, Barbara J. O'Keefe, and Ellen Wartella, 329–345. London: Sage, 1989.

———. "The Theory and Method of Articulation in Cultural Studies." In Morley and Chen, *Stuart Hall*, 113–129.

Slotten, Hugh. *Radio and Television Regulation: Broadcast Technology in the United States, 1920–1960*. Baltimore: Johns Hopkins University Press, 2000.

Smulyan, Susan. *Selling Radio: The Commercialization of American Broadcasting, 1920–1934*. Washington, DC: Smithsonian Institution Press, 1994.

Spigel, Lynn. *Make Room for TV: Television and the Family Ideal in Postwar America*. Chicago: University of Chicago Press, 1992.

———. "The Making of a TV Literate Elite." In *The Television Studies Book*, edited by Christine Geraghty and David Lusted, 63–85. New York: Arnold, 1998.

Stallybrass, Peter, and Allon White. *The Politics and Poetics of Transgression*. Ithaca, NY: Cornell University Press, 1986.

Steemers, Jeanette. "Broadcasting Is Dead. Long Live Digital Choice." In Mackay and O'Sullivan, *The Media Reader*, 231–249.

Sterling, Christopher H., and John M. Kitross. *Stay Tuned: A History of American Broadcasting*, 3rd ed. Mahwah, NJ: Lawrence Erlbaum, 2002.

Sterne, Jonathan. *The Audible Past: Cultural Origins of Sound Reproduction*. Durham, NC: Duke University Press, 2003.

Streeter, Thomas. *Selling the Air: A Critique of the Policy of Commercial Broadcasting in the United States*. Chicago: University of Chicago Press, 1996.

Studlar, Gaylyn. *This Mad Masquerade: Stardom and Masculinity in the Jazz Age*. New York: Columbia University Press, 1996.

Taylor, Timothy. "Music and the Rise of Radio in Twenties America: Technological Imperialism, Socialization, and the Transformation of Intimacy." In *Wired for Sound: Engineering and Technologies in Sonic Cultures*, edited by Paul D. Greene and Thomas Porcello, 245–268. Middletown, CT: Wesleyan University Press, 2005.

Thompson, John. "The Media and Modernity." In Mackay and O'Sullivan, *The Media Reader*, 13–27.

Trouillot, Michel. *Silencing the Past*. Boston: Beacon, 1995.

Udelson, Joseph H. *The Great Television Race: A History of the American Television Industry, 1925–1941*. Tuscaloosa: University of Alabama Press, 1982.

Uricchio, William. "Television, Film and the Struggle for Media Identity." *Film History* 10, no. 2 (1998): 118–127.

——. "Television's First Seventy-Five Years: The Interpretive Flexibility of a Medium in Transition." In *The Oxford Handbook of Film and Media Studies*, edited by Robert Kolker, 286–305. Oxford: Oxford University Press, 2008.

VanCour, Shawn. "Popularizing the Classics: Radio's Role in the American Music Appreciation Movement, 1922–34." *Media, Culture & Society* 31, no. 2 (2009): 289–307.

——."The Sounds of 'Radio': Aesthetic Formations of 1920s American Broadcasting." PhD diss., University of Wisconsin–Madison, 2008.

Waldrop, Frank C., and Joseph Borkin. *Television: A Struggle for Power*. New York: William Morrow, 1938.

Wang, Jennifer Hyland. "'The Case of the Radio-Active Housewife': Relocating Radio in the Age of Television." In *The Radio Reader*, edited by Michele Hilmes and Jason Loviglio, 343–366. New York: Routledge, 2002.

Weinstein, David. *The Forgotten Network: Dumont and the Birth of American Television*. Philadelphia: Temple University Press, 2004.

Williams, Raymond. "Base and Superstructure in Marxist Cultural Theory." *New Left Review* (Nov.-Dec. 1973): 3–16.

——. *Marxism and Literature*. Oxford: Oxford University Press, 1979.

——. *Television: Technology and Cultural Form*. London: Fontana, 1974.

Winston, Brian. "How Are Media Born and Developed?" In *Questioning the Media*, edited by John Downing and Annabelle Sreberny-Mohammadi, 2nd ed., 54–74. London: Sage, 1995.

——. *Media Technology and Society, a History: From the Telegraph to the Internet*. New York: Routledge, 1998.

Wurtzler, Steve J. *Electric Sounds: Technological Change and the Rise of Corporate Mass Media*. New York: Columbia University Press, 2007.

INDEX

actuality (as television content), 142, 143, 145, 149, 158, 159, 164

advertising, 10, 11, 13, 20fig, 23, 59, 69, 97, 101, 108, 110, 113, 118, 119, 124, 127, 132, 137, 139, 146, 148, 149, 156, 158, 171n32, 187n38; commercial broadcast model, 99, 100, 104, 116, 150, 152, 186n32, 191n118; conflicts over, 99, 101, 104, 105, 185n24; regulation of, 115; spot advertising, 157. *See also* commercials; sponsorship

Aitken, Hugh, 7, 10

Albertson, Roy, 114, 115

Alexanderson, Ernst, 5, 21, 22, 37, 38, 54, 56, 129, 177n9, 178n14, 178n15

Altman, Rick, 132

amateurs: containment and marginalization of, 4, 13, 14, 54, 58–60, 66, 88, 91, 92, 100, 117, 162, 177n1; culture of experimentation and invention, 44, 53, 54, 56, 57, 58, 63, 67–70, 75, 85, 88, 177n9; encouraged to seek credentials, 58–61; heterogeneity of, 58; national organizations of, 117; point-to-many uses by, 4; purported identities of, 51, 56, 58, 69, 70, 91, 178n12; subordinated to engineers/electricians, 52–56, 90fig, 91; television transmission, 88, 92. *See also* dx-ing

American Marconi Corporation, 4, 117

American Radio Relay League, 117

American Society of Composers, Authors, and Publishers (ASCAP), 96, 97, 98, 99

American Telegraph and Telephone Co. (AT&T), 1, 4, 5, 11, 29, 32, 34, 42, 48, 52, 174n84; Bell television demonstration, 40; toll broadcasting, 99; WEAF (station), 5, 98, 117

Amos 'n' Andy Show, The (radio, later television program), 110, 114, 118, 155

Armstrong, Edwin, regenerative circuit, 28, 69

Arnold, John, 26, 178n14

Arnold, Matthew, 106, 160

articulation(s), 160, 161, 163, 164, 184n5; of corporate liberalism, 7; of engineering, 28; of an essence or nature of television, 2, 13, 43, 91, 144, 157, 158, 160, 162, 164; of gadgets, 68, 87; of hierarchy of expertise, 59; of national broadcast models, 121, 123; of production norms, 152, 155, 196n67; of

progress, 29, 30, 31, 39, 40, 44, 56; of public and private, 100; of quality, 9, 43, 93, 94, 96, 100, 104, 105, 107, 109, 111, 112, 118, 119, 129, 140, 192n2; of technical populism, 68; of television programming as distinct from technology, 136–137; of television technologies, 12, 13, 17, 24, 28, 31, 49, 160; of television to adjacent media, 30–31, 40, 130, 139, 140, 145, 147; of television to human perception, 30–31, 130; of an "unconscious" audience, 149. *See also* Hall, Stuart

Arvin, W. B., 22

ASCAP. *See* American Society of Composers, Authors, and Publishers

AT&T. *See* American Telegraph and Telephone Co.

audience(s): adapted for television, 15, 111–114, 150, 156; attentiveness or lack of, 67, 77fig, 79, 80, 83, 91, 114, 129, 131, 132, 137, 146, 150, 155, 165, 181n84; broadcasting effects on, 110, 127, 128, 132, 141, 149, 186n34, 194n46; critics' dissatisfaction with term, 23; disciplining of, 54, 55, 71, 91, 107, 108, 133, 137, 162, 165; for early television, 38, 42, 133, 137, 151, 177n124; as fans, 62, 67, 72, 83, 102, 108, 162, 179n33; fragments, 14, 15, 162; institutional assumptions and constructions of, 12, 14, 16, 40, 46, 49, 51, 54, 62, 65, 67, 69, 71, 79, 89, 92, 93, 98, 106, 108–116, 124, 131, 132, 144, 149, 158, 159, 162, 164, 181n84, 185n12, 190n91, 193n15; investment in broadcasting infrastructure by, 124, 125; as "invisible fiction," 65; mass, 12, 91, 106–109, 111, 112, 129, 149, 163; measurement and feedback, 107–110, 138, 139, 144, 150, 153–156, 195n47; negotiations between public and private, 72, 73fig, 85, 111, 192n1; paedocratic imaginings of, 14, 65, 67, 89, 114, 115, 189n75; participation by, 92, 108, 129, 131, 142, 145, 146, 162, 199n12; passivity, 13, 14, 54, 67, 69, 71, 72, 80, 149; protection of, 64–66, 48, 114, 163; quality and, 96, 98, 99, 106–116, 127, 162, 163, 197n93; rural, 101, 102, 106, 111, 187n47, 192n129; studio, 146, 155, 156; tastes, 2, 12, 15, 79, 92, 95, 100, 109, 110, 112, 115, 129, 134, 139, 155, 158, 165, 193n24

ABOUT THE AUTHOR

PHILIP W. SEWELL is an assistant professor in the Program in Film and Media Studies at Washington University in St. Louis. He writes about media, technology, and the structure and politics of cultural institutions in the United States.

CPSIA information can be obtained at www.ICGtesting.com
Printed in the USA
BVOW03s0438030114

340814BV00004B/9/P